DEEP WATER

by

DON SCHOLLANDER

and

DUKE SAVAGE

illustrated

D1529359

CROWN PUBLISHERS, INC., NEW YORK

Third Printing, June, 1971

© 1971 by Donald A. Schollander and Michael D. Savage

Library of Congress Catalog Card Number: 78–147318

Printed in the United States of America

Published simultaneously in Canada by General Publishing Company Limited

All photographs are from the private collection of Mrs. Martha Dent Schollander

To M.S.S.
our "agent"

CONTENTS

DEEP WATER

part one

The Dream Olympics:
Tokyo, 1964

DON WITH COACH GEORGE HAINES

I

"It was the best of times.
It was the worst of times. . . ."

I SWAM IN THE BEST OF TIMES—the great years of swimming.
There were great competitors—Murray Rose from Australia,
Roy Saari and Steve Clark from the United States, Hans
Klein from Germany, Bobby McGregor from Great Britain.
We changed the sport of swimming—we were the pioneers of
modern competitive swimming—and we had all the fun and
excitement that goes with trailblazing.

I won National Championships and Olympic gold
medals and I was voted the best athlete in the world—amateur or professional—when I was eighteen. I set thirty-seven
American records and twenty-two world records. I was in the
swimming Hall of Fame when I was nineteen.

I remember so much that was good—good friends, travel
all over the world; I saw things I would not otherwise have
seen. And I remember much that was bad. When I talk about
the bad side it is not to mourn what might have been—because nobody ever had it better—but because I had the
chance to see so much. I think there are things that are
wrong. I think they should be talked about.

When I was eighteen and had just become the first
swimmer in history to win four gold medals I talked at
hundreds of banquets and high-school assemblies and press
conferences, and didn't really have a great deal to say. I
would describe Olympic episodes and tell stories about a few
Olympic personalities. Now, after two Olympics and a lot

3

that has happened in between, I want to tell what it was really like to be an "amateur" in the world of sport and an Olympic competitor.

The fact is that "amateurism" is dead. And the crowning event of sports—the Olympic Games—is in danger of dying. The 1968 Olympics came very close to being canceled, and the diseases that threatened it have not been cured. They are all still there, and the next attack may kill the patient.

When amateur rules were set up almost a century ago, sports were not so competitive or so widely popular as today. Amateur sport was recreation, not a business—and an amateur was truly an amateur. He probably worked out two or three times a week for a total of about four hours—as much for exercise as to train for competition. There was no such thing as a swimmer who swam every day or an amateur coach who did nothing but coach amateurs.

Johnny Weissmuller was the first swimmer to train every day and to have a coach who was just a coach. He was the first "professional amateur."

Today, in top-level national and international competition there is no such thing as a real amateur. The concept is a contradiction. A guy working out four hours a day six days a week isn't an amateur. Today the pressure is so great, the schedule is so demanding, the training is so intense that you sacrifice everything else for your sport; you sacrifice as much as any professional. More. The only difference today between the amateur and the professional is that the amateur supposedly does not earn money from the sport. (The rule is becoming famous in its breach.) In amateur sports today there is no place for sentiment, or hoping for the best—no room for boyish, starry-eyed belief in good sportsmanship or good luck. You'd never make it to the top. You would not survive. You compete against people from other countries who are professionals, and you must be able to think and to handle yourself like a professional. In every sense, in training and in competition, you *are* a professional.

I left home at fifteen and went to Santa Clara, California, to become a professional amateur. Seven years later I retired. If a professional football player retires at thirty-five and says he's glad not to have to go in there every week and get clobbered—he's tired—you can understand it. If a professional fighter retires at thirty and says he's been taking too many punches for too many years—he's had it—you can understand that, too. When I retired I was twenty-two. A swimmer does not get punched or clobbered—no cuts, no bruises, no broken bones—and I was an "amateur," not a "professional"; but I had had it. I was tired. And I had been tired for three years.

Deep Water was written to tell about what it was like. The training and the competition. The erosion in sports as they became the pawn of internal power struggles and of international power politics. The good side of the Olympics and the bad. The rewards. The costs.

2

WHY DID I DO IT?

In the beginning, swimming was nothing special to me. When I was seven my family moved to Lake Oswego, Oregon, a suburb of Portland, and in Lake Oswego, in the summer, that was all the kids did: they spent every day at the lake. And when I was seven, eight, nine years old that was what I did, too—went swimming every day in the lake.

When I began to train and to enter races I was nine, and I did it because it was fun. I spent about an hour three times a week at the pool, and training was just instruction in kicking, breathing, strokes, in freestyle, backstroke. But even then, in the races, I wanted to win. And I did win. In swimming, the kids compete in age groups, and when I was ten I was swimming against kids who were nine and ten, and I won. While I was ten I held the national record for the twenty-yard backstroke for boys ten and under and Oregon state records in that age group for backstroke, freestyle, and butterfly events. And it was fun.

At eleven I moved into the next age group. I was always very small for my age and now I was swimming against eleven- and twelve-year-olds who were much bigger—and better. Suddenly I was no longer winning. And I wanted to quit. Swimming wasn't a very important sport to me—football, baseball, basketball, those were real sports—and it wasn't fun anymore because I was losing. I really wanted to quit.

Well, my mother and father took a stand on that and told me that I couldn't quit just because I was losing. "Once you get back on top, if you don't like swimming, you can quit," they said, "but not while you're losing. We don't want you to be a quitter."

By the time I was twelve I had grown and then I started to win again. And I must admit that this continued to be the motivating factor. After that I kept on winning. If I hadn't won I don't think I would have stayed with swimming. It was fun because I won.

Any child is influenced by his family and I was certainly influenced by mine. My father, Wendell Schollander, was a star football player in high school and in college, and my mother, Martha Dent (Perry) Schollander, was a swimmer who doubled for Maureen O'Sullivan in the early Tarzan movies. We were a sports-oriented family and I always loved sports and was good at them. Sports were so important to my parents that when I was in the first grade and the teachers wanted to push me ahead a grade my parents wouldn't let them because they thought it would hurt me in sports. "He's small for his age now," they said. "If he ever wants to do anything in athletics, he would be too small for his class." A year later the same thing happened and again my parents refused. "He might do well in athletics. Leave him where he is."

Thinking of my early childhood I can see traits in myself that were later important in competition; certainly this desire to win was one of them, and also traits like the ability to adjust and to take care of myself and a fair amount of self-confidence. My mother says that even when I was a little kid she could leave me for an afternoon in some new place and I would find things to do and be okay.

As a child I was very much of a loner, very much on my own. Part of our land in Lake Oswego was thick woods that ended at a seventy-five-foot cliff, and when I was only seven or eight I'd go off into the woods with my dog until it was dark. My parents used to worry about me—hell, I was playing on this cliff!—but they still had enough confidence in me to let me do it and I must have sensed this because I was confident, too, that I could take care of myself. In top competition where you are constantly up against unexpected situations and when every man is out for himself, this confidence is important. Your competitor is out to get you any way he can, short of foul play—and you are out to get him. You have to feel, absolutely, that you can take care of yourself, whatever happens, and you must have confidence in your own judgment—the courage, once you decide on a strategy for a race, to stick to it. Without that kind of self-confidence you're vulnerable and your competitor will get to you with a psych-out or with his own race strategy. And you will lose.

Some of these traits I was probably born with, along with a certain natural ability. I think the competitive drive came, partly at least, from my early home environment, especially my father's influence. I have always felt that an episode in his early life had a strong influence on mine.

In high school, in Fargo, North Dakota, my father was a star football player. He made high-school All-American and wanted to go on to one of the Big Ten universities where he could play top college football, but his own father, a very domineering man, refused to send him. My grandfather was on the board of regents at North Dakota State in Fargo and he wanted my father to go there. For three years at North Dakota State, my father played great football but coming from such a small college, he was never considered for All-American and always felt that he had been denied his chance. I think this had a tremendous influence on his life—and on mine.

My father is actually very much like his own father— domineering, aggressive, what David Riesman terms an "other-directed" father; he is the typical father that you find when you analyze an achievement-oriented child. He was a pusher. Though he wanted us to be very good at sports, swimming wasn't what he had in mind. When my brother Wendell and I were just little kids, my father would spend hours with us out in the yard teaching us complicated football plays. I knew how to run pass patterns by the time I was seven.

You have to understand how it is with this "other-directed" father. He's the superego that rides over the ego with the carrot out in front of him saying, "Go get it, boy." And I'm the horse trying to get that carrot. So he's setting up goals, and at times this can be very frustrating; if a father like that pushes too hard, a son will rebel. I was saved by the fact that I did well in sports, so he didn't have to push too hard.

My mother was the love in the family. She would make any sacrifice for her boys. Any tenderness I have I got from her. I was very close to both my parents and still am, as close as I could be for not having spent any time with them since I was fifteen and a half.

As a child I was very competitive in all sports—football, basketball, Ping-Pong, anything. I was so puny—I went through a period when I got sick all the time—and I was always trying to make up for my size with speed and intelligence. Every time my brother and I played each other in any sport we ended up in a fight. It was only his natural kindness that kept him from killing me because he was three years older and about a hundred pounds heavier. I'm sure my father's goals had a lot to do with my attitude, but I also think I was sort of insecure because of my size.

Actually, my parents never said, "We want you to win." They said, "Just do the best you can and we'll be happy." But I understood that they wanted me to win, and I think one reason I did so well in sports was that I was searching for that pat on the back: I wanted recognition from my parents for being a good athlete. I didn't get it from my father as a swimmer—not at first, anyway.

Later I wanted recognition from my peers—from girls, and from guys my own age. And then, later still, from George Haines, my coach at Santa Clara, who was a very great influence in my life.

3

WHEN I WAS A FRESHMAN in high school, I had to make a big decision—whether to go out in the fall for swimming or football. To me, football was really a sport—and swimming just wasn't that important. There was more glory in football, and all my friends were going out for football; at fourteen, you know, this is important.

At that time I was just coming out of a really low period in my life. In grammar school, because I was a good athlete, I'd been a popular little kid. I was vice-president of my class and had lots of friends. Then in the seventh grade, the other guys started to go out at night—just the guys together, or sometimes to parties with girls—and I didn't go out because I was so small and very shy. And I couldn't hang around with them after school because by the seventh grade I was swimming every afternoon. So I didn't feel part of the crowd and I began to pull more and more into my shell. In the eighth grade things got even worse. I turned all my frustrations to schoolwork and made straight A's—and was far from happy.

But toward the end of that year I grew quite a bit, and also began to do well in swimming. My name or my picture would be in the paper when I won and because of that, things picked up at school. Then in the ninth grade came this big decision between swimming and football. I loved football —much more than swimming—and football was a more important sport; after that long low period I especially wanted to be popular. My father was all for football, but my mother was afraid I'd get hurt because I was so small.

Then suddenly my father changed his mind. He said, "You could probably become a pretty good football player, Don, but you could become one of the best swimmers in the state. As a freshman in football, you'll be on the freshman football team, but in swimming you might even go to the state finals."

I was disappointed and I still had my doubts but I agreed to give swimming a try for one year. "But if I don't do anything," I said, "or if I don't like it—I'm going to switch to football."

Well, I made the varsity team and I began to win. Again it was fun because I was winning. In high-school meets there were no age groups, and when I was fourteen I was competing against swimmers who were seventeen and eighteen—

juniors and seniors—and I was winning. I swam mostly freestyle, in the sprint, but actually I'd swim anything—backstroke, butterfly. They would switch me from one event to
another, anywhere I seemed to have an advantage. If I
thought I could win the butterfly, I'd swim that. If a really
good butterfly man came along whom I couldn't beat, and it
looked as though I could win freestyle, I became a freestyler.
I hate to put it down to this level, but this is the truth. This
is the way it was.

I went to the state finals that year and won two races;
while I was still a freshman people were beginning to say that
I was probably the best swimmer in the state of Oregon.

Suddenly I was very popular at school again. I was confident in the sport of swimming and I began to gain confidence
outside the sport. Then at fifteen I really grew and in my
sophomore year I began to win, not only at the high-school
level, but against anyone in the state. At senior meets I was
winning against college swimmers, too; from the depths in
the seventh and eighth grades I'd rocketed right up. I was
getting good grades; I was doing well in sports; I was very
popular in school now; and I was going out with one of the
best looking girls. I was at peace with the world.

And right at that point, when I was fifteen and a half,
my parents asked me if I wanted to leave home—to try to
really do something in swimming.

I can still remember the day my mother brought it up.
It was in November, 1961, and we were in the dentist's office,
waiting for me to be drilled on. She said, very offhand, "Don,
have you ever thought about leaving home—to swim?"

Well, at first I *completely* rejected the idea! I said,
"What are you talking about?" I didn't want any part of it.

That night the three of us discussed it, and my father
put the decision squarely up to me. He said, "You can stay in
Oregon and be the best swimmer in high school or college—
the best swimmer in this area—and never really reach your

full potential. Or you can leave Oregon and go where there's a real challenge and see what you can do."

And I said, "No. Hell, no! I don't want to go anywhere. I want to stay here—stay with my friends. Swimming isn't that important."

That was when my father told me the story about how he had had to go to North Dakota State and how he had always felt he had been denied a chance to see what he could really do. He wanted to give me that chance if I wanted it. But to have this chance I would have to leave Oregon. Did I want to give it a try?

And I didn't know. The truth was I was beginning to wonder whether I could become good enough to make the 1964 Olympics. But on the other hand I was so happy now at home; I was extremely happy that year. To give all this up just for swimming—I thought, God, is it worth it? To go away and have to make my name all over again: be alone, be a new kid in a new school, live with a strange family—this was something I wasn't looking forward to.

For a month we kicked it around and finally I said, "Okay, let's see what it's like."

Then came the question of where I should go. I said, "Well, if I've got to leave here, I don't really give a damn where I go."

My father suggested a prep school in the East, but my mother wanted me to go to California where I'd be closer to home. In the end I said, "If I'm going to leave home for this, I want to choose the best and California certainly is the big league of swimming. That's where all the stars are born." And if I was going to California I had already chosen the place. When I'd gone there to compete, I had noticed that one club whose swimmers really seemed to enjoy themselves was Santa Clara and that their coach seemed like a lot of fun and a man I could work for. His name was George Haines. At Christmas we drove down to talk to him..

And on January 21, 1962—I'll never forget the day—I

moved. It was snowing when we left Oregon; and it was snowing—for the first time in twenty-seven years—when we got to Santa Clara.

To this day I see that decision—leaving my family, my friends, leaving Oregon—as the biggest sacrifice of my life.

4

IN OREGON I had done well just training an hour a day because everyone else was training an hour a day, too: but in California, where everyone was training three hours a day, I was in another league. At Santa Clara I began two-a-day workouts, something entirely new for me: an hour and a quarter in the morning before school, two hours after school.

Also at Santa Clara I began serious interval training: swimming repeats of specific distances and timing each repeat. (If you are swimming ten 100-meter repeats, you swim a hundred meters and stop to check your time on the wall clock, swim another hundred, check your time again—ten times.) Interval training enables you to chart your own improvement and, more important, it helps develop a sense of pace, one of the most indispensable talents in competitive swimming. With a sharp sense of pace—a built-in, intuitive speedometer—you can gauge very closely the speed you are going at any point in a race. Without it, you can never really be sure of yourself or your strategy in tough competition.

Any healthy fifteen-year-old can run hard for 100 meters. Swimming hard for 100 meters is like running fast for a quarter of a mile, and it requires a kind of endurance that is carefully built up over a long period of time. In training, probably the most important single factor is building endurance.

At Santa Clara we arrived at the pool at 6:30 A.M., and

George Haines, striding up and down with a megaphone, would order a 500-meter warm-up swim. Five hundred meters is a third of a mile. Then we would swim another 500 meters "pulling," using only the arms. Next, 50-meter repeats, probably ten. Then another 500 meters with a kickboard, working only the legs. Next, 100-meter repeats, probably five. Another long swim, more repeats, breathing drills, turning drills, starting drills. One more long swim and we had worked an hour and a quarter and were through for the morning. In the afternoon we were back for more of the same. At the peak of training we were swimming about eight miles a day.

Amateur?

In top competition a whole new ingredient enters swimming, one that you never know until you reach this level—pain. You learn the pain in practice and you will know it in every race. As you approach the limit of your endurance it begins, coming on gradually, hitting your stomach first. Then your arms grow heavy and your legs tighten—thighs first, then knees. You sink lower in the water because you can't hold yourself up; you are actually swimming deeper in the water, as though someone were pushing down on your back. You experience perception changes. The sounds of the pool blend together and become a crashing roar in your ears. The water takes on a pinkish tinge. Your stomach feels as though it's going to fall out—every kick hurts like hell—and then suddenly you hear a shrill, internal scream.

In a race, at the threshold of pain, you have a choice. You can back off—or you can force yourself to drive to the finish, knowing that this pain will become agony. It is right there, at the pain barrier, that the great competitors separate from the rest. Most swimmers back away from the pain; a champion pushes himself on into agony. Is it masochistic? In a way, yes. When it comes it is oddly satisfying because you know it had to come and now it is there, because you are meeting it, taking it without backing down—because you enjoy the triumph of going through it, knowing it is the only way you can win. It's those last few meters of the race, while you're in agony, that count. If you can push yourself through that pain barrier into real agony, you're a champion.

In Santa Clara, George Haines found me a place to live in the home of Mrs. Ruth Macedo, a widow whose three sons were away from home. It was a small house, one of many all alike in a development. I had a small room—twin beds, a desk and chair, and a dresser. I spent a lot of time in that room.

The first night after my parents left, I wondered if I would be lonely. And I *wasn't* lonely. I had misgivings, certainly, but the hardest part was back in Oregon, before I moved, knowing that I had to leave all my friends. By the time I got to Santa Clara I was resigned to it, and my feeling was not one of homesickness but more, Look at the sacrifice that your parents made and that you made to do this, so you'd better do damn well and have something come of it. The first week I was there I got up and did all kinds of exercises—push-ups, sit-ups—before going off to early morning training. I'd made the sacrifice and now, damnit, I was going to work, and if nothing came of it, I was going to get myself back to Oregon.

I never really had any close friends in Oregon again. I hardly ever got home. I would try to go back for the Thanksgiving dance and the Christmas parties, and I tried to keep in touch with four or five of my closest friends—but every year I grew further away from them.

That semester—the rest of my sophomore year—was hell. Academically, Lake Oswego High had been a great school and Santa Clara High was not as good. I didn't feel at home with Mrs. Macedo and except at mealtime I stayed mostly in my room. I had no friends at school and I didn't have time to make any friends—I was putting in so much time swimming. Most guys in the swim club went to different high schools out in the suburbs and trained at a later hour.

And I was resented at first in Santa Clara—more by the parents than by the kids. Santa Clara is a swimming town, and swimming parents are like stage mothers. I had come down from Oregon and George Haines was coaching me—an outsider—and I was beginning to win.

I finally found a girl I liked—a swimmer named Chris Fairbairn—and I went with her for a couple of years. And my first friend was another swimmer who might have resented me but never did, Mike Wall. Tall, about 6 feet, 1½ inches, with the solid build of a swimmer, streaky brown hair, Mike is very self-contained, very much his own man. He had moved to California a few years earlier from Atlanta, Georgia —he still had a southern accent—and when I arrived he was the best younger middle-distance swimmer there. I quickly became a threat, but this never seemed to bother him. He was my closest friend in Santa Clara and to this day we're almost like brothers.

I wished I could have seen more of my parents. Today I feel that because I went away at fifteen and stayed away, my parents don't really know me. You know, between the ages of fifteen and eighteen a person goes through many changes, and my parents were never there to see these changes. I wished I could have shared some of the frustrations with them and some of the happiness. I wished I could talk to them more. I wished I could go home in the summer. Today it bothers me, not that I don't know them very well, but that *they* don't know me very well.

I was never sorry I made the move and the reason for that was George Haines. George was about thirty-eight then, and looked much younger: a tall, tan, good-looking man with a swimmer's build and squint lines around his bright, blue eyes. One reason George was so successful and, I think,

became one of the great swimming coaches was because he
stayed very close to his kids. To me, when I first came to
Santa Clara he was more than a coach—he was a substitute
father. Later as we worked together and as I grew older, our
relationship changed and we became very good friends.

George was a tough coach, but he seemed to know all
there was to know about swimming, down to the smallest
refinements of technique. He was one of the first to divide
the swimming season into three parts: the first part, quantity
swimming—overdistance—swimming thousands of meters a
day to build endurance that would last all year; the middle
part, half-quantity, half-quality, still building endurance but
also stressing technique; and the end of the season, before the
championship meets, pure quality swimming, all technique
and polishing.

George knew, too, that swimming could be a tedious
sport—all those repeats up and down the pool—and he
worked to keep it interesting. If he saw that we were dragging, he would change the workout, which very few coaches
do. Most coaches plan a workout and stick to it. But George
knew us so well—and this was important—that he could see
when something was wrong and he would move quickly to
make changes. Or, if we were tired he might take a longer
rest between repeats, and during that time he would horse
around a little, to take our minds off how tired we were.

That first year at Santa Clara George really tried to be a
father to me. He would ask about my schoolwork, and
whether I had any problems. When I finally found a girl he
took me aside and said, in effect, your parents aren't here and
I'm responsible for you and I'm going to give you a man-to-
man talk. And he did. From the start, I think, George had
faith in me and I certainly had fantastic faith in him. Until
then I'd been swimming mostly the 100-meter freestyle—the
"sprint"—and the butterfly, but George said, "You could
become a good middle-distance man. Why don't you try the
200 and the 400 free?" And I said okay. Then later he had me

swimming the distance event—the 1,500. He would tell me, "You can do this, you can do that," and I believed him because I felt he was the most knowledgeable swimming coach at the time. Plus I just adored him. He was such a wonderful man.

I don't think spectators or even sportswriters ever really know all the fine points involved in different sports. At Santa Clara I was beginning to learn—not only about pace and pain and technique—but about the psychology of competition. When you get the eight fastest swimmers in the country or in the world into a pool for a race, they are so nearly equal in ability that mere ability is no longer the deciding factor. A race is won on strategy and psychology and very often by psyching-out a competitor long before the race and some distance away from the pool.

A psych-out can be complex or simple. It can be worked a minute before the race or it can be continued carefully over several days. It can be directed against a single rival or against the entire field. The techniques vary, the objective is always the same: to convince your competition that you are certain to win this race. In a psych-out you always make a show of confidence, while you work to undermine the confidence of your competition.

One of the first psych-outs I saw after going to Santa Clara was a simple poolside ploy. After everyone was on the starting blocks, a man delayed the race for just a minute in order to retie the strings of his swimsuit and with that simple trick probably had every other man worrying, a little at least, down the whole first lap, about whether his suit was tied, when he should have been concentrating totally on the race. This is a very crude psych-out and would never work in national or Olympic competition.

A poolside ploy that I used more than once was to make a conspicuous show of total confidence and lack of concern over an important race. Before the race I would be standing near the pool talking with someone, perhaps a reporter, and when my race was announced I would appear not to hear the call, and while the other swimmers were taking off their sweats, loosening up, I would just keep talking. They would announce the race again—or someone would yell over to me that my race was beginning—and finally when I knew that all my competitors had noticed that I wasn't there, I'd turn around and say, "Oh, hey! I'm on!" and walk over to my block and get ready to race. My purpose was to create the impression that I thought I could win hands down. With that much confidence you can psych-out everybody in the pool.

A psych-out of a single competitor can be worked for a period of several days before the race by discussing his real or imagined weaknesses. "I watched you work out today. Do you always start kicking like that before you hit the water? Doesn't that slow you down?" And, the next day, "I'm amazed at the way you begin to kick early like that. I'm really amazed." On the starting blocks, you hope, he'll be worried about kicking too soon, and if he *is* worried, he will have a bad start.

Swimming is an individual sport—either *you* win or *you* lose—which makes swimmers particularly vulnerable to psyching-out. Every good competitor knows that competition is 20 percent physical and 80 percent mental, and he studies his opponent to learn the weaknesses through which he can reach him to shatter his self-confidence. Once a competitor has doubts, he can't win.

From the time I went to Santa Clara to the end of my swimming career, I saw the whole range of psyching-out techniques—some of them pretty dirty—and I never again swam an important race without trying to psych-out my competition. I learned early that a race is won in the mind.

Was it worth it—working like hell, giving up so much— to get into that cutthroat world? Yes. Even without the medals and acclaim I won, it would have been worth it. You get so many intangibles out of swimming: discipline, confidence, experience. Whenever I lost I would ask myself why I lost—whether the reason was some weakness in myself. In swimming you're alone a lot in the water with time to just think, and because of that I feel that I've gotten to know myself well.

And I think I've learned a lot about human nature—just by competing against other people. Before a race, I would try to figure out what the other guys were like. Were they followers or leaders, confident, worried, cautious, easily riled? And I would try to plan my race strategy around their personalities and their weaknesses. And the smart ones were doing the same to me. Over the years in swimming I think I got to know people—and to understand myself.

5

In April, 1962, three months after I moved to Santa Clara, I went to the Spring National Championships. These championships are the climax of the winter swimming season, when most teams train in an indoor pool 25 yards long, and so the races, too, are held in a 25-yard pool and are measured in yards. They're called the short-course Nationals. In the summer, most teams move outdoors to a 50-meter pool, and at the Outdoor Nationals—the long-course Nationals—the races are measured in meters. In international competition and in Olympic competition, the races are also measured in meters—you break world records only in meters—and for these reasons the Outdoor Nationals are much more important.

I went to those 1962 Spring Nationals just for the experience. I didn't expect to do very well since this was my first meet in top competition. Murray Rose, the great Australian swimmer who had been the star of the 1956 and the 1960 Olympics, was entered, and Roy Saari, a high-school senior from El Segundo, California, who was coming up fast, was expected to be the star of the meet. Murray Rose was nearing the end of his career, but this meet was the beginning of a long rivalry between Roy Saari and me. Actually Roy and I look very much alike. He is Finnish and I am Swedish, and we both have blond hair and fair skin. Saari learned some of his tricks from Murray Rose, who was the first swimmer to really use psychology in competition—including psyching-out—and I, in turn, learned from Saari. For years after this meet, although Saari is a few years older, we were very friendly but very competitive.

I had gone to watch the Spring Nationals before, when they were on the West Coast—and all of a sudden, there I was, competing in them. I swam the qualifying heats for the 220-yard freestyle and I made the finals. My God, I never expected it! Everyone was really surprised—this unknown kid making the finals of the National Championships. Then in the finals, I got third. The next night, in the 440, I took third again, and came within .4 seconds—less than half a second—of winning. Saari was the high-point winner in the meet, but before the meet I was completely unknown, and for me to get two thirds, well, people thought that was kind of remarkable. It was at that meet that I realized that I had a good chance of making the 1964 Olympics. I would only have to be the fourth fastest 200-meter man in the United States to make at least a relay team. And here in 1962 I was already third.

A month later, in May, as a member of a five-man American team, I went on my first foreign trip—to Japan. I love Japan, it has always been lucky for me, and in their national amateur swimming championships that year, I won the 200-, 400-, and 800-meter freestyle and swam on a winning relay team. For me, it was the beginning of a long string of victories in Japan.

Then, at the Outdoor Nationals that summer, I won the 200-meter freestyle, and for the first time I became a national champion.

I went home for a week in June and another week at the end of that summer, but otherwise I stayed in Santa Clara and trained. This was to be my life for a long time. Except when illness forced it, I never really went home again.

For me there was a relative disadvantage in the indoor 25-yard pool, compared with the outdoor 50-meter pool because at the time I was only 5 feet 7 inches. In races of approximately equal distance—for instance, 200 meters or its near equivalent, 200 yards—there are twice as many laps in the shorter indoor pool. A man six inches taller has a six-inch advantage on each lap—four feet in a 200-yard race. I tried to compensate for this by developing quick hard turns and the following year—April, 1963—at the Indoor Nationals, I took first in the 200-yard freestyle and second in the 500.

Three months later came a real giant step forward. At the Los Angeles Invitational, in July, 1963, I became the first man anywhere to swim the 200-meter freestyle in less than two minutes. The papers compared it to Roger Bannister breaking the four-minute mile. My time was 1:58.9.

I felt now that the 200-meter free had become my race, and it was another year before anyone else anywhere broke the two-minute barrier. I never went over two minutes again in an official championship meet.

A month later, in August, 1963, at the Outdoor Nationals, I made two firsts—the 200-meter free and the 400-meter free—and took second to Roy Saari in the 1,500-meter free. I was the high-point winner for the meet.

6

THE UNITED STATES is the only country in the world whose government does not financially support its Olympic Team. This is not the result of any International Olympic Committee (IOC) rule. The United States government simply does not do it. It never has. Our Olympic Team has always been supported by private contributions. Nobody has given me a satisfactory explanation of how this policy evolved or why it should be considered more ethical or more sportsmanlike. If there were ever sound reasons for it, I think the realities of today's Olympics have made them obsolete.

In my opinion the United States government should, like every other government, provide funds for its Olympic Team. The fact that it does not affects the team all through the Games and goes back even to the method by which it is selected.

Our procedure for choosing our Olympic Team differs from that of any other country. Most countries—at least all major countries—send large potential teams into a training camp for six to ten months and then select their official team on the basis of the athletes' overall performance during that time. The United States chooses its swimming team on the basis of performance in a single, four-day meet called the Olympic Trials, held only six weeks before the Olympic Games.

For the athlete this is a one-shot deal. At the Trials, you take first, second, or third in your event—or fourth for a relay—or you don't make the team. If you have an off day, that's tough. If you're sick, it makes no difference. There is absolutely no way you can be on the United States Olympic Team without making it in the Trials. No matter who you

are—even if you're the best in the world in your event—if you
don't perform that one day, the day of your event at the
Trials, you don't make the team.

In 1960, Jeff Farrell, a swimmer who held the world
record in the sprint—the 100-meter freestyle—had an appendicitis attack a week before the start of the Olympic
Trials. About ten days after his operation, he managed to
swim his event and came in fourth, which put him on the 4 x
100 relay team only. At the Olympics, there was no way he
could compete in the individual 100-meter event. And yet at
the time, everyone—the coaches, his competitors, everyone—
knew that he was probably by far the best 100-meter swimmer in the world. By the time of the Games he had recovered
completely and would probably have won the gold medal.
Here's a guy who was the best, but there was no way he could
be put on that team.

Why do we do this—select our team this one-shot way
with only enough time left to send it to training camp for
one month? There are several reasons. First, the United
States Olympic Committee (USOC) claims that it cannot
afford to support a team in training camp for more than one
month. Second, most United States athletes wouldn't give up
their jobs or their schooling to go into camp much longer
than a month. Certainly not for as long as six to ten months.
In most countries, Olympic athletes have finished school and
are on a government-supported payroll. (This involves a
whole separate subject—the varying definitions of an "amateur" throughout the world.) The third reason is that the
international Olympic rules specifically limit the time of
Olympic training camps. The rule states that no one is
eligible for Olympic competition who has given up a job or
school for special training in a camp for longer than four
weeks. Most countries put the rule book on the top shelf of
the closet and close the door.

As a swimmer I object to these trials. I object to the one-shot policy and I object to the timing of the trials. We force our best athletes to "peak"—to give everything they've got—just to make the team. Then after having taken the best out of them just fighting each other, we ask them only six weeks later to peak again for the toughest competition in the world, the Olympic Games.

In swimming, the focus of a peak is not just a single race. It is an entire meet—for as many events as you are swimming—and it takes a lot out of you. Today, peaking in swimming is a carefully worked out procedure. For several months before a major meet you train very hard, swimming four or five hours a day, covering 9,000 to 12,000 meters. (In the summer of 1964, I swam two hours in the morning, an hour in the afternoon, and two hours in the evening.) Then four or five days before the meet, you stop this intense training and you begin to peak. You reduce training time to a half hour or an hour a day, just enough to stay loose. You change your whole way of life. You adopt the schedule that you will keep during the meet. You get up at the same hour each morning after going to bed at the same hour each night. You try to swim each day at the hour at which you will swim your event. The purpose of all this is to accustom your body to conditions as close as possible to those of the race, even to working in the water after so many hours of sleep and after so many hours of being awake. You do nothing that will dissipate your energy. If you're at school you cut down on studying, you give up dates, you rest in the afternoon. You read, you watch television, you eat and sleep. You indulge in no outlet for your tension, and that tension builds and builds inside you. The idea is that in competition you're just going to explode. Finally, just before the meet, you shave all the hair off your body. This is partly for physical reasons, because tiny drops of water collect on the hair and make you less streamlined; but it is partly psychological, too, even symbolic. With this final gesture you feel that you've done everything you can to get ready for this race. The idea of peaking works—and it drains you—totally.

Normally, American swimmers reach a full peak twice a year, for the Indoor Nationals in April and the Outdoor Nationals in August. Physiologically and psychologically it is almost impossible to peak three times in less than three months. In 1964, American swimmers were faced with the Outdoor Nationals at the end of July, the Olympic Trials at the end of August and, six weeks later, the Olympic Games.

In April, 1964, a few months before the Olympic Trials, George and I decided on a strategy that we felt could really pay off for me but involved quite a risk. At the Indoor Nationals that year I took two firsts—in the 200 and 500—and came in second to Roy Saari in the 1,650. Flying home after the meet, George and I talked for three hours about how we could plan for the three meets coming up so close together: the Nationals, the Trials, and the Olympics.

You couldn't peak for all three, and we knew that some of the best American swimmers would skip the Outdoor Nationals and that others would enter them but would not peak. They would swim through them and save themselves for the Olympic Trials. But a peak at the Trials still meant two peaks very close together because the Olympics were coming up only six weeks later. And two peaks in six weeks is tough.

Finally George and I came up with a fairly daring idea. What if I peaked for the Nationals in July, and then did *not* peak for the Olympic Trials? This would be taking a real risk. To make the Olympic Team, I would only have to finish third in my events, but in any event at the Olympic Trials, the top four or five men finish very close together—the fifth man sometimes less than a second behind the first—and a peak could make the difference. But if I could do it—make the team without peaking—then I would be much better off at the Olympics. The decision was up to me. I could play it safe and peak, as everyone else would do, to be sure I would make the team, or I could gamble and risk losing everything to shoot for bigger victories at the Olympics.

George and I weighed the odds very carefully. We considered the competition—their recent times, the progress they could be expected to make, the way they would probably perform under the pressure of the Trials. We made the decision that day on the plane. I would peak for the Nationals, for whatever psychological advantage that victory might give me. And I would take a chance at the Trials that I would get at least thirds. It was a risk and we knew it, but it was a calculated risk. I thought I could do it and George thought I could, too.

At the time this was a pretty radical strategy. I don't think anyone had ever considered not peaking for the Olympic Trials. Later, after the risk paid off and people heard about it, they called it the "Strategy for Gold."

That summer George and I made still another change in my Olympic plans that actually increased the risk. In the Nationals you can only enter three individual events, and for the past two years I had entered the 200, the 400, and the 1,500. I'd been winning my middle-distance events—the 200 and the 400—but I was finishing second to Roy Saari in the distance event, and I began to doubt if I could win the Olympic gold medal in the 1,500-meter. In July, before the Nationals, I wanted to make a change in my events. "George, instead of going for the 1,500 this year," I said, "I'd like to try the 100-meter sprint."

"You're not a sprinter," George said, quite honestly. I hadn't done much with the 100-meter since I came to Santa Clara.

"Well, I think I have the speed," I said. "I've done some pretty good splits in relays. I think I can do it."

If I wanted to try, it was all right with George, and so,

that summer, for the first time, I swam the 100-meter race in
the Nationals—and I won. I took first, too, in the 200 and the
400, and was high-point man in the meet—a good feeling, but
not so good as it would have been in another year because I
knew a lot of people hadn't peaked and I had. And I was very
much aware of the fact that the Olympic Trials were only a
month away, and that I was on the far side of a peak.

Now the question was how many events I was going to
shoot for at the Trials. I was a middle-distance swimmer, but
in the 1964 Olympics there was no 200-meter free—only the
400. It was definite now that I would try for the 100 and the
400, the question was whether I should go for the 1,500, too.
And from the results of the Nationals I didn't know because I
had passed it up.

Actually the 100 and the 400 are considered a much
more difficult double than the 400 and the 1,500. No middle-
distance swimmer in recent history that I could remember—
no one since Johnny Weissmuller—had ever dropped down
from the 400 to win the 100-meter, and no 100-meter man
had ever gone up to the 400. A sprinter sometimes goes up to
200 but never to 400. The two races are just very different
and training for them is different. In the 100-meter, the
emphasis is on speed, in the 400, on endurance. In the 1,500
the emphasis is also on endurance, obviously, and the 400 and
the 1,500 are a fairly common double. But I had made up my
mind to swim the 100. The only question was whether to go
for the 1,500, too.

George felt that I could certainly handle the 1,500 all
right, and my parents thought I should try it. But I didn't
know. When we left for the Olympic Trials in New York,
four weeks after the Nationals, I still didn't know what I was
going to do.

I finally decided against it because I thought that the
range from 100 to 1,500 was just too great. The 100 is a
sprint. The 1,500 is like a marathon. I felt that it just

couldn't be done. Besides, I didn't see anybody beating Roy Saari in the Olympics in the 1,500. And I did think, knowing the competition, that I could win the 100. Even though I didn't have the experience in the race—and I certainly didn't have the best times—I actually thought I could do it.

It's easier to decide on a calculated risk than it is to live with it. The week before the Olympic Trials I watched everybody at Santa Clara easing off, lounging around, getting really psyched up, shaving down before we left for New York. Then when we got to the Trials I was so nervous I couldn't sleep; I realized what a chance I was taking. By not peaking for this, I could conceivably have blown it all. I might not even make the team. Psychologically it really got to me. I just couldn't sleep for four or five days.

I didn't take any firsts at the Olympic Trials, but I did manage seconds in my two events. In the 100-meter I finished behind Gary Illman, an old friend from Santa Clara, and in the 400 I was second behind Roy Saari. This gave me two individual events and automatically put me on the 4 x 100 meter relay (four men each swimming 100 meters). It was easy to win a spot in the 4 x 200 meter relay, and there was a possibility of my swimming a fifth event because normally the sprinter who turns in the best time in the 100-meter finals at the Olympics swims the freestyle leg of the Olympic-medley relay.

As far as I was concerned, I was delighted with two seconds, but other people wondered what had gone wrong. Everybody said, "What's happened to Schollander? Is he going downhill? Is he clutching under pressure?" At the Nationals I'd been high-point winner, and here, four weeks later, I couldn't manage first place in even one event. Everybody was saying, "What the hell is wrong with him?" It didn't bother me because I knew what I was doing—and George knew—but it was kind of surprising the way my stock really went down at those Trials.

7

AFTER OUR TEAM WAS PICKED, we were sent to training camp at Los Altos, California, for four weeks before leaving for Japan. Until this time every man had been training with his own individual coach. Throughout the rest of the world, most teams go into training camp six to ten months ahead of time.

Very few other countries bother to distinguish between professional and amateur athletes. Russia and other Communist bloc nations, we are told, take their best athletes into the army where their year-round assignments are to train at their sports. In France the best athletes have good jobs on paper—jobs at which they do little or no work—in order to permit them to concentrate on training. Even Australia, one of the few countries that still holds a firm line between amateurism and professionalism, sends its Olympic team to camp for a long pre-Olympic training period. (This difference in training-camp policies was a very important factor four years later in 1968 when the Olympics were held in Mexico City at high altitude. By the time our team was selected, other countries had been training teams at altitude for six to ten months.)

In 1964, we were very much interested in the Australian swimmers. Dating back to the first Olympics after World War II, there was a history of rivalry between Australian and American swimmers. In 1948 and 1952, the Americans were on top. Then, at the 1956 Games in Melbourne, the Australians just annihilated the Americans and everyone else. They had new styles, new techniques of training—everything new— and they completely dominated the Olympics. Then the Americans got busy studying the Australian methods: the

Australian crawl, training techniques, psychological aspects, even the food the swimmers ate. Murray Rose, the hero of the 1956 Games, was a vegetarian, so everyone began to study the effects of diet. At the 1960 Games, it was a toss-up as to which team was better.

Australia's pre-Olympic policy is to send a big potential team into training camp, and to keep everything that happens there very secret. They don't give out any of their times. When you plan a race against them, they're an unknown quantity. In 1964, the Australians went into training camp and we didn't hear a word about them for six months. We didn't know what the hell they were doing. But they had all our times from the Nationals and from the Olympic Trials, just one month before the Olympics.

I don't know what those guys from other countries do in camp for eight or nine months. Ours were four dull weeks. All we did was eat, sleep and swim, eat, sleep and swim. No dates—even the girls' Olympic Team wasn't around. They were training in Los Angeles and, according to their letters, having a great time. In our camp, we had training rules, bed checks, everything; they kept telling us that our country was depending on us, the officials were depending on us, and on and on. . . . Usually we were so tired that we didn't even horse around very much. We would watch television or listen to the radio and go to bed. The whole time we were there we went to one movie—"The 1960 Olympics." We were up there at a really nice resort, Ricky's Hyatt House—nice food, nice training camp, great place to go swimming—and getting unbelievably bored with the whole thing.

Then someone came up with the idea of giving us a battery of psychological tests. The results were supposed to help the coaches to help us during the Olympic Games. If the tests showed that a guy was easily depressed, they could work with him one way; if they showed another guy was too easily keyed up, they could handle him another way.

The tests took four hours. We came back one day from morning workout, so tired, really beat, and after lunch all we wanted to do was just fall into bed, and they said, "All right, now you have to take these tests for four hours." All through them you could see guys yawning, just so bored. Steve Clark, the captain of the Yale swimming team, would answer questions for half an hour, and then read a magazine for a while and then go back to the questions. Guys would go out and have an ice-cream sundae and then come back. Or some guy would say, "Look at question forty-three!" And everybody would look and question forty-three would say something like, "Would you rather go to bed with your girl friend or read a good book?" Roy Saari, who was at USC then, just answered every sex question in the affirmative.

Well, the results came back, and out of all the teams that had ever taken this test, we were found to be the most *oversexed* team anywhere. We were the most oversexed, under-cultured, temperamental, and easily bored team ever tested. So from then on we had a reputation to uphold: hell, the most oversexed team . . .

By the end of the month training camp really began to get to people—the boredom, the hard work, the tension of training every day with guys you might be competing against in Tokyo for a gold medal. Whenever I trained for the sprint, I would be in the pool with Gary Illman, and when he had a great day, I would know it. This begins to get you down. People were edgy, irritable. Little squabbles broke out all the time.

One night about ten of us packed into a car after that 1960 Olympics movie. Mike Wall piled in next to me and, just kidding around, I tweaked his ear; he got ticked off and hit me in the face—not hard, but it scratched me. Then I got ticked off and really rapped him on the back of the head, and if we hadn't been so packed in we would have gotten into a real fight over nothing. Toward the end of camp, when we were all on edge, squabbles like this blew up out of nowhere. Until the end of the Olympics, Mike and I didn't talk to each other. And that shows what the Olympic pressure is like, and the effect it could have even on a very close friendship. After the Olympics were over we finally sat down together and straightened the thing out.

At the end of the four weeks we went down to Los Angeles, and it was great just to be able to let off steam, see girls again, go to a party for the Olympic squad.

I remember it was the end of September and everyone had gone back to school. I was going to Yale but not until the second semester because of the Olympics. It was fall—the football season had started—and here we were still swimming. I remember thinking how strange it was—it still seemed like summer to me, just a long summer season.

In Los Angeles the whole Olympic Team was assembled and everyone was given luggage and uniforms. And lectures. We were told that the world would be watching us, that other athletes would be judging us. We were told how to conduct ourselves in Japan. Two people representing the State Department lectured us on handling political questions. If somebody approached us and said he wanted to defect from his country, we were instructed to say, "I can't talk to you about it, but I'll take your name and my manager will give it, in strict confidence, to the proper American authorities," and then we'd forget about it. At the end of an hour and a half lecture, we began to realize that, in addition to athletic competition, there were political and propaganda overtones at the Olympics.

From Los Angeles the Olympic Team was flown to Tokyo in four different planes, with each individual team split up so that if one plane went down, no team would be wiped out.

Until now, the Olympic Committee had taken very good care of us, but there was a lot wrong with that plane ride.

For one thing, it was a night flight and we knew it would be pretty crowded so we probably wouldn't get much sleep, which meant our whole schedule would be upset. It would be morning when we arrived in Tokyo and missing a whole night's sleep could really set us back at a time when we couldn't afford it, physically or psychologically. This thought bothered us even before we left. As it turned out, I was up forty-eight hours straight, and I was wiped out for the next three days. All I could think was that for four weeks we'd been doing everything possible to get ourselves tuned up to this really fine condition, only to have it knocked for a loop— two weeks before the Olympics—by the travel arrangements.

We were the first athletes to board the plane in Los Angeles; the USOC (United States Olympic Committee) officials were already on, sitting in all the good seats—the window or aisle seats—so that we had to crowd in between them. A couple of guys griped about it and said, "What goes on here?" And some official explained, "We had extra seats and these officials are paying their own way." We felt that we could have used that space, especially on a night flight, and that probably a lot of women on board weren't officials but officials' wives.

We would have noticed these officials under any circumstances, but we were particularly aware of them because we'd heard so much about the AAU-NCAA feud. The AAU has jurisdiction over most amateur athletic competition in the United States and has heavy representation on the United States Olympic Committee. The NCAA (National Collegiate Athletic Association) has jurisdiction over all college athletic competition. The feud between the two began when the NCAA accused the AAU of poor organization, of wasting money, and of freeloading—passing out free foreign trips to its officials by sending them abroad with the athletes, letting the officials ride on the athletes' backs. The AAU, in turn, accused the NCAA of trying to pull off a power grab. The feud got very hot and developed into a bitter power struggle. The NCAA announced that any athlete who competed under

DON WITH HIS MOTHER, MARTHA DENT SCHOLLANDER, AND
JOHNNY WEISSMULLER

DON WITH THE SULLIVAN AWARD

AAU jurisdiction would be barred from NCAA competition. This meant that anyone who went to the Olympics would lose his athletic scholarship, if he had one, and probably couldn't go to college. Then the AAU said that anyone who competed under the NCAA couldn't represent the AAU. So if an athlete went to the Olympics under the AAU he would lose his scholarship; if he kept his scholarship and competed under the NCAA, he couldn't go to the Olympics. What a great choice.

By 1963 it looked as though the United States wouldn't have an Olympic team, so Congress started an investigation and the AAU and the NCAA put the feud on the shelf. Between Olympics they take it down and dust it off and get going at each other again.

After the plane took off, I remember a kind of subdued feeling and I thought, "We're on our way. The next time we see Los Angeles, the Games will be over and we'll be winners or losers."

I couldn't sleep on the plane so I spent the whole time talking to people. If I sat next to a wrestler, I'd ask him about wrestling. If I was with a track man, I'd ask him about track. I was really interested in what they had to say about their sports, and I was probably also thinking I might learn something from them. I kept moving around, talking to different people. I figured if you just sat alone you'd start thinking. You could get so fatalistic about something like this and start to say, "I wonder what's going to happen, I wonder what's in the cards"; and I didn't want to do that.

I was eager to get there and to see Japan again; I had been there twice—in 1962 when I was only sixteen, and again in 1963—and I was fond of the Japanese people. And they were good to me. The Japanese like young people—they love children—and I was so young then that when I won they sort of made a favorite of me. I had never lost a race in Japan.

Looking back on it, I guess I felt sort of like a gladiator

going into the arena, wanting to get into the fight and yet nervous about actually going out to face it. I was anxious to get there and to do well, and yet I was scared.

The plane put down in Tokyo and for a second I had that fatalistic feeling in my stomach. Outside it was daylight and hundreds of reporters and photographers and spectators were there to greet us. We pulled ourselves together and straggled down the ramp. I hadn't slept at all and I was one tired guy, coming down that ramp with the rest of the team. Then all of a sudden I heard it, all around me there were Japanese people and they were shouting, "Schollander! Schollander!" They remembered me! The guys laughed and kidded me about it but I felt good. I felt at home.

8

AT EVERY OLYMPICS the athletes live together in the Olympic Village. The purpose of this is not only to assure equal treatment for everyone—the same quality in accommodations and food—but also to promote international harmony. Through living together and through competition in sport, it is hoped that people from different countries and cultures will get to know each other and to understand each other better.

In Tokyo, the Olympic Village was built on the site of an old United States naval base, about six miles from downtown Tokyo. Living quarters for the athletes consisted of a few three- to five-story apartment buildings, and several one- or two-story houses spaced along a winding road. To one side was a large dining-hall complex. Every Olympic Village has eight or ten different kitchens and dining halls to cater to the food habits and requirements of people from different cultures. Off by itself, in one corner, was the women's area with its own gate, its own dining halls, and its own guards. Many countries don't send women's teams. Out of approximately eight thousand athletes, there were about one thousand women. In the center of the site was an international building open to everyone for relaxation and recreation where, it was hoped, athletes would meet and talk and get to know one another. The entire Village was surrounded by a high fence. At the main entrance, on ninety-four flagpoles, flew the flags of the ninety-four participating nations.

The American team was in a four-story building, with the swimming team on the fourth floor. During any important meet you never room with anyone you will be competing against, no matter how close a friend. In the 100-meter free, I would be competing against Gary Illman, a good friend from Santa Clara, and against Mike Austin, from Yale. In the 400, I would be up against Roy Saari and John Nelson. By now Saari was a good friend, but rooming with him was out of the question when we would be competing for a gold medal. As the event drew closer, there would be psyching-out efforts—directed even against people on your own team—and rooming together would make it that much easier. Actually, before an event, competitors avoid each other as much as possible. I roomed with Carl Robie, a butterflyer, and with Dick Roth, who swam the individual medley.

This rivalry between members of the same team has prompted people to ask, "Do you feel in the Olympics that you are swimming for yourself or for your country?" Actually that's a good question. At the Olympics you see the excessive pressure to win that is put on the athletes of many countries— the Russians, for example, although they are not the only ones. Some of these athletes say that the Americans do not suffer this pressure, that we compete for ourselves, and that is the reason we do so well. To a certain extent, this is true. In a race, I viewed all the competitors the same—my teammates or those from other nations. In the 100-meter I expected my toughest competitors to be Gary Illman from the United States and Bobby McGregor from Great Britain, and I wanted to beat one as much as the other. I wanted to win, but I was rooting for Gary to take second. As an American you are certainly aware that you are representing your country, but you also want to win as an individual. After the race, when you're up there on the victory stand, you're happy because it's a victory for your country—not for yourself. It's sort of paradoxical: you swim for yourself, but after you've won, you're happy because it's a victory for your country.

Most of the American teams, especially during the first week we were there, tried to get around and meet people. We felt that athletes from other countries were waiting to see what Americans were like, and we wanted to try to create goodwill. We also wanted to meet people from foreign countries. I'd never met anyone from Russia or from Nigeria, I'd never known an athlete from India. I really went out of my way to meet people and talk to them.

Actually the Olympic ideal of bringing together people of different nations and cultures depends very much on each individual and whether he makes the effort to communicate with other athletes. Some people were so concerned about the Olympics and about their own events that they just sat home and rested. I felt this was bad because you could psyche yourself right out. If you weren't enjoying yourself, you wouldn't be relaxed.

Some teams made it a policy to keep to themselves. The Russians, for instance, seldom went out. In 1952, their first year at the Olympics, the Russians stayed apart in their own separate village. In 1956 they stayed in the Olympic Village, but they were still not allowed to go out and talk to people. In 1960, they were allowed to mingle, but only if they were accompanied by a representative from Russia. Then in 1964 they were free to go out and mix with other people but they chose not to. At least not very much. We rarely saw the Russians around the Village.

But even those of us who did get out and meet people knew that as the Olympics drew closer we were not going to be as friendly to them, especially if we were going to compete against them. The Americans shared a dining hall with the British and the Colombian teams, and I used to go down to talk to Bobby McGregor, who swam the 100 free. Bobby was a tall, sharp guy with dark hair, very friendly, with lots of confidence. Most sprinters are nervous, but McGregor was always very cool. The first week we spent a lot of time together and became good friends. But the week before the 100-meter race, our friendship stopped. We hardly ever saw each other. The morning after the race, we got together again and talked for about three hours.

Japan went all out to prepare for these Olympics. Many countries that host the Olympics will just use existing facilities and probably modernize them. The Japanese constructed all new facilities. They used their best architects and built magnificent modern buildings. The swimming stadium, in marble, was the most perfect and most beautiful stadium I had ever seen. They built new freeways, a new subway system, a monorail. They worked for five years to prepare for these Olympics and spent hundreds of millions of dollars. I don't think they ever regretted any of it. Knowing the Japanese people as I did, I felt that this was a matter of national dignity. They're a very proud people, and I think this was an effort after the war to regain respect in the community of nations. They had made great strides since the war, and they wanted other people to come to Tokyo to see what they had done. I think they felt that being able to host the Olympic Games was the most important thing that had happened to Japan since World War II.

9

THERE WAS A PERIOD of two weeks between our arrival in
Tokyo and the opening ceremony on October 10, and during
the two weeks you could feel the pace and the tension picking
up. Every day new teams arrived, the Village became busier,
reporters showed up from newspapers and magazines from all
over the world. Every day there were more press conferences
and more interviews published in the newspapers. Every day
you could read another expert's opinion on who would win
and who would lose. You could see people beginning to get
edgy.

I decided that for the next few weeks I would work to
keep complete control of everything in my life that it was
possible to control: schedule, health, training, relaxation
and, above all, my emotions.

Of these, by the time you get to the Olympics, training is
probably the least important. But I still tried to train every
day at the same time—the time of the race. I would talk to
George to be sure I was working on the right things. Before
every session we would decide what we wanted to accomplish
that day, and afterward we would ask whether we had accom-
plished it and decide what to work on the next day.

I tried to take care of myself physically: to go to bed at
the same time every night, to get up at the same time every
morning, and to get plenty of sleep. I had been in Tokyo
before so it was easy to resist the urge to see the town. I took
more vitamins than I had ever taken before in my life, just
because they might do me some good and they couldn't do
me any harm. I tried to eat the right food, not for reasons of
health but for fuel. Before a big race, you think of yourself as
an engine; if you're going to go well, you need good fuel.

And yet one of the biggest problems was that the food was so great. The Japanese had hired two hundred of their best chefs and put them into this little Olympic Village, and the chefs loved it. They were used to working in big hotels and they loved cooking in these little kitchens. So many people began to gain weight that the American officials put a scale in the dining room and made us weigh in. I decided to take off a few pounds so that for the race I'd be lighter than my training weight—like taking lead out of a horse's saddle.

I made up my mind not to let anything upset me. The Japanese had provided bicycles to help us get around the Village, but there were never enough. If I couldn't find a bicycle, I would wait or walk. I was careful to take the right bus to training, so that I wouldn't be too late and have to hurry, or too early and have to hang around. If I couldn't get into the pool exactly when I wanted to, I told myself it didn't matter. Whatever happened—that was fine with me. It rained a lot that week; if I got caught in a rainstorm, it was no big thing.

With all the rain, people all around me began to come down with colds. I was taking every precaution—sleep, vitamins, food, wearing towels around my neck, caps on my head—and then, a week before the opening day, I came down with a sore throat. That really almost psyched me out. I thought, Oh, hell! Am I going to be sick for the Olympics? After everything has worked so well, is *this* going to throw me? You're so conscious of everything: food, health, psychological aspects, both psyching-up and psyching-out. As it turned out, the sore throat didn't do me any physical harm, but I almost did psych myself out with it. And for other people it was good psych-out ammunition against me. Everyone kept saying, "How do you feel? I hear you've been sick. *Have* you been sick? Gee, you look lousy. You *are* sick, aren't you?"

Many men on the team didn't see girls at all during the Olympics. They just shut themselves off completely. But I met a girl named Patience Sherman, an alternate on the women's team, and I think she helped me relax. We'd take short trips around Tokyo, sit around and talk, or walk around the park after breakfast, just laughing and relaxing. At a time like this you have to be able to laugh, so I was lucky to have somebody like Patience.

Most of my competitors didn't agree with me and didn't go out at all. We heard that the English girls hadn't been allowed out on dates for ten months. All this pent-up emotion is the reason for the wild orgies that you hear about after the Olympics. If you hear of anyone breaking training *during* the Olympics, chances are it's an alternate, but when the Olympics are over, the athletes who have trained so long and so rigorously just have to break out and blow off steam. And they do.

10

THE OLYMPICS would last for two weeks and most of the swimming events were scheduled for the first week. My first race, the 100-meter freestyle, was on Sunday, October 11, the first day of competition.

This was my schedule:

> (1) 100-meter freestyle
> heats: morning, Sunday, October 11
> semifinals: night, Sunday, October 11
> finals: night, Monday, October 12
> (2) 4 x 100 meter relay
> finals only: night, Wednesday, October 14
> (3) 400-meter freestyle
> heats: morning, Wednesday, October 14
> finals: night, Thursday, October 15

(4) 4 x 200 meter relay
      finals only: night, Sunday, October 18

There was a possibility of a fifth event—the 4 x 100 medley relay—depending on the outcome of the 100-meter free. The American who swam the fastest time in the finals of the sprint usually swam the freestyle leg of the medley relay.

In all the relays, the United States first team swims only the finals. An alternate team swims in the heats. This gives the alternates a chance to swim in the Olympics and it means one less race for the finalists, who are probably swimming several other events. The alternate team is always strong enough to qualify the United States for the finals.

My first race was the 100-meter and I began to concentrate on it totally. In this event I was an underdog. I didn't have the experience that comes with swimming a race hundreds of times, as I had in the 200, for example, so that you know it inside out, and I hadn't shown impressive speed over that short distance. My time in the Nationals had been far off the best on record. When the predictions came out, most experts picked me to finish fifth, or third at best.

And yet, because it was my first event, I felt that this race could make me or break me for the rest of the Games. If I won, I would be "up" for the rest of my events—my confidence would be flying high. If I lost, I would be "down." That sounds temperamental, but I have seen an early race work this way on swimmers. So this 100 free took on much more importance than just another event.

In training camp I had worked mostly on building endurance for the 400. In Tokyo, I concentrated on everything I needed for the sprint—quick starts, quick turns, quick bursts, speed—and I found that I was providing my competitors with psych-out ammunition. They began to work on me: "Do you really think you can swim the 400 and the 100?" "That's a tough combination." "What ever made you decide to try that?" "You're really working to get up speed, aren't you? Do you think you can do it—in a week?"

An enormous amount of psyching-out goes on at the Olympics. You make a conscious effort to stay immune to it, not to let it get to you, and as your event draws closer you go out of your way to stay clear of it altogether. You avoid your competitors, you avoid friends of your competitors, and you eat only with your closest friends—all to keep psyching-out opportunities directed against you at a minimum.

For every race, you plan a strategy; you decide ahead of time how you intend to swim it. Once the race begins, to stick to your plan you must have confidence in it and in yourself. And you must have a very fine sense of pace—that built-in time clock that is indispensable to a champion swimmer. You develop a sense of pace by swimming the laps so many times that at any point you know automatically, without calculating or thinking about it, exactly how fast you are going. For instance, if someone told me to get into the water and swim 400 meters, in sixty-five seconds for the first hundred, sixty-nine seconds for the second hundred, sixty-nine for the third, and sixty-eight for the last hundred, I could get in and do it, give or take two-tenths of a second on each split, and I could think about any damn thing I pleased —the weather, the news, anything—I wouldn't have to count the seconds or strokes. I've done 100-meter splits so many hundreds of thousands of times; I just have to decide how fast I want to swim and I can turn myself on automatically at that speed and think about something else.

Without this sense of pace, you can become an easy victim in the pool to someone else's strategy. You may have planned to start the race very fast and you may be doing everything right—swimming at exactly your planned speed. But then, halfway down the first lap, you see something you didn't expect. You think you are going fast, but someone is way ahead of you. Without that built-in time clock, you can panic. You think, Man, I must be going slower than I thought because he's not a fast starter and he's way ahead. I'd better get going. And you take off after him. You've probably become the victim of his strategy. He's made you swim the race the way he wanted you to swim it—not the way you had planned, the way that is best for you.

If you have a sharp sense of pace, his early, unexpected lead doesn't bother you. You just think, He's going too fast, he's going to die. You ignore him and swim your own race. Without a sense of pace, the cleverest strategy in the world is useless.

All swimmers have a favorite way of swimming a race and most sprinters like to go out very fast—for two reasons. One reason is simple: the 100-meter is a short, fast race, and if you can get an early lead it is not impossible to hold it. The other is that in the sprint it is important, for a technical reason, not to be too far behind at the 50-meter turn. In this one race there is a condition at this wall that does not occur in any other race. If three or four fast swimmers reach this wall and turn at nearly the same time—which is what usually happens—they kick up so much water that they create a strong wash that backs up against the wall. Any swimmer who is even a split second behind turns right into this wash. And swimming against it is like swimming against a rip tide. This wash is peculiar to the sprint. In a longer race the swimmers are not going as fast and, as a rule, are swimming according to different race plans so that they rarely turn at exactly the same time. In the sprint, because of that wash, you can't be too far behind at the turn.

This is in contrast to the way I have always liked to swim a race. I have always felt that there are advantages to holding back for the first part of the race. For one thing, if you're in the lead and you turn your head to see where someone else is, you're not as streamlined—you slow yourself down. Also, it's bad psychologically to see another man gaining on you. But if you go out slow and then move to come from behind, you will probably succeed. You have conserved your energy and they have spent theirs. And momentum is on your side—you are going faster at that point than they are and you are still picking up speed; you are accelerating and they are decelerating. And there is always the psychological effect. When they see you coming up, there is a good chance that they will think, Oh, God, here he comes! and then they will try to speed up and their stroke technique will become less efficient.

A strategy is designed, ordinarily, to outwit one or two major competitors during the race, enough to force them to abandon their own race plans and swim the race your way. But when I considered the men I would be up against in the finals of this Olympic 100-meter event, I realized that I wasn't looking for a strategy to use against just one or two men. I was going to be in there against the seven fastest sprinters in the world, including Gary Illman, who had finished first at the Olympic Trials, Alain Gottvalles of France, who held the world record, Hans Klein of Germany, the first man in the world, after me, to break the two-minute 200-meter barrier—a great swimmer and a really great competitor—Bobby McGregor, the British sprinter, a tough man to beat in any pool, and Mike Austin, the other American, a very experienced sprinter who had just finished Yale. All five of these men had turned in better times regularly than I had ever made in the sprint. For all five the 100-meter was the only individual event they were swimming at the Olympics and it was all they had trained for. All five were much more experienced in the sprint; they knew the race better. And they were older than I was and outwitting them wouldn't be easy.

And yet I felt that the only way I could win was with strategy. Not a strategy designed to throw off one or two men. I was the underdog. I had to think about beating everyone in the pool. I needed a complex strategy tied to a general psyching-out of the whole field.

Among all the probable finalists in the sprint, I was the only last lap swimmer. All races are arbitrarily divided into sections called splits, and times are recorded for each split as well as for the entire race. In the 100-meter, there are two 50-meter splits. I knew that most of the others liked to go out fast and try to hold their lead in the second split. I was the only one who liked to make my move in the second lap, and they would all know this. They would know my split times just as I knew theirs. I tried to put myself in their place and to consider what they would think about me and my probable strategy. Historically, I was a last lap swimmer and they would know that. And, for me, a strong last lap made sense because more than any of them I had endurance. I was a middle-distance and distance swimmer. If I took off on the second split of a 100-meter race, I certainly wouldn't die on the last 5 or 10 meters. I would last. Everything in my record suggested that I would try to win on my last lap.

So I began to talk about my second lap. Whenever someone would ask me how things looked in the 100 free, I would emphasize my second lap. I would say, "Well, I'm a middle-distance swimmer and I may not have much speed, but I have a good last lap." Or, "You know, I'm a come-from-behind swimmer. I've always got my last lap." Even my friends began to talk about my last lap. I wanted everyone in that race to think that if he was going to beat me, he had to do it early—because he would never do it on the second lap.

As the opening day drew closer, I could see other people getting very edgy, practically saying, "Oh, my God, if I don't win . . . !" I made a conscious effort to stay loose. And I did. Certainly I wanted to be mentally up for my race; I wanted to be excited about it, but not so excited that I would be nervous and upset. I concentrated even more on living on schedule—training at the right time, sleeping at the right time, and always protecting myself against psych-out ploys. With only a couple of days to go, I started eating more carbohydrates. Carbohydrates give you fast, quick-burning energy, the kind you need for the sprint. I was peaking very carefully, trying to keep everything under control, building inner tension without peaking too soon, worrying about the event, certainly, but guarding against letting anything touch my confidence.

I never had any trouble sleeping during the Olympics, but I have to admit that those last few nights, when I went to bed, I would say to myself, "You've worked for this a long time. You've done everything right. You're ready. Now think and keep cool and don't blow it. Just get in there and see what you can do."

I I

ON SATURDAY, October 10, a Japanese newspaper ran the headline, "THE GREAT DAY IS HERE," and that afternoon, at Tokyo's National Stadium, the eighteenth Olympiad began, with all the famous tradition and pomp and color of the opening ceremony. On flagpoles rimming the stadium flew the flags of the ninety-four competing nations. In the center above the scoreboard were the Japanese flag, the flag of the city of Tokyo, and then the Olympic flag. On the scoreboard, lights spelled out the words of the Olympic creed, written in 1896 by the father of modern Olympics, Baron Pierre de Coubertin: "The most important thing in the Olympic Games is not to win but to take part, just as the most important thing in life is not the triumph but the struggle."

Thousands of athletes paraded around the stadium, many of them in colorful native costumes. Some delegations, like the American and the Russian, were very large. Some were very small—a flag-bearer and three men from Madagascar; one athlete and one flag-bearer from Liberia; one athlete and one flag-bearer, wearing yellow robes, from the Cameroons.

Then the emperor of Japan declared the Games open.

You can imagine how the Japanese people felt, with the teams from all the nations parading before the emperor in their national costumes, and thousands and thousands of people from all over the world in Tokyo, sitting in the stands. The Japanese people were crying because for so long this had been their dream and finally the day had arrived. The Olympic flag was raised and eight thousand pigeons were released. Then a Japanese University student, who was born near Hiroshima on the day the atom bomb was dropped, carried in the Olympic flame and lit the Olympic fire that would burn for two weeks until the closing ceremonies.

The next morning I swam my first race—the qualifying heats for the 100-meter freestyle. Waiting for my turn, I watched two or three earlier heats and saw that most swimmers were taking out the first 50 meters in 25.1 or 25.2 seconds. I probably could have breezed down easily in 25.4 but I took the first lap in 25.9, and in the 100-meter a half second is a big, big difference. Then I came hauling back fast enough to qualify, closing a big gap in the last lap.

In the semifinals that night, mine was the second or third heat, and one of the other swimmers in the same heat was Alain Gottvalles, the Frenchman who held the world record. Ever since his arrival in Tokyo, Gottvalles had been doing a lot of talking—too much, we felt. He had made derogatory remarks about the American swimmers, calling us machines. He laughed at all our training rules and boasted that he drank a bottle of wine and smoked half a pack of cigarettes every day and still broke world records. This might have been his way of psyching us out, but he was pretty arrogant and I didn't think he was that good even if he did hold the world record. He hadn't ever done much else.

That night the eight of us were sitting on a long bench in a corridor between the locker room and pool, waiting for our heat. This was the first time I had ever been this close to

Gottvalles and I could see that he was nervous about the race. He seemed like a pretty high-strung guy. Actually, I was pretty relaxed because I thought I could make the finals without any trouble. I was standing at one end of the bench, moving around a little to stay loose, talking to another swimmer. Every now and then I would glance at Gottvalles, and I began to get the feeling that I bothered him, so I moved a little closer. Then I saw that this upset him, so I moved closer still, until I was standing right over him. He moved away, farther down the bench, and I began to edge up to him again. Finally he got up and headed for the locker room and went into the bathroom. And I followed him. He stepped up to a urinal and although there was another one free, I stood behind him and waited for him. When he finished he turned and almost ran out of that bathroom. I wouldn't have horsed around like that in the finals but that night I thought it was sort of a cool thing to do. He had talked so much and he was so arrogant, and I wanted to see if it would work.

Now you can put your own value judgments on that, but that's the kind of thing that goes on all the time at the Olympics. In fact that's a mild psych-out ploy, compared to some I've heard about. Psyching-out is part of the game. You've got to be able to take it, and you've got to be able to do it. Training, conditioning, natural ability are not enough —with only those you won't win. In Olympic competition a race is won in the mind.

There is no way you can tell the whole story of how a guy wins at the Olympics—if you are going to be honest—and still make him look like a 100 percent nice guy.

In the semifinals that night, I took out the first lap again in 25.9 seconds—at the turn Gottvalles had a half-body length lead on me—and then I blasted out again and passed him on the last lap.

The list for the finals was shaping up about as we had

expected: Gottvalles from France, Hans Klein from Germany, Bobby McGregor from Great Britain, Illman, Austin, and me from the United States. In his semifinal race, Gary Illman set a new 100-meter Olympic record.

As I came downstairs after my race that night, I heard Bobby McGregor around a corner in the corridor, talking to a reporter. Bobby was saying, "Oh, yes, Schollander has by far the fastest second lap of anyone in the 100 free. But remember that both laps count. It's possible that somebody will get out so far ahead that nobody will catch him."

I stepped around the corner and Bobby knew I had heard him. And I knew that if Bobby was talking about my last lap, the others were probably thinking about it, too.

This sort of thing goes on at the Olympics much more than sports fans would like to think. Competition becomes very cutthroat. People will go to very great lengths to win a gold medal. I know a girl who in 1960 felt that a swimmer from another country deliberately jumped on her during training as she came into a turn. The other swimmer said, "Oh, I'm sorry. I was pushed." Well, it's a pretty frightening thing to be jumped on in the water, and during Olympic competition people just don't go pushing other people into pools, unless there's a reason for it. When something like this happens, especially under the pressure of Olympic competition, it can unnerve you for several days. You associate that wall with the incident, and for days your turns are affected.

In 1960 another girl had a disagreement with a whole group of girls, and she lived in fear that they would try to sabotage her. Apparently they kept the fear alive deliberately—in a fairly vicious way—and it worked. Both of these girls were favored to win gold medals, and neither of them did. Both of these examples, I think, were particularly vicious. A certain amount of psyching-out is part of the will to win, and I would never apologize for a psyching-out technique that was within the bounds of decency. You are not doing anything to your competition that they would not do to you. You are there to win, and you fight to win with everything you've got, including your mental ability. If someone goes beyond the limits of decency in working a psych-out on you, you have to be able to take it. But there are limits beyond which you yourself do not go.

The finals were scheduled for eight o'clock the next night and Mike Austin, Gary Illman, and I were supposed to leave together for the stadium by car at six thirty. We always liked to get there early so that we wouldn't have to hurry before a race. We started down the stairs together at about 6:15. By now the pressure was really on, and we were pretty quiet, just thinking about the race. When we reached the stairs, Mike said he'd forgotten something and went back to his room. Gary and I started down the stairs.

When we reached the second floor I remembered that I'd forgotten my warm-up towel and went back up to get it. As I walked past Mike's room I could see him there, sitting on his bed. When I passed his room again on my way back I didn't see him but I could hear that he was still in there. I didn't stop because I didn't want him to think I'd come looking for him.

Downstairs I waited with Gary in the car and as time passed—at least ten minutes—I could see that this delay was getting to him. I told myself to stay cool. Still Mike didn't show, and I began to wonder what he was doing up there. Maybe he was looking for something. Maybe he was nervous and wanted to be alone for a few minutes to calm down. Or—was this a psych-out?

After about twenty minutes, he showed up. By now Gary was pretty sore and I wasn't so cool myself, but I probably would have been much more upset if I hadn't suspected that it might be a psych-out ploy. To this day I don't know why Austin went back up to his room or what he was doing there for twenty minutes.

* * *

At the pool, Mike and Gary got right into the water, and George came over to ask me how I felt. Before getting into the water, I always like to swing my arms to loosen up, get my blood going and my heart beating faster, so now I started swinging my arms in wide circles, faster and faster, and I shouted, "I feel great, George!" I felt good, but not that good; I was pretty nervous. But I stood there, swinging my arms, making racing car noises: "Rrrmmmmmm! Rrrmmmmmm! I feel terrific, George! Rrrmmmmmm! Rrrmmmmmm!" George stared at me as though I'd flipped and said, "Are you all right?"

"Are you kidding, George?" I said. "I've never felt better in my life. Rrrmmmmmm! Rrrmmmmmm!"

People began to look at me as much as to say, "What goes with this kid?" It wasn't that I was so young that I didn't know what I was doing. I knew what I was doing. I was trying to make Mike and Gary nervous by acting as though I wasn't nervous, and by horsing around I buoyed up my own confidence.

Once we got on the starting blocks, I wasn't horsing around anymore.

The 100-meter freestyle is a short, fast race, and in the Olympic finals the first and the eighth man could finish within one second of each other. Everything has to be perfect—the start, the turn, the end. At the finish, you should be accelerating and you must come in "in phase." Your touch to stop your clock must be part of the downward motion of your final stroke; if you come in "out of phase" so that your hand falls short of the touchplate, then you have to take another stroke and four guys will finish ahead of you. That's how close it is. In the 100 free, there is no time for mistakes.

The best start is the quickest start. When the starter calls, "Swimmers to your marks," you start to come down forward on the balls of your feet very slowly and then, in position, you stop. The starter will not shoot the gun while any swimmer is still in motion. (If you look at a line of swimmers balanced over the water just before the gun goes off you wonder why they don't fall in.) The perfect start is to come down so slowly—moving slower and slower—so that you are the last man to reach this position—only an instant before the gun goes off. The perfect start is one in which you have not actually stopped; in which, although you appear to be perfectly still, there is still the slightest, imperceptible forward motion, if only in your muscles, so that when the gun goes off you still have momentum to be the fastest man off the blocks.

Waiting for the gun, I came down very slowly. I was determined I was going to keep that imperceptible forward motion going and be the first man off the blocks. If I went too soon, then I would just cause a false start. Either way, I'd be ahead. If it was a false start, it would just add to the pressure and I honestly felt that I was in better control of my emotions than the other guys in the race. I wasn't trying intentionally to cause a false start, but if there was one, it would be all right. If I was able to come down so slowly, so accurately timed, that my motion never actually stopped, although it seemed to—if I could get away with this—I'd be off first and that would be great.

I edged forward, slower and slower, just barely moving, just short of stopping, and then just before the gun sounded someone took off. There was a false start, but it wasn't charged against me. Someone else had gone too soon. Maybe he was trying to do the same thing, I don't know, maybe he was just nervous. As a result the pressure piled up, and that was okay with me.

A second time we came down slowly, slowly, into position, just barely moving, and the gun sounded and we were off.

And I just blasted out that first lap. This was my strategy. All week I had worked to convince everyone that I was a dangerous man in the second lap. In the heats and in the semifinals I had held back at the start and shot ahead in the second lap. Now I burned up that first lap, hoping to be right with them at the turn. I hoped that for an instant they would panic and think, What's wrong? Did I go out slower than I thought? If he's right here with me now, what will he do to me in the second lap? After burning up this first lap, there would be no way I could turn in a terrifically fast second lap, but only I could be certain of that. The others couldn't be sure whether I had gone out very fast or whether their own sense of pace was off.

In lane six, Austin was just going wild on that first lap. He went out so fast—he must have figured he would get as big a lead as he could and then try to hold onto it. But you just can't do that, not even in the 100-meter; you have to save something for the second lap. At the turn he was a half-body length ahead of me, but I was certain he couldn't last.

Actually everyone went out fast—Illman, McGregor, Klein, Gottvalles—everybody tore up that pool on the first lap. And at the turn, I was with them. In the heats and semifinals I had gone down in 25.9, now I was down in 25.3.

For me, Illman had seemed like the man I would have to beat, but coming out of the turn, Illman suddenly ran into trouble. As eight men streak down the pool they create big waves in the water that quiet down again after they have passed. But at the wall you turn around and you go right back through these waves before they quiet down. This is not the wash at the wall, this is choppy water—*waves*. After the turn you absolutely must hold your breath for four strokes; you must stay streamlined and keep your head down and knife through those waves. Illman knew this as well as anyone, but for some reason, after two strokes, he turned his head and breathed. I saw this later on films. You can see that he was a little ahead of me and you can see him turn to breathe. And as he turned his head he hit a wave and just bounced—and dropped almost a foot behind me. Just like that. Boom. I don't know whether he had swallowed water or whether he was momentarily upset at seeing me in the next lane right with him. But it threw him for a second and he had to recover, and I pulled further ahead of him.

Going back, on the second lap, because I breathe to the right I could see the field to my right, and I could see that I was ahead of all of them and pulling away. But I couldn't see McGregor, to my left, in lane two. Ten meters away from the wall, I actually had the thought—and I'll never forget it—I'm going to win! I'm going to win! But at that point, although I didn't know it, McGregor was actually ahead of me. With 5 meters to go he was still ahead. He had gone out so fast that, if I had not gone out as fast as I did, there would have been no way I could have caught him. But he had gone out too fast, and during those last 10 meters he was decelerating and I was accelerating. And I just touched him out. I *just* touched him out—by one-tenth of a second.

12

THE STORY OF THE OLYMPICS is the story of people. Besides the victories and the gold and silver and bronze medals, as the days passed you began to hear such great stories about people who, one way or another, showed the real spirit of the Olympics—the will to win in the best sense of the word.

One of them was about my roommate, Dick Roth. Dick was supposed to swim the 400-meter individual medley—a really tough event in which one man swims all four strokes—backstroke, butterfly, breaststroke, and freestyle. Three days before his event he had an attack of appendicitis. He was rushed to the hospital and for a whole day the doctors observed him and then, that night, decided to operate. But Dick refused to let them. As an excuse to get them to delay it, he said that his parents were arriving the next day and he wanted to wait for them.

It was the next day that I won the 100-meter free, and when Dick heard about that he got really excited. Later on, he told me that, at the time, he thought, If Don could win that I'm going to get out of this hospital and swim. I've been the best in my event for two years and I'm going to win. He hadn't gotten any worse overnight and they put off the operation, but just being in bed was hurting him; he wasn't training and he was getting weak. He got out of the hospital the day before his event and he swam in the heats, qualifying only sixth out of eight. He was so weak he just barely made it, and after the heats he was completely exhausted. He spent the whole next day in bed. We were all upset for him because we knew that, after two days in the hospital, his chances of winning were slim. He looked just terrible and we didn't think he would do a thing. Well, he went out and swam one of the greatest races I have ever seen. He won and set a world record and that record lasted for four years. Two weeks after he got back to the United States, he had another attack and this time they operated and took out his appendix.

Al Oerter, who was Olympic discus-throwing champion in 1956 and 1960, was trying to win the gold medal for the third consecutive time. One day during workout, about a week before his event, he collapsed in pain as a chronic cervical disc injury flared up. For a week they treated him, but on the day of the event he was still in agony. They taped him up and did what they could for him and he went out to compete. His first throw was terrible and he just collapsed with pain. After the throw they packed ice on his ribs. When it was time for his second throw, they took off the ice, and he tried again. This guy had been enduring such great pain all day long. It had taken a tremendous effort just to make the finals, and I imagine many people counted him out. But on his second and next-to-last throw, something within this man—call it the will to win—made him get up there and he just bent over and gave it everything he had. And that discus just flew. He won the gold medal and set a new world record.

And there was an African runner in the heats of the 10,000-meter run who had fallen about two laps behind the runner in next-to-last place. A lot of people who fall that far behind will give up and quit. But this guy stayed with it—he just kept running. Everybody was finished and off the track and he kept going to finish his race. Then, during the last lap, the people started to applaud him. They applauded and applauded and when he finished they cheered as though he were the winner of the gold medal. He really caught the fancy of the Japanese people because he had stayed with it, competing for the sake of competition, and this was what the Olympics was supposed to be all about. From then on, for the remainder of the Games, this runner was a hero. He met the emperor, he was on national television. Everyone was so taken with him because he'd showed the true spirit of the Olympics and even then—although these were called the "Dream Olympics" and there was never a word of public criticism—everyone knew that the true spirit of the Olympics was eroding.

And then there was the story of Billy Mills and the 10,000-meter finals. The United States had never won the 10,000-meter race and nobody expected Mills to win—he was practically unknown. But when he came around the turn on the last lap, he was ahead. The fans just went wild. Then Ron Clarke, the famous Australian runner, pulled even with him and they were neck and neck down the back stretch. And then a third runner, from Tunisia, came up behind them. He was so tired that he couldn't go around them so he went between Mills and Clarke and pushed Mills out of step so that he fell back into third place. People were so upset they were screaming, but Mills just picked up his step and started fighting back. He gained on Clarke and passed him. And then coming down the home stretch, he closed the gap on the Tunisian and pulled ahead to win the gold medal.

And in 1964 you heard another kind of story, too, that told you something else about the Olympics.

A Russian girl, Irina Press, was a favorite to win the shot put, and when she lost, she just broke down and cried bitterly. Finally a newspaperman said to her, "Why are you crying like that? We realize you lost, that you're unhappy, but you're in hysterics!"

And she said, "You don't realize how much this will cost me in my job, in my salary, when I get home!"

There was another Russian girl, Elvira Ozolina, who threw the javelin. This girl was just beautiful. Everyone in the Olympic Village noticed her because she had long, blond hair that hung all the way down her back; she was just so beautiful with this magnificent hair. And then she lost her event. The next day she went to a Japanese hairdresser and told her to shave her head. The Japanese girl refused to do it so the Russian girl grabbed the scissors and cut off her own hair—and then the Japanese girl did shave her head. The Russians denied that it happened. I heard the story from some American girls who were in the shop at the time.

The fact is that Russia—and not only Russia—puts enormous pressure on its athletes to win at the Olympics. By various means they support their athletes year round, to permit them to train. They offer them inducements to win—lots of carrots—and they reward them for victories.

This is not simply a question of national pride. The Russian government is acutely aware of the enormous propaganda value of Olympic victories. This is something that other countries understand very clearly, but America does not understand at all. We simply do not realize that the Olympics are so much more important to other people all over the world than they are to us. We Americans are more interested in professional sports, and to us the Olympics are a bunch of amateurs. Americans watch the Olympics on television because they are curious to see what happens and they hope we do well. But if we lose, well, we're just amateurs and it doesn't matter very much. If we lost in basketball, for instance, they would just say, "If we could send in the Boston Celtics, there would be no problem with that gold medal."

Americans do not at all grasp the fact that in other countries the people are as much interested in their Olympic teams as we are in our professional teams. Sports are important to these people, just as important as they are to Americans, and most countries do not distinguish between professional and amateur athletes. Their Olympic teams are their professional athletes. These are their national sports heroes. The Olympics are televised all over the world, and all over the world people watch them the way we watch the world series. This is the source of the propaganda value of the Olympics—an interested, eager, worldwide audience.

Furthermore, it is an audience that can be reached on the level of sports. Many of these people may not understand the subtleties of communism or democracy or the arms race, but they do understand sports. And they understand when someone wins. They don't read about it in the papers or hear it in a political speech. They see it on television—with their own eyes. This is the one area where they can see Russians and Americans actually confronting each other. They watch a Russian and an American boxing each other for a gold medal, or running or swimming against each other in race after race. And they don't just think, Well, the best man wins. They think, The strongest country wins. Russia is always telling emerging nations, for example, that it has a better system, that the United States is soft and corrupt. If the Russians really clobber the Americans in the Olympics the whole world sees it and Russia just says, "You see." The

Russians regard the Olympics as a golden opportunity every four years to show their superiority. To them, the Olympics are a showcase to the world.

13

THE DAY AFTER the 100 free I was on cloud nine because I felt my toughest event was behind me. I felt good about winning and I felt good about the way the Japanese people had cheered me the night before. After my race they had mobbed me as though I were one of them, and someone told me that the Japanese people had sort of adopted me. I had come to Japan when I was fifteen, completely unknown, and I had had my first big victories there and things had gone so well for me ever since. The Japanese people felt that I got my start there and that Japan was lucky for me. They even used my name and address in a school textbook to illustrate how to address letters in English. I think this genuine affection on the part of the Japanese people was very good for me. I have always felt that I swim better when there are people around who care whether I win—someone besides my parents because I know that they care. I think that having Patience at the Olympics helped. And I was always aware that I wanted to win, partly at least, for George. But I think that having hundreds of fans among the Japanese people had an effect on me. It's hard to define, but somehow all those people on your side pulls something extra out of you.

I had a day off the day after the 100-meter, and I took a long time at breakfast and talked to Bobby McGregor. Now that the event was over we were good friends again. I took a walk around Tokyo with Patience, and everywhere we went the Japanese people congratulated me. I felt so good that whole day.

Then the medley relay affair blew up in my face.

The medley relay is a 4 x 100 meter event, 100 meters each of backstroke, butterfly, breaststroke, or freestyle, a different man swimming each stroke. On the American team it has been an unwritten rule that the swimmer who turned in the fastest time in the 100-meter freestyle finals at the Olympics would swim the freestyle leg of the medley relay. An exception to the rule is that if all three American entries do poorly in the 100-meter finals another sprinter might be given a chance by means of a time trial.

Just after we arrived in Japan, the coaches called a meeting of the swimming team and told us how some of the relay teams were to be picked. For the medley relay there would be swim-offs to choose the butterflyer, the breast-stroker, and the backstroker because there were no 100-meter races in those strokes. The freestyle spot would go to which-ever sprinter—Mike Austin, Gary Illman, or myself—turned in the fastest time in the 100-meter free, or to Steve Clark, the Yale swimming captain, if he could lead off the 4 x 100 meter freestyle relay with a faster time than any of us had gone in the 100-free finals.

I had the feeling at this meeting that the coaches didn't believe that any of us—Austin, Illman, or myself—would do much in the sprint. The head swimming coach, Jim Counsil-man, had remarked a few times that the 100-meter freestyle would be the toughest race for us to win, and many people felt that Steve Clark was actually the fastest 100-meter man on the American team. At the Olympic Trials he had only made fourth, but it was a fact that he had bursitis five or six weeks earlier and many people believed that it had hampered him.

My own feeling, which was shared by almost everyone, was that if in the 100-meter finals the best that any of us did was third or fourth, then they would certainly be justified to give Steve a chance at the medley spot, but that if one of the three of us won the 100 free, he should automatically be on the medley relay team.

Even then, two weeks before the sprint, I really thought that I would win it and that they would have to put me on the medley relay team. After I won it and set a new Olympic record I thought the matter would be settled.

The next day I found out that it wasn't settled. They still wanted to give Steve a time trial. I was really stunned. I told George that I felt I'd earned the spot on the medley team. I also said I didn't think it was fair to compare a guy's time in the sprint finals with another guy's time leading off a relay. For many reasons, technical and psychological, you can usually turn in a faster time leading off a relay than you can in an individual event. The pressure is not the same. In an individual event you don't swim for time—you swim to win. In the individual finals there would be stronger swimmers than in the lead-off of the relay (in a relay every team saves its fastest man for the anchor leg), and stronger swimmers create more turbulence and slower conditions in the pool.

I didn't enjoy arguing this way—Steve had been a good friend of mine for a long time—but I really felt I was right. Then suddenly somebody said to me, "You're going to win four gold medals, anyhow. What do you care whether you get one more? What's the difference between four and five?"

I didn't think it should be brought down to that level. I thought it was a question of justice. Certainly in the back of my mind I was aware that this could mean my fifth gold medal. And it wouldn't be just one more gold medal—it would be an *unprecedented* fifth gold medal. No swimmer had ever won four gold medals at an Olympics, but nobody in history—in any sport—had ever won five. But this wasn't my arguing point. I felt that I had earned the spot on the medley relay team.

A lot of controversy developed out of this incident.

Many sportswriters criticized the coaches for denying an American the chance to win five gold medals and pointed out that the Russians would have given anything to have had a five gold-medal winner. People came up to me and suggested that Counsilman, who is head swimming coach at Indiana University, was sore at me for choosing Yale over Indiana. I wasn't sure whether the coaches thought about any of this or not—it was possible. Probably they just felt that Steve was a great sprinter, which he certainly was, and that he deserved at least a chance to swim the medley relay.

My time from the sprint finals was 53.4 seconds. That night Steve led off the 4 x 100 meter finals as planned and turned in a 52.9 and that was that. My time, swimming the anchor leg, was one-tenth of a second slower—fifty-three seconds flat. I was disappointed, even though that relay gave me my second gold medal, but as far as George, Steve, and I were concerned, the incident was closed.

Only the press wasn't ready to drop it. After the relay I went upstairs to the practice pool and took a long time swimming down, just being by myself, swimming. When I finally got out of the pool, George came up to me and said, "You'd better hurry up. Get back to the Village and get some dinner and go to sleep. You've got the finals of the 400 free tomorrow." I told him that I'd promised to see a reporter from *Time* magazine after the relay, but George vetoed that. He told me to forget it and get back to the Village. Then just as I was leaving somebody came to tell me that the reporter was waiting. Well, I'd promised to see the man, so I started over to talk to him, but then I thought, No, George was pretty emphatic about going right home. So I sent the reporter a message that it was late and I had a big race tomorrow and I would see him tomorrow night after the 400 free. I don't know how the message was delivered, but the reporter interpreted it to mean that I was sulking and wasn't talking to anyone and he was pretty ticked off. He found George and I heard from someone standing near them that he said,

"Haines, where is that son-of-a-bitch Schollander?" George was upset, anyway, because he was caught in the middle between Steve and me. And, the way I heard it, he said, "If you say that again, I'll flatten you!" Whatever anyone said or didn't say, the reporter left mad. The next day I found him and explained what happened, but by then he had filed a story. In the next issue *Time* reported the American victories, including mine.

> . . . by week's end, only a tidal wave was going to keep [Schollander] from winning his fourth gold medal . . . in the 800-meter relay. That ought to be enough to satisfy anybody, but when a newsman showed up for his appointment with the No. 1 star of the 1964 Olympics, Schollander refused to talk and closeted himself in a room. Why? He was so disappointed that he was practically in tears. He wanted to win five gold medals—something nobody had ever done in the history of the Games. He probably would have, too, if Teammate Steve Clark hadn't beaten him right out of a spot on the U.S. 400-meter medley relay team. . . .

Even then I knew that you had to expect a few lumps from the press. I had had them before and I would have them again. On the whole I have no complaints—the press has been good to me. But the effect of this story lasted a long time. More than once after I got to Yale, arriving late for my freshman year because of the Olympics, some wise guy asked if I'd had any crying spells lately.

14

IN A WAY I was more nervous before the 400 free than I had been before the 100. In the sprint, I had felt that a lot was at stake because it was my first race, but I was a dark horse and if I lost, it wouldn't be an upset. In the 400, I was the favorite. The pre-Olympic predictions had been split between Roy Saari and me, but then Roy had lost to Dick Roth in the individual medley, which he had been favored to win, and people thought that he would be down. I knew that a competitor like Roy Saari wouldn't give up that easily. He might not be riding high, but he would be mad and out to make up that loss. In my planning, Saari was still my competition.

In the 400, strategy can be more complex because it's a longer race. It's never easy to force an experienced competitor to swim your race, and the longer the race, the harder it is to control it. Even if momentarily you throw a competitor off, he has time to recover.

In planning a race your strategy can range from doing the unexpected at some critical point in the race to swimming the whole race in an unpredictable way. For example, when I began to swim, the accepted strategy for the 200 free was to swim the first 100 meters very fast and the last 100 meters a little slower. After I held the world record, because I was expected to care about "times," people expected me to go out fast, so for a while I began to "jam the pace." I would take it easy at the start and other people would see that they were right with me and think they were going very fast. Then, on the second split, when I suddenly blasted ahead they thought they must be dragging, getting tired.

Then when I figured they were catching on to that strategy, I switched and began to blast out at the beginning. You have to keep changing your strategy so that people will never be quite sure about what you're doing. And you have to guard against letting someone else's strategy affect your race. If a competitor is way ahead of you, you can't let yourself think, I'll never catch him at this speed, I'd better get going. You must trust your sense of pace and have confidence in your race plan and stick to it.

Nobody knew all this better than Roy Saari, who was a master strategist with a superb sense of pace. I could remember a 500-yard race, in April, 1963, when Saari burned me badly with strategy. Saari likes to go out fast, taper off in the middle, and then close fast. Normally I like to go out slow and finish fast. In that race I went out at my usual pace and Roy took it out a little faster than I had expected and had a good lead on me after the first 100-meter split. Then he slowed way down, really jamming the pace. When I pulled even with him I told myself that I wanted to save something for a strong finish and that if I'd caught him here I had probably been going too fast. So I slowed down a little, and he slowed down a little more—and I slowed down still more. By this time we were both way off the pace. Roy knew what he was doing, but I had let myself get confused. Then he confused me even more. As a rule you start to go all out in the last 100 yards of a 500-yard race, but Roy came blasting out of the turn with 150 yards still to go. When I saw him take off, I thought, Have I miscounted? Are we just 100 yards away? I'd better get going. In the split second it took me to think that, he opened up a body-length lead. He knew what he was doing every minute, but I had let him confuse me— and he won.

Later that same year—1963—in Japan, I was able to throw Roy with strategy during a 400-meter freestyle, and what happened then influenced my strategy at the Olympics. At that time you still had to touch the wall with your hands at the turns, so nobody ever used the flip turn; they touched and then pushed off with their hands. The flip turn—pushing off with your feet—gives you more thrust but it also takes more energy. There was a gain, but not enough—as long as you had to touch first with your hand—to be worth the energy you spent. Nobody flipped turns, except possibly the last turn in the race, when you had only 50 meters to go and getting a big jump at the wall could make the difference. Well, in that 1963 race, Roy and I swam the first length neck and neck, but at the wall, I flipped the first turn—something that had never been done—and I got a body-length lead on him. It threw him for an instant—he couldn't believe that I had actually flipped the first turn—and then he had to really work to catch me over the second length. He did catch me, but he had worked too hard to do it, and I had the advantage for the rest of the race.

Now, coming up to the Olympic 400 free, I felt Roy and I were so closely matched that whoever won would do it on strategy. I thought about how Roy would try to swim the race, and I decided that he would take it out fast and try to force me to go along with him. Also I figured that he would expect me to flip the first turn, so he would flip it, too. And, I decided, he might even flip the second turn. This was something that had never been done before. You can't spend the energy flipping all the turns unless everyone else is spending it, too, but Roy had endurance and I thought he might try it. I thought he would take the second lap fast, flip the turn, and try for a psychological advantage right there by coming out of that second turn with a very big lead on me. I decided to flip both the first and the second turns.

The night of the race, we went down the first length together and we both flipped the first turn. Coming back toward the 100-meter wall, Roy was to my left. He breathes to his left, so he couldn't see me, and I breathe to the right so I couldn't see him. But I could see that I had a full body length on the three guys to my right. So I knew that Roy and I were both taking this race out fast. I still thought that this was probably the most important length in the race—Roy's strategy would be to try to win it here—coming out of this second turn. I considered the possibility that he might really take off on this length to get a big lead and then increase it still more with a flip turn, so that by the time I got to see him again he would be way ahead of me. My strategy was just to be with him—not behind him—coming out of this turn. I wondered whether I should speed it up a little. I was tempted to step it up, but I wanted to save as much as I could for the last 100 meters. I finally decided, since I had at least a body-length lead on everybody I could see, that Roy and I had both been going quite fast and that he probably had not stepped it up enough to pull ahead of me.

I reached the wall and flipped the second turn. As soon as I could breathe—I'll never forget it—I saw that I was a body length ahead of the men in lane 4 and lane 3. And there in lane 2—taking his first breath at exactly the same instant that I breathed—was Saari. We looked each other right in the eye. He had flipped his second turn and still we were neck and neck. He had no lead, and in that instant I felt I would win.

On the second 100-meter split I didn't move any further ahead of the other guys in the pool, but I noticed that I was pulling out a little on Roy and I wondered what he was doing. On the third split, going down, I saw that I had almost half a body length on him and now I thought I could risk slowing down a little. If he was trying to jam it, that was all right; it was possible that we had gone out too fast. Coming back on the split, I took just one breath to the left; I saw that I was still ahead of Roy, but the rest of the field was passing him and beginning to catch me. That meant Roy was tired. At the 300-meter wall, the guys on either side of me—Allan Wood from Australia and Frank Wiegand from Germany—turned with me. Over the last 100 meters they had made up a body length on me and now, whereas I had been coasting just to stay ahead of Roy, suddenly I had to worry about these guys. I hadn't even been thinking about them, and they had caught up with me. I thought psychologically they were probably flying because they were gaining—that really charges you up—and I had been taking it easy.

Murray Rose was broadcasting the race for television, and at that 300-meter mark, he said, "No world record is going to be set in this event. Schollander will have to come back in 1:02 to do it, and no one has ever done the last 100 that fast."

But because my second and third splits had been so slow, and because these guys shook me up, I came back in something like 1:01.4, so I did break the world record. But that just happened. The most important thing is winning the race, and the purpose of strategy, always, is to win, not to break the record.

My final race was the 4 x 200 freestyle relay, on Sunday, October 18, the beginning of the second week of the Olympics. The 4 x 200 is usually the last race in a swimming meet, a kind of grand finale. Supposedly this event is an indication of a swimming team's overall strength because it requires four good 200 men, and 200 meters is an interesting and difficult length that calls for both speed and endurance—plus a good sense of pace.

Altogether the American team had taken fifteen gold medals in swimming, and we wanted to finish a great meet with a victory in this final event—the big relay. But in this 4 x 200 we were faced with a serious threat from the German team. The Germans had decided to really concentrate on this race and they had scratched their best 200-meter men from every event for three days preceding it. They were training at special hours, off somewhere in special pools. Hans Klein, the German anchor man, was a very good friend of mine and for two weeks before, I had seen him regularly around the Olympic Village. For five days before the relay, I didn't see him once.

We knew about the Germans' intense concentration on this race and it did have a psychological effect on us. Then they began to work on us through the press—to try to psych us out. They gave out comments such as, "The German team is rested and the American team is tired. In this relay the

THE FIRST GOLD MEDAL

DON WITH HIS FOUR GOLD MEDALS

WINNERS OF THE 400-METER FREE STYLE—TOKYO, 1964

Americans are under great pressure to win in order to maintain their country's impressive record. The German team is the underdog, but we've been training hard for this relay and we are going to win it." I read that Hans Klein had said that in the anchor leg, if he could just go off with me, or even a little behind me, he would beat me. Hans was a good friend and still is, but before this event he was more concerned with his race and with his country's prestige. The papers pointed out that Klein was a strong 200-meter man and that he was rested, while I was probably pretty tired. This effort to psych-out a whole team through the press was unusual. And it got to us a little. It smacked of confidence. And a lot of what they said was true.

When we took a good hard look at ourselves we were a little worried. Steve Clark, our lead-off man, was primarily a sprinter, although he had won his place on this team easily enough. Gary Illman, who would swim second, had lost his big race—the 100 free—and although he had won a gold medal in the 4 x 100 relay, he was having trouble getting psyched-up. Our number three man was Roy Saari, who just had not been able to get going at all. Obviously there was something wrong with Saari that week—he had not yet taken a gold medal—and by now he was really depressed. And I was the anchor man, and I was tired and beginning to be harassed by publicity.

The coaches were concerned about the entire team, but their biggest doubts were about Saari and they were seriously considering replacing him. They were thinking of putting someone in there who was not down and who had not already been in three events. When I heard about this I was really upset, and I told George that I thought it would be very unfair not to let Saari swim this last race. Even though Roy and I had been competitors for years we were good friends, and when I heard that they were thinking about replacing him, I went to talk to him. When I asked Roy if he thought he could handle his split, he said that he felt that he could, but he knew about their doubts and he seemed almost apathetic.

I decided that Saari really deserved to be on that team. Damnit—here was a guy who had worked so hard for so many years—he should have won at least three gold medals, and if we took him off that team he wasn't going to win any. I felt he had earned a place on the 4 x 200 team even more than I felt I had earned my place on the medley relay team, and I knew how I felt when I was bumped. I don't feel this way about every swimmer just because he has a few records in the book. I've known guys who looked good on paper that I never thought were good competitors. But Roy Saari was a great competitor. Regardless of his performance this past week, he was still one of the two or three best swimmers in the world, and I just didn't see how they could take away his place in this relay.

So I went to bat for him. I said, "You guys took me off the medley relay and I thought I'd really earned a spot on that team, but that's done now. You could have argued forever about whether Steve or I was actually a better 100-meter man. But there's nobody you can put on this team who would be better than Roy Saari." We talked about it for a while and finally the coaches left the decision to the rest of the team and the three of us got together. Steve and Gary certainly weren't against Roy, and when I felt so strongly that Roy should swim, it was okay with them.

And it worked out all right. It was our last race and we made it. Clark led off and gave us a small lead and Illman increased it a little. I watched Saari go out third, and then I glanced over at Hans Klein getting ready for his anchor leg. I could see that Hans was charged up for this race much more than I was. I had been peaking for seven or eight days now, and I had been swimming a lot of races and I was tired. I hoped Saari would come through and he did. We had a body-length lead by the time I took off. I knew I didn't have to go wild. If I did the anchor leg in just under two minutes, Hans wouldn't be able to catch me. But then I thought that this was the last 200 meters I would swim in these Olympics, and I didn't want Hans to outsplit me. I didn't want to lose even part of the lead the other guys had picked up. It was a matter of pride. I figured I could give it everything I had just one more time.

That was the first time that I had thought about a race in just that way. I had won so much—now I had so much to lose. At that moment—just before I went off on that last leg— I knew swimming had changed for me. I understood something that would be true for many years to come: I would be swimming, not only to win, but *not to lose,* and that people would be swimming not only to win, but to beat Schollander.

I went down and back that 200-meter leg in 1:55.6, two seconds faster than my own world record. The American swimming team won its sixteenth Olympic gold medal and I became the first swimmer in history—and only the second athlete—to win four gold medals in one Olympics.

part two

Who Owns a Champion?

DON WITH HIS PARENTS BEING INTERVIEWED BY NEWSPAPER
AND TELEVISION REPORTERS IN A VIP ROOM ON HIS ARRIVAL
FROM TOKYO

A PARADE IN LAKE OSWEGO, OREGON

15

From the San Francisco *Examiner*, Friday, October 23, 1964, by Curley Grieve, *Examiner* Sports Editor:

SCHOLLANDER IS HERO OF GAMES TO JAPANESE

Tokyo—As far as the Japanese are concerned, Don Schollander is the indisputable hero of the Olympic Games. Whether it's his almost white hair or his four gold medals or his Adonic looks, he has caught the fancy of this tight little island. . . .

J. Lyman Bingham, executive director of the Olympic Committee . . . said to me: "I want to show you the most unusual thing I have ever experienced since being in this business for 35 years." He took me to a room and unlocked the door. On one side were at least 500 packages. On the floor were three large baskets filled with letters and telegrams. "With few exceptions, these are all for Schollander," he said. "This is the greatest expression of goodwill for an individual I have ever seen in my life. . . . He is so young, strong, handsome and appealing Japan has just decided he is something of a god in a land where worship is complex religion. . . ."

At poolside Don was constantly surrounded and he could barely move when he left the Olympic Village because he was so easily recognized and his autograph was so eagerly sought. And pictures—thousands of them were shot. Even to touch him was considered as a rare privilege. . . .

Personally, in my life I have never seen anything like it and I have been around a few heroes including Jack Dempsey and Babe Ruth. . . .

When I climbed out of the pool that night I was surrounded by a mob of people—reporters, photographers, friends. Someone hung the four gold medals around my neck. The reporters fired questions at me and the photographers pushed me out onto a diving board so they could get pictures. For two hours I couldn't get out of that stadium. I couldn't move. And all I wanted to do, now that my last race was over, was get out and blow off some steam. After holding on for so long to such tight control I just wanted to cut loose. After two hours I finally broke away. For the whole swimming team this was the last race; training and competition were over and we went out and made a night of it.

It was about 4:30 when I climbed into bed. At 7:30 some photographers from *Life* banged on my door. I opened one eye. My roommates were nowhere around; I didn't know whether they had come and gone or hadn't come in yet. *Life* wanted more pictures.

"Come on back later," I mumbled.

"No," they said, "We want to get a picture up on the roof and now the sun is right. Come on. We've got your medals."

I pulled on my sweats and at 7:30 in the morning, up on the roof, they shot that picture that appeared on the cover of *Life*. They had me looking out into the sun, and I was so beat I just couldn't keep my eyes open. Finally I said, "Look, tell me when you're going to shoot the picture and then I'll open my eyes." Well, if you remember that picture, I'm looking out over the camera into the morning sun—supposedly the model of the all-American boy, blue eyes, blond hair, determined look. The only determination I had that morning was to keep my eyes open long enough for them to take a picture and to go back to bed.

For the rest of the Olympics, wherever I went in Japan I was mobbed. Some of us went to Osaka to give a swimming exhibition and at the railroad station there were about five hundred screaming kids waiting for me. When I got back to Tokyo there was that whole room piled up with gifts and letters. I took the letters home and sent the gifts to a Japanese orphanage.

On Sunday, October 25, the eighteenth Olympiad came to a close. It was a wonderful thing to see all the athletes mingling together on the field for the last time and for me, I think, it had a special meaning. I couldn't help thinking about all that had happened in the few weeks since we had arrived in Tokyo. Now I had been voted the outstanding athlete of the Olympics. And my own country had chosen me to carry the flag in the closing ceremonies at the head of our team. I was deeply moved. I feel that was the highest honor I have ever received in sport.

I went home and found that four gold medals had changed my life.

I wasn't due at Yale until the second semester in February, and I had intended to go home after the Olympics by way of Asia and Europe and take a month to travel around. But now things had changed and my mother and father thought that I should come straight home. They told me I had a responsibility to the American people whose contributions supported our Olympic Team. "You will be severely criticized if you just disappear," they said. "You have an obligation now. When you were a boy, older athletes like Johnny Weissmuller and Murray Rose inspired and encouraged you; now it's your turn to do this for other young people. Whether you like it or not, you're a public figure now and you have to come home."

I must have known that there would be some fuss when I came back to the States, but even now, looking back, I find no way I could have been prepared for the months that followed. As soon as I got off the plane the onslaught began.

I went to Los Angeles first with some friends, and suddenly I was bombarded with invitations to attend banquets, make speeches, give interviews, appear on television programs. The Pacific-AAU district nominated me as their candidate for the Sullivan award, the nation's highest honor awarded each year to an amateur athlete. I flew up to San Francisco to attend their banquet for Olympic champions and flew right back to Los Angeles for a television appearance with some other Olympic athletes on the Hollywood Palace. After that an agent offered me a screen test. I had walked on and shaken hands with someone, thereby showing great talent.

On November 1 I went home to Oregon. This was something I had looked forward to for such a long time. Since the day I left for Santa Clara—January 21, 1962—I hadn't been home for more than a few days at a time. It was always just a visit and each time I had wished it could have been just a little longer—it was always so quiet and peaceful in Oregon. Now, after all the pressure of the Olympics, after traveling halfway across the world and back, after all the sudden publicity, more than anything else that was what I wanted—peace and quiet—just to be with my family and my friends and myself, to have time to think and relax.

At the Portland Airport there were hundreds of people and a brass band to meet me when I arrived—the mayor of Lake Oswego, local and national reporters, photographers, television cameras. Lake Oswego had made it Don Schollander Day with a big parade and a reception afterward. They let the kids out of school at noon. That night there was to be a welcome home dinner and I was to sit next to Governor Hatfield. At the city limits, a new sign read, "Entering Lake Oswego—Home of Don Schollander."

You can't imagine what this meant to an eighteen-year-old—to be welcomed like this by my own town. After this

huge parade, at the reception I tried to make a speech and I couldn't. I was so touched by this warm welcome, I didn't know what to say.

After the reception I was dropped off at my house. My parents were tied up in traffic somewhere and the house was locked, so I went next door. The neighbors invited me in and fixed tea and suddenly I had such a good feeling. I sat there, thinking, This is great—just sitting here, drinking tea and talking to old friends. This is really a return to a normal life.

Peace and quiet and a normal life, it turned out, were very far away. The next day I went to a sportswriters' luncheon and, the day after that, to a theatre that was playing a movie about me, made at Santa Clara before the Olympics. I winced every time I heard the title: "The Boy Who Swims Like a Fish."

I remember the weeks that followed as a blur of ceaseless activity. There seemed to be no pause and no end to it. The telephone never stopped ringing. I spoke at luncheons and dinners. Organizations kept voting me awards, and I had to go and make a speech to accept them. I was never home.

I supervised swimming practices and held swimming clinics at high schools and YMCA's. Every day the mail brought hundreds of letters to be answered. I liked working with high-school kids and talking to them—at least that seemed worthwhile. As for the rest of it, I was eating lunch and dinner with different people in a different ballroom in a different city every day, when all I wanted to do was stay home and eat with my own family and my own friends. I wished I had time just once to take a walk by myself in the woods.

I began to feel as though I were living in a goldfish bowl. Wherever I went, people pointed me out. Kids came up to me on the street to ask for my autograph. They came to my house and rang the bell to ask for a picture or an autograph. At parties people watched to see if I would take a drink. Even my old friends watched me. Just sitting around with them I could sense that they were on guard, as though saying, "Let's wait and see what he's like now; let's see if all this has changed him." I could understand how they felt but it bothered me. And I knew I had to take the initiative to show them that things were still the same and that I cared about what *they* were doing—not just about what *I* was doing and had done. I began to wonder what I was in for at Yale where I would have to make new friendships, not just reestablish old ones. I began to realize that when you become a public figure in your own eyes you may be the same as any other guy, but in other peoples' eyes you're not the same—not until you prove that you're okay.

The thing came to a head at a party over Thanksgiving weekend with all my old friends—the people I'd known almost my entire life. By now I was making such an effort to be just one of the crowd that every time I felt someone's eyes on me, I'd polish off a drink to show that I was okay. The next morning I was a pretty hung-over guy and I decided that was the last time I was going to try to prove that particular point that way. If I was a public figure, I would have to live with it. The important thing was to be my own man.

I accepted all those invitations from adult organizations because I truly felt an obligation to the American people who supported our Olympic Team. I talked to the kids because I wanted to. I felt they should be encouraged to excel, as I had been encouraged by older champions. I felt they should know that to be the best takes a lot of will and sacrifice and hard work, but that it could be done—and that no one was doing it any other way.

If I hadn't felt these obligations, I could have turned down most of the invitations. I could have eliminated at least half of them by asking for a fee—a hundred or two hundred dollars. But I was an amateur, and in the United States, amateurs are not allowed to receive money for any activity remotely connected with their sport. As an amateur I couldn't take money for swimming, certainly, but I couldn't take money even for talking about swimming or for discussing any experiences or information or opinions that derived from my swimming, such as the experience of competing in the Olympics or the different attitudes of other governments toward the Olympics or their propaganda value which I thought the American people were ignoring. As long as I was an amateur swimmer I couldn't be a professional speaker.

Did I consider turning professional? Not really, although inevitably the subject came up. I was deluged with requests for permission to use my name or my picture to endorse products or to support organizations in health campaigns. A film company wanted to do a documentary on me, and "The Boy Who Swims Like a Fish" was playing all over the country. People began to tell me I could make a million dollars. At eighteen! In the end several companies and organizations did use both my name and my picture. I endorsed anti-drinking and anti-smoking campaigns and the products of a dairy company and a health-foods company. A nationwide insurance company used my name and picture in an advertisement urging parents to plan for the future so that their children would have the chance to be Olympic champions.

All these people had to get permission to use my name from the AAU or the USOC, and usually there was a contribution—for the AAU or the USOC. So one of these groups was richer. And the company was richer because its contribution was not nearly as large as the fee it would have had to pay a professional, and the public saw my name endorsing a product. I signed releases. Why not? I couldn't ask for the money anyway and it was harmless.

The fact is that many amateurs do make money and get

away with it—but not the ones at the top. The AAU keeps a sharp eye on them. In the years that followed I found out more than once that the AAU assumed that I was cheating and went to great lengths to check up on me. After the Olympics, the people of Lake Oswego raised money for a gift to me and gave me $1,000 as a gesture of recognition, in much the same spirit as the gifts I had received from the Japanese people. When the AAU heard about it they ordered me to return the money at once. My father explained that that was impossible; it had come from hundreds of people. In that case, the AAU said that I should donate it to the AAU! My father fought back on that issue and finally they agreed that it could be put into a trust for me to draw on for graduate school, after I'd retired from swimming.

More than once I have thought that the AAU considers this its only mission in life—to preserve amateurism in its pure, unadulterated state. During the next four years, as I was exposed to the contradictions of an unrealistic situation, I more and more began to question the whole structure and the obsolete rules of amateur sports.

Aside from the opportunity to make a great deal of money, probably the best reason for turning professional in 1964 would have been the simple fact that experience had shown that a swimmer can only expect to stay at the top for about two years. Very few people last longer than two years in swimming. And I had been at the top for almost two years then.

But I didn't want to turn professional. I wanted to swim for Yale, and I wouldn't be able to do that if I turned professional. And I was only eighteen. I didn't want to be over the hill at eighteen. I knew that if I decided to remain an amateur I had to last for four more years because swimming attracts national interest only in an Olympic year. I considered that a challenge and I thought I could do it.

Some of those invitations after the Olympics were very exciting. On December 1, together with other Olympic gold medalists, I had lunch at the White House with President Johnson.

A few days later I flew to Chicago to be guest of honor at the Eagle Boy Scout dinner, where I met Jesse Owens, the only other four gold medalist.

Then, one day early in December the AAU called to say that I had been invited, along with Gary Illman, to visit France. We were to put on a few exhibitions, swim in a few races, and have a chance to see the country. It sounded great. And—more interesting to me than to Gary—Phil Moriarty, the Yale varsity swimming coach, would make the trip with us as the AAU representative.

On December 15 I left for Paris.

16

FOREIGN TRAVEL is one of the few material awards available to amateur champions. The AAU works overtime to be sure that no money changes hands, but athletes are permitted to travel to any foreign country that invites them and pays their expenses. This can become a mixed blessing because when an athlete travels he doesn't train regularly and many athletes find that, once they are famous enough to travel, they start losing the fame because of the traveling. The invitation to visit a foreign country can come from the government, a sports organization, or even a private company, but it must be extended through the AAU, which makes all the arrangements, and it must include an AAU coach. An AAU rule states that a coach must accompany every athlete who travels abroad for any purpose related to his sport. This rule, according to the AAU, is to protect the athlete from foreign exploitation. In my career I received very little protection against exploitation from anyone and more than once I sus-

pected that the coach was there less to protect me than to
protect the AAU's first commandment—the amateur shall
accept no money.

Our visit to France was sponsored by a branch of the
French swimming federation and by a Marseilles newspaper.
On the morning of December 15, Phil Moriarty, Gary, and I
took off from Kennedy Airport. At Orly Field, where our
hosts met us, I immediately gave the French press some
cannon fodder. I had forgotten my passport! We had to spend
the night at the air terminal hotel and wait for my passport
to arrive on a plane the next morning. The French press
picked up the story and ran a big headline: "Schollander Est
Arrivé Sans Veste—et Sans Passeport!"

The schedule called for us to go first to Marseilles, where
we would spend several days, and then return to Paris. Our
party consisted of six or seven people—Gary, Phil, and I, and
a few sportswriters. In Marseilles another man joined us—a
sharp little guy with a moustache who just seemed to be
along for the ride. Gary and I called him "Dirty Pierre,"
because he was always offering us "really nice girls—you know
what I mean?" I have no idea what Dirty Pierre does but I
ran into him again in 1968 in Mexico, again traveling with
athletes.

Also, to my amazement, there was a bodyguard named
Ambrosio. Our French hosts, it turned out, had insured me
for $200,000! Later I found out that in at least one other
country I had a bodyguard without knowing it. Much later,
three years after it happened, I learned purely by chance in a
New York bar that I had been guarded in Germany. I was
having a drink with a sportswriter, and at the next table
there was a guy who was having himself a big night. Then all
at once this guy noticed me, sat up straight, and then came
over to our table and said, "You're Don Schollander."

I tried to ignore him because I'd had my troubles with
wise guys in bars before. But now suddenly this man was

completely sober. "I know you," he said, "I was your body-guard in Germany in 1965." He knew so many details of that trip that he absolutely convinced me that he was telling the truth. It shook me up a little to learn that someone had tailed me so closely for four days and I had been totally unaware of it. I wondered how many other times that had happened that I didn't know about either. I've never found out.

The misunderstandings that developed during this trip to France were a cold plunge into the problems an athlete can run into traveling abroad at the expense of the host country.

In this case, although the AAU had handled the arrangements, no one had told us anything specific about our swimming schedule, so as soon as we arrived we asked about it. We were especially interested in how much we would be expected to compete because neither Gary nor I had trained at all since the Olympics. We were told that in Marseilles there was to be a big exhibition on the nineteenth and in it we would be asked to enter one individual event and one relay. That seemed fair enough. I asked whether we would be competing against Gottvalles, and they said no, he was not entered in this exhibition. This was strange since the usual practice is for the best swimmers of the host nation to compete against foreign guests. I figured that since both Gary and I had finished ahead of him in Tokyo, maybe Gottvalles wasn't ready to take us on again—and I let it go at that.

But as soon as Gottvalles' name came up, the French reporters rushed to defend him. In Tokyo, they said, the Americans had had the advantage of three men in the race while Gottvalles had been in there alone, the only Frenchman. At first I argued with them. I tried to explain that in the Olympics it was one man against the other seven, regardless of nationality, but they insisted that there was less pressure if you had two of your own countrymen with you in the pool. There was no logic to their argument except, I suppose, that if the athlete himself believed that, it could affect his performance. Anyway, I was their guest so I dropped the subject.

At Christmas Marseilles is a big holiday spot and for two days we toured the city in a busy, festive atmosphere. After dark we did the town with Dirty Pierre. In Marseilles our hosts told us that on the day after the exhibition—the twentieth—there would be a big swimming race in the harbor. Would we like to enter it? We said no, we had never raced in cold water, or, for that matter, in a harbor.

The exhibition on the nineteenth began at around eight o'clock in the evening and just before the meet, Gottvalles turned up—but not to swim. He was there as a commentator for national television.

And in his broadcast he just roasted Gary and me. We swam in a 100-meter freestyle race against five or six French swimmers, and it just happened that Gary led for the first 90 meters and at the end I touched him out to win. Gottvalles explained (as we heard it later) that this was our usual strategy—prearranged. Gary set the pace, going out fast, and then I came along to win. We had used this strategy in Tokyo, he said, and obviously to make it work required two Americans in the pool. Alone, as he had been, I couldn't have won. Apparently his attack was so brutal that some of our French friends who had spent a few days with us resented it, and after the meet they broke a well-kept secret. They told us that we were scheduled to swim against Gottvalles the next day in the harbor race. This "Coup de Noël" harbor race, they said, was the real reason why we had been invited to France.

Gary and I hit the ceiling. We had been asked a second time about this harbor swim and again we had said no, we hadn't changed our minds, we weren't interested. Until now we had thought that it was just some little local race. Now suddenly it was important enough for Gottvalles. We tried immediately to straighten this out with our hosts. We explained that we didn't know how to swim a harbor race; we had competed only in pools. In a harbor race there were no turns, no marked distances you need for pacing. You just jumped off a boat and swam to shore. And we had no experience swimming in such cold water. We said that we felt that we should not do it. We hadn't been invited to France for this kind of swimming.

"Oh, come on," they said, "be good sports and do it."

"Well," we said, "we'd like to be good sports, but we really don't know what we'd be getting into and we don't think we should do this."

Then they said, "It's already been announced in the newspapers! Everybody will expect to see you. This harbor swim is one of the big events of the holiday season. After all, it's not so much—we're only asking you to swim 180 meters."

They really had us. They had paid our way over here, put us up in a beautiful hotel near the water, entertained us for three days, and now they were only asking us to swim one more race—less than 200 meters. How could we refuse? Already Gary and I could see the headlines about the ugly, ungrateful Americans. And as American athletes in a foreign country, we felt a responsibility to think about goodwill. We gave in and agreed to swim.

When we got to the harbor the next morning, there was a huge water show in progress—water skiing, hydroplane races, scull and crew races. It was a cold, foggy, drizzly day but already, someone told us, there were one hundred thousand people there. Back from the waterfront, as far as you could see, were colored tents and trailers, and the harbor itself was crowded with boats—sailboats, motorboats, speedboats, yachts—everywhere except in the stretch of water left clear for the races. For the first time, I realized that this was a very big deal.

The starting point for the race was a launch anchored in

the harbor, and there was a speedboat waiting to take us out to it. As we headed out into the harbor, I saw that the water was filthy—grass, seaweed, garbage floating around, rainbow-colored streaks of gasoline. With the fog blanketing it down, the stench was sickening. The thought of swimming in that muck really turned us off.

After a minute I reached over the side of the boat to feel the water. And I promptly forgot about the filth. That water was about fifty-five degrees Fahrenheit! Man, it was cold! Just swimming in that icy water could be dangerous when you weren't conditioned to it. Racing in it could be very dangerous.

As we approached the starting launch I could see six or seven swimmers already aboard. And there, off to one side, jumping up and down to warm up, dressed in his sweats and looking very confident, was Gottvalles. In that instant, when I saw Gottvalles, I caught on. Suddenly I realized that this was a setup. Gottvalles had probably been getting ready for this race ever since the Olympics, training, working out, conditioning himself to the ice-cold water. And what had I been doing for two months? Signing autographs and making speeches. I looked at Gottvalles jumping around on that launch, just waiting—just ready to eat me alive and I saw how stupid I'd been. A setup, and I had walked right into it. All these years I had been living competition, thinking about competition, and I had made it to the top. And now that I was there I had stopped thinking about it. I was busy with success and I had gone soft—not so much in the body as in the head. I had allowed myself to be set up.

I had about two minutes to figure out how to swim this race. As protection against the cold they had offered us wet suits—full-length rubber suits—but wet suits cut your speed and no one else was using them. The others had been conditioning themselves to the cold water. Gary and I turned down the suits but decided to use the headgear.

Cold water tightens your muscles and accelerates your heartbeat. I knew the thing to do was to start slowly in order to adjust to the cold before going all out, but I didn't know how long that would take and this race was only 180 meters long. Then I realized that there would be another problem if I started slowly. There were more than a dozen swimmers in this race, and the harbor wasn't roped off into lanes. This was just a free swim to shore. If you held back you could get boxed in and then if you tried to cut through you could get your teeth kicked in. But if you went too hard at the start, you could get paralyzing cramps when you were still a hundred yards from shore.

As we lined up at the starting point along the side of the launch, I looked at the boats crowded with people on either side of the narrow course and at the television cameras focused on that strip of water, and I thought that not only was Gottvalles going to beat me, but all of France and half of Europe would see him do it. At the starting line it was pretty crowded; there were other swimmers bunched together around me and around Gary, too, at the other end of the boat. I thought again how easy it would be to get boxed in. Then I saw that Gottvalles wasn't crowded! He was standing off a little, with plenty of space, alone in the bow of the boat where he could get off in the clear—clobber us—and prove what a difference it makes to have your own countrymen in the race. I looked at Gary, hemmed in at his end of the boat, and then at the guys crowding around me. And I got mad.

The starter ordered us into position and I climbed up on the side of the boat along with everyone else. Then, suddenly, I jumped back down and ran toward the bow of the boat. Somebody yelled at me, but I kept running. The starter sent them off and I was still running. I jumped in nearly a second behind the rest of the field but now there was only one man between Gottvalles and me.

I hit the water and the cold shot through me like a knife. I could feel my heart speeding up and the muscles tightening in my stomach. To my right I saw that Gottvalles wasn't taking it out very fast. I breathed once to the left and saw that Gary was getting boxed in by the French swimmers. When I breathed to the right again I saw that the one man between Gottvalles and me wasn't swimming straight toward shore but was angling over a little toward me. It looked as though I had a cutoff man.

Now I had to make a decision. To clear the cutoff man before he got in my way I would have to go hard right away. But if I went out too soon, cramps were inevitable. With luck they would be in my legs and I would still be able to pull to shore. If the cramps hit my stomach someone would have to come out in a boat and pull me from the water. So I could go all out now or I could hold back—forget it and let Gottvalles beat me—and at least be able to walk away from the race.

What do you care? I asked myself. If it means so damn much to them—if they want to beat you so badly—why fight it? This race isn't that big a thing. Let him have his day. What do you care? But, damnit, I did care! I was young and foolish enough not to want to lose. I had beaten Gottvalles once under normal conditions. I could do it again. The day would come. But I told myself that I could beat him right here in this harbor and I was going to do it. I wasn't going to be anyone's patsy.

I picked it up very fast to clear the in-between man and then I looked for Gottvalles to decide whether I should ease off. Then I realized that it didn't matter now; I'd gone so hard that if I was going to get cramps I would get them, and I decided that the best thing I could do was finish the race as quickly as possible and get out of that water.

No matter how many times you have felt the pain, you forget how bad it is until it hits. I could feel it starting in my stomach and reaching into my legs, and I was afraid that the cramps would come before I reached the beach. I kept going hard. My one thought was that the harder I went, the sooner it would be ended, and then suddenly my fingers touched the concrete landing and it was over. I groped to my feet and staggered out of the water. This is something you never do—get right out of the water; you must let your heartbeat return to normal while you're still buoyed up by the water. But I was so cold and the pain was so overwhelming that I couldn't lie still. I had to get out of that water.

A second later Gary struggled onto the landing beside me. He had made the same decision—to swim it fast and get it over with. We had finished first and second—with Gottvalles third.

Someone threw a blanket over me and two men worked at the cramps in my legs. Then suddenly Gary doubled over and collapsed as cramps hit his legs and his stomach. The officials sent for a doctor.

At Marseilles I began to ask serious questions about the AAU. Clearly this was one of the biggest swimming events in Europe and somebody at the AAU should have known about it. Somebody should have told us well ahead of time and given us a chance to turn down the whole trip if that was the price. How many other American athletes—kids who didn't know better—have been patsies in foreign countries, traveling under AAU auspices and supposedly under AAU protection? The athlete himself has no opportunity even to try to clarify the arrangements ahead of time. The AAU insists that all arrangements be made through its office. But then, as soon as the athlete leaves the United States, the AAU makes no effort to maintain any control over what happens to him. It does ask for an itinerary, but it seldom gets the whole story before the athlete leaves home and goes to another country where he is at the mercy of the people who have organized and paid for his trip.

The AAU should assert itself, politely but firmly. It should establish clearly the terms and conditions of the trip, and it should make clear that if the terms of the agreement are not respected other American athletes will not accept invitations from that country in the future. The AAU people justify this weakness on grounds that they believe in being good guests. When you're in somebody else's house for dinner, they say, you don't complain about the food. And I agree with that. But if you're in someone else's house and they want to play sick games—what then?

In Paris we ran into another kind of problem that can plague an athlete when he is a guest in a foreign country—the lack of communication in matters not pertaining to the sport. Often these are quite trivial and derive from cultural differences, but many times these misunderstandings mushroom into something out of all proportion to the incident.

At lunch one day in a Paris restaurant we were offered wine. The AAU suggests firmly to American athletes on tour that they do not drink alcoholic beverages, so we felt that we couldn't accept the wine. We didn't make a big thing of it. We just said, "No, thanks." We assumed they knew it was against AAU policy. The episode was trivial; it took less time than it takes to tell about it. But the press picked it up and ran a story poking fun at these uncultured Americans—eighteen or twenty years old—drinking milk. There was actually a cartoon of Gary and me, sketched as babies with milk bottles, but it didn't seem to be directed against us personally. It was more an attack on the uncultured Americans.

And still it didn't end there. The Associated Press syndicated the story to the United States with a different slant. Here was an eighteen-year-old who had this sudden fame and didn't know how to handle himself. The *Yale Daily News* ran the story on the sports page. The AAU didn't bother to explain to anyone that we were only following their firm suggestion. I think that since the AAU establishes the rules it should make very clear to the host country its policies and regulations under which American athletes must travel.

Before we left, the press had a final romp. We were invited to the European film premiere of "My Fair Lady," and to a dinner party before it. When we asked about what to wear, we were told to wear dark trousers and our Olympic blazers—to what turned out to be a very formal affair. The next day a French newspaper printed that we had not worn dinner jackets because our necks were too big to be fitted to formal wear. We felt like the return of the Neanderthal man!

But there were good things about the trip. We met some nice people and we saw Paris and other parts of France. I was burned a few times and I learned a lot. Maybe I was lucky. I learned to ask questions myself and to be sure I understood the answers and that mine were understood. I learned to get things straight ahead of time. Later, there were other trips that were much worse and I was armed with this experience that I had gained in France. I was never again caught so offguard—so taken by surprise that I remained silent. I spoke up. I argued. I said no. Next time around I wouldn't have done that harbor swim.

While I was in Marseilles, UPI voted me their Top Athlete of the Year award.

17

FROM THE BOSTON *Globe:*

SCHOLLANDER GOING TO YALE
—by Bud Collins

Tokyo, Oct. 23, 1964—The name on the door at Welsh 98 is Schollander, and the tenant will be checking in as a late starter in Yale's Class of 1968.

There may be a few people there to meet him, such as Yale's swimming coach Phil Moriarty. Moriarty probably has been sitting outside that door for a week to be the first in line to shake Don Schollander's flipper.

"Nothing unusual about this," Moriarty will say, his eyes gleaming like a pilgrim's at Mecca. "Just the ordinary welcome I arrange for every incoming freshman to make him feel at home." Then Moriarty will give the signal for the Yale band gathered in the passageway to strike up "Bowwow dogfish—Eli Yale!" And, after that, from within the room will come the voices of the Whiffenpoofs—standing on a table from down at Mory's—with "We are poor little porpoises who have lost our way. . . ."

A bulldog will stand erect on hind feet and lick Schollander's cheek, and Moriarty will say, "This is Handsome Dan, Don. He's yours for four years. This little cart here is for him to pull you back and forth between here and the pool. . . ."

Schollander shouldn't mean any more to (Moriarty) than the A-bomb does to the Chinese. Schollander is four first places every time he goes into the tank—unless he breaks a fin somewhere along the way—and the only reason he can't win more is that four is the intercollegiate limit. . . .

When I read that article I groaned and thought, Oh, great! It said just about everything about the way I hoped things would not be at Yale.

After France I stayed home for about a week—still without a day to myself. On January 2, a movie company came to shoot pictures for a film about the Olympics. On January 3 I spent the day with a reporter from *Sport* magazine who was doing a feature about me for the March issue. On January 4 I took off again, this time to Germany to receive an award from the Association of International Sports Correspondents—

sportswriters from sixty countries—who had voted me the World's Best Sportsman for 1964. I flew into New York a day early and made a one-day side trip to Yale to begin to get organized.

I wanted Yale to be the beginning of something new, not just another stage in my swimming career. People were saying that Yale had accepted me only because of my swimming but that wasn't true. The acceptance came in April, 1964—before the Olympics and before the Nationals. There were no gold medals then shining up from my application.

I had heard so much about athletes who reached the top so young and then had nowhere to go. Many athletes are finished young, and then so many just hang on, living in the past. It's bad enough when this happens to a baseball or football player at thirty-five, but if I let it happen to me, I would be a "has-been"—over the hill—at twenty-two, if not sooner. I didn't intend to spend the next forty years—or the next four years—reliving the glory of two weeks in Tokyo.

On the trip from Kennedy Airport to New Haven that cold winter evening, I sat in the back seat of the airport limousine and thought about all this—that I wanted college to be the beginning of something new, that I was coming to Yale as a student, not as a swimmer, and that I hoped other people would see it that way, too.

In New Haven the car pulled to a stop at the Taft Hotel and another student and I climbed out and got our luggage. He was coming in from Ireland and it turned out that we lived in the same freshman house—Welsh. For him it was a place; for me it was only an address. As we walked down the block toward the campus, there was about an inch of snow on the ground.

"You're as late getting back as I am," he said.

"Yeah," I said. For some crazy reason it meant so much that he didn't recognize me.

"What number Welsh?" he said.

"Ninety-eight."

"Oh, the last entryway, then," he said.

So that was where I was. I nodded. "How about you?"

"One twenty-one."

I took a shot at it. "First entryway?"

"Middle," he said. "Funny how we can live in the same building for four months and never see each other."

We walked through Phelp's Gate and turned in front of Welsh Hall. "Here's where I get off," he said, at his entryway. "So long."

His name was Brian McKinney and to him I was just another guy getting back late from vacation. I felt great. A year later, in Ireland again for Christmas vacation, Brian McKinney died of pneumonia. I've always wished I'd told him how much it meant to me that night to be just another guy getting back late.

I walked up a flight of stairs, knocked on the door of room ninety-eight, and met my roommate. A tall guy with dark hair, thin face, strong jaw, a swimmer's broad shoulders. Barry Wemple. He had been a swimmer at Williston Academy Prep School and was on the Yale freshman team.

"Yeah, come on in," Wemple said and walked back to his desk. Then he pointed to a pile of boxes in a corner of the room. "There's your mail. I've been saving it for you."

The room was nearly empty—just Wemple's desk and chair, a couch, a beachcomber's chair and a small table. Through an open door I saw a very small bedroom with only one bed. I looked around a minute and asked Wemple if there was someplace I could get a bed.

"Oh, yeah. I had the janitor haul it away last September. I figured it would only be in the way. I'd have had it brought back but I didn't know you were coming so soon." Tonight, Wemple said, I could sleep on the couch.

"Okay," I said. "Then how do I get the bed back?"

"You can catch the janitor tomorrow."

I wanted my roommate to treat me like any other guy. I

had hoped he wouldn't make a big thing of my Olympic success—and Barry Wemple sure wasn't making much of it.

The next day I got the bed into the room and took off for Germany. Actually Barry Wemple was a hell of a nice guy, and we were good friends for our whole four years at Yale. But when you first meet him he's very cold; he doesn't knock himself out being friendly.

The five days I spent in Germany were the most relaxed I had known since the Olympics. I went alone. I wasn't going to swim so I didn't need a coach. Hans Klein, an old and good friend, met my plane, and we were able to spend a lot of time together.

The World's Best Sportsman, 1964 award was presented to me at a dinner in Baden-Baden for European sportswriters. I felt pretty good about it because they stressed that it was for good sportsmanship as well as athletic excellence.

The German people were warm and friendly and asked absolutely nothing in return. There was no pressure—no racing. During the few days that I toured parts of Germany with Hans, nobody imposed on me. But it was on this trip to Germany that I first realized that this frantic pace at which I'd been living was catching up with me. In Baden-Baden, Hans and I went to the famous health spa for a treatment. Afterward, when I was relaxed, I suddenly realized how tired I had been lately and I was shocked. This was the first time in my life that I had ever actually had the thought that I was physically tired.

(AP) Jan. 13, 1965—Today Schollander, an 18-year-old Yale freshman, won the big one—the Athlete of the Year award in the annual Associated Press year-end poll. . . .

Schollander rolled up a huge margin in the AP voting, with 138 first-place votes and 459 points on a 3-1-1 basis. In all, 250 sportswriters and broadcasters cast their ballots.

Johnny Unitas, the great quarterback of the Baltimore Colts and the Most Valuable Player in the National Football League, was the runner-up. Unitas got 14 first-place votes and 134 points.

(Listed among previous winners of the award: Sandy Koufax, Maury Wills, Roger Maris, Rafer Johnson, Ted Williams, Mickey Mantle, Willie Mays and, two decades earlier, Joe DiMaggio.)

That first year at Yale was tough. Any hopes I'd had of being accepted as just another student, like anyone else, quickly vanished. This is something that most people starting out at college never think about. Why would they? What does it mean, after all, at college to be accepted like everyone else? It means being an unknown quantity. It means meeting people and wondering who they are and where they come from and what they are like—and going through a process of exploration to find out.

At Yale there were about eight thousand guys—every race, religion, nationality, every ethnic and economic background, every philosophy—and any one could meet any other one of the eight thousand and wonder what he was like, where he was going, and what he was all about. Except me.

I soon found out that I was the one man on campus who was different. Everybody knew me. They knew where I came from and what I did and they were pretty sure they knew all there was to know about me. Probably every guy on that campus still expected to prove himself in his chosen field. My field was settled. I had been there. I had nowhere else to go. I had a label: swimmer.

I had hoped to go unnoticed. Within a few days I began to feel like a campus monument. Everywhere I went people stared at me. Guys would point me out to each other or to their dates. I would look away and try not to be self-conscious about it, but when I looked back they would still be staring.

When I passed a group of people, before I was out of earshot, I would hear the whispers. Sometimes I would only make out my name, sometimes a few cynical remarks, like "I wonder if he's had any crying spells lately." In the co-op I overheard, "Schollander is no different from you and me. He gets up in the morning, brushes his teeth, eats his breakfast, and then goes to the swimming pool for the day."

In the Commons—the freshman dining hall—people would stare at me while I ate. I would sit there, usually alone because I hadn't had time to make friends yet, and I would be painfully aware that four or five guys at a nearby table were obviously discussing me. Not knowing anybody is hard enough, but when people have read about you in *Time, Sports Illustrated, The New York Times,* the *Yale Daily News,* and have seen your picture on the cover of *Life,* and when you're sitting there all alone with no one to talk to while they stare at you, it can be pretty miserable. Especially when you're a freshman at college and starting late and only eighteen.

Almost from the start I began to get hate letters, wishing me a short, unhappy stay at Yale. Little kids telephoned me and I would talk to them for a minute, but some of them kept calling me for four years. High-school girls called and offered to come over to see me—offered openly their services in bed. Homosexuals telephoned me. They would breathe over the phone about my nice body and then ask me to come over for a drink. That really shook me. After a while I realized that half of them were serious and the other half were playing sick jokes.

On top of everything else, the movie "The Boy Who Swims Like a Fish" was a co-feature at a downtown theatre.

> *Schollander didn't imagine that he was a "campus monument." Long before he arrived, he was a legend at Yale. We had all read the* Time *article. We had seen his picture on the cover of* Life *and he looked too straight, too all-American. Again and again we had read about him in the* Yale Daily News.

Part of the problem, once he arrived, was that he showed. If he had had brown hair, his life would have been easier. But with his famous blond hair and all-American good looks you couldn't miss him—and nobody did.

There were people who wanted to see how they stacked up against an Olympic champion—not in swimming, but in everything else. When grades were posted guys would check their own grades and then look to see what Schollander had done and you would hear, "Schollander pulled an 85. Not bad—for a jock." If he was alone on the campus on a Saturday night, you would hear, "The great Schollander hasn't got a date."

Actually it was only a minority that made him feel so conspicuous. The majority of the guys were ready to accept him for whatever he turned out to be. Some said, "You've got to admire the guy for what he's done. I feel sorry for him, walking into this place being who he is." Others even said, "He's probably a hell of an interesting guy."

But for four years, as long as he was at Yale, he was the most famous college student on the East Coast. Little kids called him until the day we graduated. I remember one—Mike—who called him at least once a week during the last two years when we shared a phone. And you don't really believe the stories about the homosexuals and the sick jokes until you've taken one of those calls. The hate letters that I saw were on Yale stationery.

Even as a junior and senior, when things should have cooled down, he was still conspicuous. In Poughkeepsie, on one of our trips to Vassar, a Princeton student who was drunk wanted to fight him just because he wanted to beat up Schollander. In April, 1968—senior year—while we were playing touch football on the Cross Campus, I heard a passing student say, "There's Schollander playing football. I hope he breaks his leg."

"*Hey, Don,*" I said, "*Some kid hopes you break your leg.*"

He just grinned. "Is that what he said?"

By then he hardly noticed. He had risen above it. But as a freshman—eighteen, alone, a world figure with no friends, no manager, no protection—he was watched and harassed and he felt it.

D.S.

18

MY BIGGEST PROBLEM was time. Even before classes began, the rat race started again. I returned from Germany on January 13, spent one night in New Haven, and took off again the next day for a pair of engagements in Ohio—a Touchdown Club dinner in Columbus and a National Swimming Institute dinner in Cleveland. Back in New Haven, I actually had a few free days to begin to find my way around Yale. The other guys were all taking exams, which only reminded me that I was still an outsider, starting college one semester late. But on January 21 I went to New York to tape "To Tell the Truth." Then I returned to New Haven, and three days later went back to New York—as guest of honor at the B'nai B'rith sportsmen's dinner. Then back to New Haven.

On February 1, classes began and I found myself taking sophomore courses. Most freshman courses were full year courses that couldn't be started in the second semester. The dean advised me to take five sophomore courses and make up my freshman requirements the following year, a decision that left me less than overjoyed because I'd already figured I'd be in for some academic troubles, coming in new this way in the second semester.

In my first small discussion class—most courses were large lecture courses—the professor helped these fears along. First he had trouble getting my name straight; then he wanted to know what I was doing there; then he needled me a while for not knowing some work that had been covered during the first semester; and finally he told me that he really didn't think I could keep up with a sophomore class.

A week after classes began, I was traveling again. On February 8, I went back to Oregon for "Don Schollander Day," which involved addressing a joint session of the state legislature and attending a reception afterward.

I came back to Yale on February 9, and five days later, on February 14, I went to Milwaukee to formally receive the Associated Press Top Male Athlete of the Year award.

A week later, on February 21, at the New York Athletic Club, I received another honor—the AAU Sullivan Award, which is given each year to "the amateur athlete who, by performance, example and good influence, did the most to advance the cause of good sportsmanship during the year." For this award not only sportswriters and sportscasters cast ballots, but also amateur sportsmen, including Olympic athletes.

On February 27, I was back in Oregon, this time to open the State Easter Seals campaign, of which I was honorary chairman. Back to Yale on the first of March.

On March 11, I was named winner of the first annual ABC–*Sports Illustrated* Grand Award of Sports. I was selected over such competition as pro-football star Jimmy Brown, all-American basketball star Bill Bradley, and Notre Dame football quarterback John Huarte.

With every passing week, time was becoming a more serious problem. I had a scholarship job in the Yale news bureau, where I spent two hours, five afternoons a week, writing to hometown newspapers about their local students at Yale. Then, every day at five o'clock I had swimming practice. I was managing to study about four or five hours a day, whereas other freshmen were averaging seven or eight hours.

When I did have a few hours to study I was constantly interrupted—not only by those nut calls from kids, girls, and sick jokesters, but by what seemed to be the entire working press of the East Coast. Yale officials had asked me—as part of their "town-gown" goodwill effort—to give special consideration to the local press and to speak at local high schools if I was invited to do so. And I did. But it was much more than the local press. It seemed as though, when I got to Yale, every magazine and newspaper that had been too far away to call me in Oregon decided to reach me in New Haven.

I was falling far behind in my studies. Anyone else with my schedule would have depended on weekends to catch up, but I was never there on weekends. I would be off somewhere getting an award.

Many of these awards—the UPI award, the AP award, the Sullivan award, and the ABC–*Sports Illustrated* Grand Award of Sports—were great honors, and anybody would have been proud to receive them. And I was, too. But with some of the others, I really had a conflict. It seemed that people from organizations all over the East were calling to tell me that I'd been voted an award and asking me to set a date when I could come and get it and make a speech. I couldn't find any way to get out of it. I wasn't mature enough. I needed an agent or somebody to handle these requests. If I said I couldn't come, they'd ask why not. And what could I say— that I had to study?

So I'd go. I'd get back Sunday night and stay up late to study, go to four classes Monday morning and then collect the pile of mail that arrived in my box every day. I'd spend nearly an hour trying to separate the important letters or letters from friends from the fan letters and the hate letters. I began to consider a fan letter an imposition because I had to give two minutes that I couldn't spare to answering it. The evenings were mine, except for Wednesday, when there was usually a swimming meet, and weekends when I was usually away. Evenings I studied, trying to accomplish in three hours what most guys were doing in eight. By eleven most of the guys would start to hack around, and I wanted to hack around, too, and try to make some friends, which I wasn't doing because I had to study. Then it would be Friday and I'd be off again on the banquet circuit.

I had heard of universities providing a secretary to a student celebrity who was deluged with fan mail and speaking invitations. But at Yale this was not the policy. I think, even more than a secretary, I would have been grateful if Yale had given me some protection against the harassment, some excuse to refuse these invitations—because I had started late or because I was on a scholarship—anything, just as long as someone in the administration would back me up if anyone checked.

I didn't have many dates my freshman year. On the few weekends I stayed in New Haven I used to walk across the campus around midnight after the library closed. I would see all the guys walking with girls or hear the music coming from some party. I used to look forward to the weekends I could spend at Yale but then I would get so depressed. I realized that I wasn't having any fun at college.

Invitations began to arrive from almost every country in Europe, asking me to visit during the summer. Ordinarily I would have been thrilled, but as they piled up, along with the American invitations, the summer just began to look like an extension of the nightmare.

At a dinner in Chicago I asked a professional football player if he went to very many of these things.

"I do the banquet circuit about five months every year," he said.

"How do you stand it?" I asked.

He just stared at me, then grinned, "money."

Barry used to ask me why I accepted all those invitations and I honestly didn't know. In a way I still felt an obligation. What could I say to these people, "No, I don't want your award . . . ?" I knew how much it meant to them and I couldn't say it.

Every time I went to one of these banquets I met a couple of company presidents who had come to listen to me, and I used to think that there was something pretty mixed-up about that. I thought I should be listening to *them*. During those months on the banquet circuit I was offered dozens of jobs that would be waiting for me when I finished Yale, if only I said the word. I would listen to these men and thank them and I would think there was something faintly insane about all this. I had hardly started at Yale. I didn't know anything yet. At that point I was worried about whether I could even survive the first semester of my freshman year.

19

If I was a marked and pressured man on campus it was worse in the pool. I was swimming regularly on the Yale freshman team and I kept telling myself that I ought to get into condition, but I never had the time. I would turn up at a meet and swim my events—almost mechanically. I never thought about the race in advance. I always had too much work; I was always running; I was always tired.

My attitude toward swimming was changing, a fact that hit home suddenly at a minor meet with a prep school—Williston. I'd been so busy I hadn't thought much about the race ahead of time, but when I got to the pool that Saturday afternoon, I saw that the stadium was jammed. The reason

for the excitement was one very good swimmer on the Williston team, Jim Edwards, who had just missed making the
Olympics in the 100-meter. Suddenly it hit me: first, I was
terribly out of condition, and, also, I might actually *lose* to a
prep-school swimmer in front of a packed stadium. Yale
would win the meet by thirty or forty points anyway; the
team victory was not at stake. Nothing was at stake—except
my pride and my record. For the first time I swam for no
other reason, no other goal, except *not to lose.*

Before the race I did everything I could to psyche that
guy out; I put on a great show of confidence. Swimming the
race I gave it everything I had. And I just barely touched him
out. I won on my reputation, really, and I knew it. Edwards
was afraid to pull too far ahead of me too early in the race.

That night, alone, I walked around the old campus for a
long time and thought about how my life had changed and
how I had changed. For years—all those years, as far back as I
could remember—I swam to win. Because I loved to win. And
I had always believed that was one of the reasons I won—because I swam to win. Now I was swimming only *not to lose.*

The Harvard meet was scheduled for March 13 in Cam-
bridge. For at least a month before it I'd heard about Bill
Shrout, a Harvard freshman who had gone undefeated all
season. And I'd heard, too, that Harvard fans were just waiting to see what he could do against me. Bill Shrout at
Harvard was Jim Edwards at Williston all over again—only
worse. And I was worse. I still hadn't had time to get into
condition. I was away every weekend in February, and I was
falling even farther behind in my work. And more and more
I was aware of the long line of guys, psyched-up and in peak
condition, just waiting to knock me off. Shrout at Harvard
was next in line for his turn at bat.

Some time before the day of the meet I had to turn out
two papers that were due the following Monday and study

for a one hour test scheduled for that same Monday. I was really pushing the work and couldn't even think about psyching myself up for a race. At one point during the week before that meet I was suddenly so overwhelmed by the work load and so frustrated by my own fatigue that I didn't see how I could swim at all. I really felt I was going to lose. Five months earlier I'd been a champion—on top of the world. Now I felt I couldn't cope any longer with the pressures and confusion that championship had brought.

Then one night, unexpectedly, George telephoned me. I started to tell him about my swimming, but once I began to talk I poured out everything. I told him about the academic pressure at Yale, the pressure of being on display, the pressure of the public demands that made it impossible to get into any kind of shape. I told George I was in terrible condition, something I had never known before. I told him I was worried about the change in me—I was swimming only not to lose. I said I felt I was going to be beaten in the Harvard meet, not so much by a better swimmer but by everything else—by my own success and the consequences of it.

George listened while all the confusion that had been building up in me for weeks came rushing out. Then he talked—quietly and firmly. He told me that my performance this year depended not so much on my training this year as on my training last year. Last year, he said, I was probably the best-conditioned swimmer in the world and last year's training would pull me through. Anything built up so carefully over such a long period of time, he said, would only break down very slowly.

Then, very seriously, he warned me that I'd better get back to Santa Clara and strict training that summer. He knew from experience that if a swimmer went a whole winter without serious training and then took off the summer, too, he would fall too far behind in the sport ever to catch up again. I made up my mind that I would go to Europe for just two weeks—to Germany, Switzerland, and Belgium where I was already committed—and then get back to Santa Clara.

The stadium at Harvard was packed with a noisy, excited crowd. A kind of fever had built up about this meeting between Shrout and me. The Boston sportswriters had played up the freshman meet over the varsity meet. A television station was covering the freshman meet only. The public loves an underdog, and there was real excitement in the prospect that undefeated Bill Shrout might knock me down. For me, I had changed public roles quickly and the new one of a Goliath whom people were waiting to see get it right between the eyes was not a very happy one. And yet I knew it was true. Ninety percent of that crowd wanted to see me get killed.

All winter I had been swimming mostly the 100 and the 200. Shrout had been swimming the 200 and the 500. Now Jim Barton, the Yale freshman coach, asked me to go up to Shrout's distances for the Harvard meet and swim the 200 and the 500. I agreed to do it. What else could I do? The reason for all the excitement—the only reason the meet was being televised—was that I was supposed to be meeting Shrout. Again I had the feeling of being swept along by public demands against which there was no protection and little I could do.

The whole meet turned out to be a hideous mix-up. The usual practice at these meets is not to submit names in advance but to announce the contestants in each race just before it begins. When the 200 was announced, I was in it and Shrout was not. I thought maybe he was avoiding me in the 200, which has always been considered my best race, to go after me in the 500. He probably knew that I wasn't in any kind of shape for an endurance race. I could sense the disappointment in the crowd so I tried to swim a good race—to give them something. I set a new NCAA freshman record for the 200, but actually it wasn't much of a record and I didn't have to go all out to do it.

Next came the 50-yard freestyle. Shrout was in that. I was not. I hadn't swum a 50-yard race in years. The crowd grumbled, there was talk that I was avoiding Shrout. Shrout swam his 50-yard race and he won. Then came some diving events and some other swimming events.

Then the 100 free. Again Shrout was in it and I was not. To me it was clear what had happened. The Harvard coach had figured I would swim the 100 and Shrout had dropped down to my event; Jim Barton had asked me to go up to the 200 and the 500, even though I hadn't done them all year, because they were Shrout's usual events. The crowd understood none of this. They only knew that once again I was not going to meet Shrout and they started to boo me. At first there were a few scattered boos and hisses and then more and more people picked it up. For a few minutes the race was delayed because of all the commotion in the stadium. Then, at last, the crowd calmed down and Shrout won the 100 free easily and got a roaring ovation.

I felt badly about the mix-up, so when the 500 free came up I tried first to make it a close, exciting race—to pull the other swimmers with me. When I saw I couldn't give them a close race, I tried to swim as beautifully as I could. Nobody was interested. Finally I decided to swim as fast as I could. I really knocked myself out and I broke another NCAA record and received some polite applause, mostly from the Yale people in the crowd.

When I pulled myself out of the pool after the 500, I noticed a slight twitching in my arms. This had never happened to me before. I had been tired after races, but never so tired that the muscles in my limbs started to give out. It wasn't a serious twitching, but it betrayed more than normal fatigue, even after a long race. For a minute I was puzzled. I looked at the twitching and thought, That's strange, and then I forgot about it.

The final event of the meet, just two events after the 500, was the 4 x 100 freestyle relay. Even in top condition I wouldn't have been entered after swimming 500 yards only ten minutes earlier. I was glad that for me the meet was over. I had really gone all out to break that record and I was exhausted.

But after the 500 Jim Barton asked me to swim the anchor leg of the relay because Shrout was swimming it for Harvard. I thought he was joking.

"Yeah, right," I said.

"I'm serious," he said.

I couldn't believe it! Shrout had been resting for five long events—at least half an hour—and I had just gotten out of the pool after swimming 500 yards. And during the entire afternoon Shrout had swum a total of 150 yards (50 plus 100), while I had swum 700 yards (200 plus 500). I told Jim that Shrout would kill me if I tried to do that anchor leg. By now some of the Yale varsity swimmers were coming out of the locker room and they couldn't believe that I was being asked to swim the anchor leg of a relay ten minutes after swimming the 500 free. A couple of them even said, "Jim, are you kidding?"

But Jim was serious, and in a way I knew how he felt. He was a rookie coach—this was his first year at Yale—and this was an important meet. A lot of fever had built up, and probably he felt that he should have straightened out the races ahead of time. At any rate, he pressed me to swim the relay and finally I agreed. Also I guess I didn't like the idea of people booing me and saying I had ducked meeting Shrout.

I hoped I would go out either way ahead of Shrout or so far behind him that I couldn't be expected to catch up—in a close race, I knew, he would murder me.

We went out almost together; I had a small lead of about a yard. By the 50-yard wall he had closed it and we were together. On the third lap he went ahead. I knew he was

PREPARING TO DIVE IN AN INTERCOLLEGIATE MEET

going to outsplit me; I was just trying to hang onto the race
for Yale. Until the final turn I just held in there, trying not
to fall too far behind. Then, on the last 25 yards I pulled out
everything I had left in me and managed one final spurt. It
was enough to catch up and just touch him out to win.

He had outsplit me—by a fraction of a second. When
they announced the split times the Harvard fans went wild. I
hardly heard it. All I could think of at the end of that race
was how tired I was.

A week later vacation began and all I wanted to do was
rest. I thought how great it would be to just go somewhere
and sleep in the sun. I'd have been happy just to go home to
Oregon and sleep for a week. But I spent the vacation in New
Haven. I had a couple of speaking engagements in the East
and I had a lot of work to catch up on—and the Spring
Nationals were to be held at Yale on April 1 to 3, during the
last few days of vacation. Also *Life* was sending a reporter and
a photographer to New Haven to do a story on me. They
wanted to cover me at the Nationals and then through a few
days of "life at Yale" after classes started again on April 5.

Those 1965 Spring Nationals were the most frantic I
remember. I'd asked Patience Sherman to come up to visit
me and I was damn glad to see her. At that point I needed a
date and a good friend and Patience was both. But the days of
careful peaking—a regular schedule, plenty of rest, no diver-
sion, no wasted energy—were gone. All through the Nationals
I was entertaining the reporter and photographer from *Life;*
even when they are the nicest guys in the world, this takes a
lot of time. They are there to get a story, and they put in a
full day's work every day. During my senior year, a reporter
from *Sports Illustrated,* Gil Rogin, a great guy, came to New
Haven for the same purpose. By that time I had a dozen
roommates who helped talk to Gil and it still took a lot of
time. Freshman year, when *Life* came, I was on my own.

The *Life* reporter and photographer followed me wherever I went. They came to my room at seven in the morning
and took pictures of me getting dressed. They took pictures
of me eating, swimming, racing. After school began, they
came to classes with me and to the dining room. I was
flattered that *Life* wanted to do a whole article on me, but
having these guys taking pictures of me all over the campus
was embarrassing.

For the Spring Nationals I was entered in three relays
and the 200-yard freestyle, in which I managed to set a new
indoor record. After that race a couple of people said that I
had all the conditioning and the style and the power that had
brought me four gold medals in Tokyo. But I knew better. I
was tired. I was tired all the time now.

> *This is not an exaggeration. In the photographs
> taken at this time, which appeared in the April 16, 1965,
> issue of* Life, *Schollander looks exhausted—even sick. In
> the picture of him holding Handsome Dan, a heavy well-
> rounded bulldog, he looks much older than eighteen. He
> has dark circles under his eyes, a lifeless smile, and a
> drawn look on his face. He looks as though he can hardly
> lift the dog.*
>
> *In a picture taken in the Yale swimming pool after
> winning the 200-yard freestyle in the Spring Nationals,
> again he has the dark circles, the tired smile, the drawn
> look. He looks as though he shouldn't be in the water.
> And yet he did win the race against very tough competi-
> tion—the best in the country—and he set a new American
> record.*
>
> *One must ask the question: What was the indefin-
> able something that made him able to do this? (Just as
> he was able, in the relay at Harvard, to find that last bit
> of energy for a spurt—to win.) He was physically ex-
> hausted and he had been out of condition for a long
> time. It was more than technical training because others*

in the pool had had the same quality of technical train-
ing for as many years, if not more. The fine line between
the winner and the rest of the field is supposed to be so
thin that his physical fatigue should have made him
finish last. And yet he won. Was it only the will to win?
Everyone in the pool wanted to win. Then how can one
define the special ingredient, the special quality—unique
in Schollander—so that, when everything logical said he
should have been last, he was still first? I think no other
swimmer in our century has had this quality to this
degree. Others have seemed as promising—others have
shown flashes of brilliance—and have failed when, logi-
cally, they should have won. Schollander won even
when, logically, he should have failed. Whatever it is,
however it is defined, it is beyond simple addition or
complex logic. It is the quality that sets him apart, above
the rest, a special quality of greatness that made him
unique.

D.S.

20

By MID-APRIL I felt I had reached rock bottom. Physically I
felt rotten. And no matter what I did, I couldn't catch up on
the work. With exams just a month away I was actually afraid
I might flunk out. I was turning down all new invitations
now but my schedule was still cluttered with old promises. In
April I had to reopen the World's Fair in New York. On May
3 I was due in New York again to receive the National Academy of Sports Award.

In mid-April the *Life* article hit the stands and suddenly
I had a whole new set of problems. The article quoted me:

"If I just wanted to swim, I would have gone to USC." Also, "I like not having girls in class here. They so often proved to be phonies back in high school, turning on all that charm." I certainly know that USC isn't just a swimming school and God knows I have no objection to girls turning on the charm. We had talked about these things and if this was what the reporter had gotten out of it, it wasn't the impression I meant to convey. I was deluged with letters. All my friends at USC wrote that they didn't like what I'd said and I felt that I had to answer them. The girls I knew in high school—and even their mothers—wrote to tell me they weren't phonies, and I had to write back to tell them I didn't think they were phonies.

Another quote that really bothered me was a comment on Japan. The *Life* people had asked me if I wasn't practically a god in Japan. I said that I was popular there but that the Japanese make a great deal of sports figures. They were sort of teasing me about it and they said, especially swimmers, especially ones with blond hair. I thought they were kidding and I said, yeah, yeah. They asked me if I wouldn't have had it made if I lived in Japan; I could probably retire, and all I'd have to do would be to sit on a Yamaha motor scooter holding a transistor radio and a camera. I had just laughed and said, "Yeah, well I don't know, yeah, I guess so." They quoted me: "If I were in Japan I'd be tempted to quit right now. I'd have it made. The Japanese idolize sports figures, particularly swimmers who are young, American, and blond. All I'd have to do there would be to have a picture of myself listening to my Sony portable or riding a Yamaha and I'd be a rich man. But here I'm no celebrity." That upset me because it made me look as though I thought I could take the Japanese people—and the Japanese had been so good to me.

When I read the article I felt that I'd really blown the interview. But I learned something from it. I learned that in an interview you have to weigh every statement carefully before you make it and be sure that you're clearly understood. I learned that when you say yes to a statement, that becomes your statement, and you can't assume that certain things won't be printed. I learned that reporters are human and don't necessarily know what's in your mind, and you have a responsibility to be absolutely clear. Actually *Life* wasn't that unfair to me and I learned a good lesson and I remembered it.

My last exam was in sociology, and I stayed up all night studying for it. At five in the morning I remember I was looking out the window, watching the sun come up over the old campus. I stood there thinking about all the things the old campus was supposed to mean to a freshman—things I had missed: touch football in the fall, snowball fights in the winter, stickball in the spring, the freshmen riot held every year on the first Thursday in May. I was at a banquet in New York the night of the first Thursday in May. I thought about all the friends you made on the old campus before your class split up and went into residential colleges. Lots of guys had gotten together and were moving in groups of four or six. Barry and I were sticking together—by now we were good friends. We were going into Berkeley College, but we hadn't even been able to find two other guys to fill a four-man suite. I thought that morning about the "road trips" to Smith and Vassar I had had to turn down to study or to go somewhere and make a speech, and about the bull sessions over coffee after dinner I had had to pass up because I just didn't have time. Next year, I thought, somehow I would get on top of all this. Next year when I came back to Yale, I would settle in as a student. I wouldn't be transient again.

A few days later, on June 8, I went to the White House for the second time, to a reception given by President Johnson for the presidential scholars—the outstanding high-school seniors from all fifty states. Famous people in many different fields had been invited so that the students could talk to them. And I was supposed to be one of the famous people they might like to talk to. I talked most of the time to John Glenn, and I kept thinking that I was only a year older than the students and that I really belonged on the other side of the fence. I was really one of the kids, interested in talking to these important people.

The next day I went home to Oregon. I was still going to Europe but I had stayed firm in my decision to limit my trip to three countries, Germany, Switzerland, and Belgium. I could have left from New York, and I should have, but months earlier I had promised to be the grand marshal of the Portland Rose Festival, the biggest event of the year to the people in Oregon, which was to begin on June 12. So I went six thousand miles out of my way to be in a parade. For the first time in my life I slept on a plane. And when I got home all I wanted to do was sleep. George called me in the morning before I was to leave for Germany and reminded me that he wanted me back at Santa Clara right after I left Belgium. I said I would be there.

I landed in Würzburg on the sixteenth and went right to sleep. I was scheduled to compete against Hans Klein the next night. In January I had told Hans that I wouldn't be in condition to race against him in this meet. He had laughed and said, "Neither will I; neither will I! We'll probably swim the slowest race in history." But he was in condition and he beat me—badly.

After the race Hans came into the locker room, really upset. He didn't want me to think it was a setup. He said he hadn't really trained for this meet; he hadn't expected me to be in such terrible shape. I told Hans I thought I was sick and he agreed there must be something wrong with me. But what could Hans do?

By the time I reached Switzerland I felt rotten. I spent the whole first day in bed, resting. The second day I worked out a little and then joined the rest of the party on a trip up into the nearby Alps. I've always loved mountains and this was something I really wanted to see. We drove part of the way up into the mountains and then took the chairlift to the top and walked to the very summit. It was one of the most beautiful days I've ever seen—and one of the most magnificent views. But when we got home that night I was so tired I couldn't believe it. In the morning I asked to see a doctor.

In Berne a doctor examined me and said that I was probably coming down with a cold. But by now I knew that my rate of recovery after a swim was too slow, which indicated an infection, and I insisted that there *was* something wrong with me. The doctor insisted there was not. I told the people promoting the race that I was too sick to swim. They took me to a specialist who assured me that I was well enough to swim. I was beginning to suspect that I might have mononucleosis, but the doctor said I didn't have mononucleosis. The promoters pointed out that they had an investment in me and it was my duty to swim since two doctors had assured me there was nothing wrong with me.

So I swam. I swam 200 meters in two minutes, seven seconds, ten seconds slower than my normal time. I still came in first because in Switzerland swimming is not a major sport. Then after the race, I tried to pull myself out of the pool and could not. I tried again. I got halfway up and then my arms gave out and I slipped back into the water. I just hung onto the edge until a couple of people pulled me out. They rushed me to the hospital.

My world was very quiet at last.

part three

Russia, 1966

21

WHEN I WOKE UP in the hospital the next morning, a doctor told me that I had glandular fever, which is the European term for mononucleosis. I thought, Good, and rolled over and went back to sleep. For four or five days I lay there; I remember thinking, in the rare moments when I was awake, how good it felt just to lie in that bed and sleep and not have to catch any planes or answer any telephones or make any speeches or swim any races. Nobody was asking me to do anything.

For four or five days my condition grew worse. My temperature went as high as 104 and the drugs didn't seem to affect it. The doctor suspected that hepatitis was setting in. That scared me. I knew that hepatitis was a common but dangerous complication of mononucleosis, and that people died of hepatitis. At that point the AAU got concerned and considered sending a man over to look into what had happened. My father made reservations to fly over. Then my fever broke and the AAU stayed home and my father stayed home and I was okay. I simply woke up one morning feeling fine. Obviously one of the drugs had worked, but I remember thinking, Hell, all I needed was a little sleep—because once I got it I felt great.

By the time I could sit up and read I had hundreds of letters and telegrams from all over—Europe, America, Japan. This was the good side of being a world figure. Of all of them I remember one from my old friend Carolyn Wood of Portland: "Dear Don—America just honors its heroes to the point of destruction."

* * *

Three factors can contribute to the end of a swimmer's career.

One—*Too long a layoff*. Swimming changes and progresses very quickly. New swimming techniques, new training methods, new psychological approaches are constantly being developed. A good swimmer must be in continuous contact with a good coach and with other good swimmers. To remain a good swimmer, he has to stay with the sport, no matter how great he already is. Being away from it for as long as six or eight months can finish you forever.

Two—*Age*. Few swimmers last more than two years after they reach the top. Most swimmers peak at about eighteen or nineteen and last until about twenty or twenty-one. Swimming is physically such a demanding sport, and takes so much time and dedication, that swimmers just run out of energy and motivation.

Three—*Disease*, which not only causes a long layoff but takes a physical toll. If a swimmer comes down with any debilitating disease—hepatitis, scarlet fever, "mono"—which hinders his swimming for physiological, not to mention psychological, reasons, for two months or more, then his chances of swimming well again are almost nil. Endurance built up over the years vanishes. You have to start all over again and it's just too tough. It's a long road back and it's hard to convince yourself that you can do it or that you even want to try.

I had already been away from serious training for too long. And I had been at the top for more than two years. Now, with mono, I had all three destructive factors working against me and it was pretty generally accepted that I was finished.

I spent two beautiful weeks in that hospital. The Swiss were very kind to me. I had cute Swiss nurses and many of my European friends and some of the American families living in Germany and Switzerland came to visit. The wife and daughter of the American consul in Berne visited almost every day and they brought me fruit and cakes and little gifts. The hospital was nestled in the mountains and my room had a terrace overlooking the Alps. I spent a lot of time on that terrace, thinking.

I wondered if I was finished and I figured that I probably was. I knew what sickness could do to a swimmer—especially after a layoff—and I wasn't kidding myself. Even more, I wondered if I cared. I suppose I did care. I had enjoyed swimming and I had enjoyed competing. I liked the people involved in sports. I had enjoyed winning, and, much as I complained, I enjoyed many of the rewards that winning had brought me. I had visited many places that I would never have seen. I was thrilled at some of the awards that came my way. People have said that I was the best thing that ever happened to swimming because I made it an important sport—but swimming was good to me, too.

Still, I had mixed emotions. I was tired of swimming, tired of training, tired of fighting to save my swimming reputation. I was tired of publicity and of obligations. And I was just tired—physically tired.

I have never felt, and I certainly didn't feel then, that swimming was my whole life. It was no tragedy if my swimming career was over. It had to be finished some day, so what if the day had come a little sooner than I had expected. It was just the end of a stage in my life—not the end of the world.

Just before I went home the doctor came in to talk to me and he looked so obviously troubled that I thought I was in for some bad news. The bad news was that I wouldn't be able to swim all summer.

I just thought, Boy, put that in writing.

I hadn't been home for the summer in four years. I flew into Portland late in the afternoon—over the Columbia River Valley gorge—and, with the sun just beginning to set, to me it was the most beautiful sight in the world. Oregon has always meant something special to me; I love the tall trees and the mountains. Our home in Lake Oswego was in the middle of thick woods and high mountains, and to me it represented everything that was beautiful and peaceful and quiet.

That whole summer, I just slept all night and lay in the sun all day. On days when I felt particularly strong, I drove my neighbors' boat while they water-skied. Now and then I went to a movie—the early show—and came straight home afterward. I ate my meals in my own dining room and slept in my own bed for two whole months.

I began to read a great deal: psychology, Russian literature, the stock market. I even bought a stock—I invested $300 in Lear Jet—and with money at stake I really studied the market. I remembered all those company presidents who used to come to listen to me and I thought, Too bad *I* wasn't listening to them.

I missed George Haines and Mike Wall that summer but I didn't miss swimming. It wasn't until the week of the National Championships that I began to get restless. Then I started to get publicity, a different kind of publicity from before. People referred to me as a "former great," and I read in the papers about my career that had "climaxed in Tokyo and ended in Berne."

That made me mad—to hear again and again that I was all washed up. To me, I wasn't over the hill. To me it wasn't a question of whether I *could* win again, but of whether I wanted to try. I believed that if I tried I would win. As far as I was concerned, I had never fallen—no one had ever beaten me—I was just taking a forced rest.

When the Nationals began that summer, I was the meet record holder in the 100, and the world record holder in the 200 and 400. At the start of the meet, the press wrote that many young swimmers were after my records that summer. But not one of my records fell. No one did in 1965 what I had done in 1964.

DON WITH JOHNNY WEISSMULLER IN LAKE OSWEGO, OREGON—
SUMMER, 1965

22

BACK AT YALE that fall I couldn't believe what one case of mononucleosis had done for me! Now that I had a reason to turn down all those invitations I was a free man. Now I had *time*—for dates, football games, parties, plays, special lectures, "road trips" to Smith and Vassar. I had time to study and my grades jumped. I joined a fraternity—Deke. At the end of the year I was elected a class representative to the Yale Co-op Board of Directors, and also secretary-treasurer of Deke. Barry and I, who had made no close friends the year before, moved with nine other guys for junior year. We had a combination of suites that became legendary—seven bedrooms, a living room, a den, and a bar.

But if my college life was great, my swimming was not. The problem was that I was starting all over again—from the bottom. I had to build up all over again the kind of endurance I had always been able to count on. I needed good hard overdistance training—thousands and thousands of yards—to learn to feel at home again with the pain, to go through the pain barrier and push it farther and farther back until I was on top again. I needed the kind of training I had had at Santa Clara. And Yale just didn't go about it that way.

By December, when swimming practice began, I was feeling fine. I was rested and strong and I was really looking forward to good tough workouts. The first day out, I realized that I wasn't going to get them at Yale.

At Santa Clara the first third of the season was devoted to quantity swimming only—overdistance—to build up endurance that would last all year. Yale did very little overdistance work. At Santa Clara, and everywhere else on the

West Coast, it had been routine to use circuit training, in which everyone is swimming all the time, going off at fifteen-second intervals and swimming up one side of the lane and down the other—no one hanging around wasting time. Yale did not use circuit training. The fact is that the Yale program produced good sprinters; but I was both a sprinter and a middle-distance swimmer, I needed that overdistance work, and I wasn't going to get it.

I saw that swimming just wasn't big business on the East Coast, which in one way was fine with me. But nationally I was still going to have to compete against guys who were training at colleges where swimming *was* big business. I told myself that I was at Yale for an education and that swimming came second now. And yet I had made it known that I didn't intend to retire; I had refused to admit that I was finished at nineteen, and I knew that other swimmers would be watching me. And I knew, too, that those other guys, with more intensive training programs, were going to move even further ahead of me and they would know it, too. Nobody was going to wait for me. I was in danger of losing a big psychological advantage. At the first big tournament they would see I hadn't come back; that, training at Yale, I was falling even further behind. After the first big race they would think, He's behind and he's losing ground—now is the time to finish him off.

I managed to win the races I swam for Yale that year, but that didn't mean I was back in condition and I knew it. The best swimmers—Wall, Roth, the new blood—were all out West, or at Indiana with Jim Counsilman, where swimming was big business. And Yale didn't compete against them. They were in a different league—in more ways than one. Even the records I broke didn't mean that everything was all right. I'd gone almost as fast in practice at Santa Clara.

The real test would come at the first postseason championships—the National Collegiate Athletic Association

(NCAA) tournament—the Collegiates—where I would have to compete against the nation's top swimmers who had been in intensive training all year. I knew I wasn't in any shape to win and I was worried.

Then, two weeks before the Collegiates, I took a serious blow. I came down with Asian flu. For a whole week I lay in bed in the infirmary, really depressed. I figured this was the end of the line. There was no way now that I could get ready for the NCAA meet. And losing my first important races after mono would put me at a tremendous psychological disadvantage. Once your competitors think they have your number they don't pay so much attention to you any more. They don't worry if you jam the pace, they don't watch you so carefully. Once they think they can beat you, it's a lot easier for them to do so.

In the end I was saved by power politics. While I was in the infirmary, Yale was suspended from the NCAA for refusing—quite correctly, I think—to honor a new NCAA rule requiring athletes to maintain certain averages in order to compete for their college. The other guys were disappointed that we wouldn't be allowed to swim in the Collegiates—they actually thought we could win them—and I didn't tell them that USC and Indiana would murder us. I hated to see the NCAA making power grabs again, but, personally, I was relieved to get a reprieve.

It was a short reprieve—just two weeks—until the AAU Spring Nationals in Brandon, Florida. After a bout with flu I wasn't ready for the AAU meet, either, but I tried to psych myself up. I told myself I had an advantage because everybody else had just peaked two weeks earlier for the Collegiates. I told myself I still commanded respect, that I only had to make a show of confidence.

The first race was the 500-yard freestyle. In the qualifying heats Mike Wall was swimming in the next lane and Mike knew that I always went just hard enough to qualify—

no harder—in the heats. For the first 400 yards he stayed with me, depending on my sense of pace, figuring I'd get us in under the wire. But after 300 yards I was dead tired. After 400 yards Mike realized that we were way off and he took it out on his own. I finished way behind.

When I came in Mike looked at me very strangely, and said, "What the hell happened to you?"

I was really in pain—and so tired I could hardly breathe. "I just couldn't do it," I snapped back.

Mike apologized, and then I felt badly for having snapped at him. I was mad at myself, not at Mike. Then his father came over and said, "What happened to you guys? I don't think either one of you made the finals." Mike just said we were tired, and then Mr. Wall took a good look at me and I guess he understood and walked away. Mike made the finals and I did not. I'd missed by less than a second.

I just lay back in the pool until I began to catch my breath. All I could think of was that I had barely been able to swim 500 yards. I couldn't understand what had happened, and I didn't fully realize what this could mean. Finally I got out of the pool and put on my warm-up suit.

Then it happened. Jim Counsilman walked up to me and shook my hand and said, "Well, Don—at least the pressure is off you now."

I stood there, dumbfounded. I couldn't believe that he'd said that. Then another coach came up and shook my hand and said, well, I'd had a brilliant career. And another: it was too bad it had to end this way, but I'd been the best for a long time. And another—and another.

It was like a funeral. I'd missed those finals by less than a second, but it wasn't a miscalculation: I just hadn't been able to do it. I was tired. And it was obvious to everyone here that I was tired. For a minute I just sat there thinking. This was the first time I'd lost a championship race in many, many years, and I sat there telling myself that I hadn't been able to swim 500 yards and wondering whether it was the flu and the lack of overdistance training at Yale, or whether I really was over the hill at nineteen. Maybe I was like every other swimmer. I'd had my two years and I'd had mono and I was finished.

Then I saw George coming toward me, and I thought, miserably, What can I say to George?

Well, George walked up to me, took a quick look around to see if anybody was watching, and then said, "I know I'm not your coach right now, but your stroke is really off." He sort of squinted and shook his head. "I mean, it's *really* off! Your streamlining is out in left field. You're making work for yourself. No wonder you look so exhausted."

Suddenly everything was all right again. The only man whose opinion I really cared about didn't tell me what a great career I'd had. He told me that my stroke was off. And then he showed me where it was off and how I could correct it. I was coming out of the water at the wrong angle and this was something I couldn't have felt myself. I'd have seen it if I'd seen pictures but I hadn't seen pictures. A minute ago, psychologically, I had hit rock bottom. Now that George told me the problem was a technical one, my spirits skyrocketed, which probably made as much difference as the correction in my stroke.

The next day I won the 200-yard freestyle. Then some people said, "Maybe he's not finished." But not as though they meant it. I think many of them thought it was a final flash in the pan and that I was, in fact, all done. On the third day I finished second in the 100 and by then I guess I wasn't entirely sure myself.

I would find out that summer, I knew, when I got back to Santa Clara. And I would find out at the Summer Nationals, always the most important meet, where I would be competing against the nation's best, and actually the best in the world. The old swimmers that I knew would be there—tough, experienced, and highly trained; and there would be a whole new crop—young, red hot, and highly trained. It's strange at nineteen to be talking about a new young crop but it was true. I was painfully aware that it was almost two years now since I had competed against the best.

23

I REMEMBER the first day of practice at Santa Clara that summer—June, 1966—as though it were this morning. We turned out at eight o'clock in a fog so thick you couldn't see from one end of the pool to the other. Standing behind the blocks, George knew we were still alive only because every minute or so we showed up and turned. Every now and then somebody would emerge out of the fog and disappear—going the other way in your lane in his place in circuit training. Occasionally when you turned you heard George encouraging you or coaxing you on or yelling at you.

We started with a 1,000-meter warm-up swim. When I began I wasn't even sure I could still swim 1,000 meters— especially at the Santa Clara pace. At the end I wasn't even breathing hard and I felt better. Then we went into kicking drills, pulling drills, sprint drills, more distance work, breathing drills, more sprint work, another long swim. That first morning we swam about 4,500 meters, nearly three miles. *That* was overdistance. For the first time in much too long I felt that I was back in swimming.

After practice, George told me that it was all still there; it was only a question of beating it out of me. And then I knew I was all right.

About a week later I called the AAU offices in New York to ask whether I could still go to Poland and Russia with the

United States swimming team being sent over that summer. I'd been invited to make the trip in April but I had declined. Originally the State Department and the AAU had planned the trip to last three weeks, ending just a couple of weeks before the Outdoor Nationals, and I had felt I had to stay with George and train. But now the trip had been cut to ten days. I was making good progress in Santa Clara, and George and I thought that some foreign competition might be good for me. The team was filled but the State Department agreed to add me as an extra.

The team going to Poland and Russia met in New York on July 7: eight men, seven girls, a girls' chaperone, and a coach, Don Gambril from Pasadena City College and the Los Angeles Athletic Club. It was a good team, although not the best we could have sent to Russia. Many of our top swimmers had turned down the trip because of the Nationals, feeling that they could travel any time and that it was more important to win a national championship.

Some of the swimmers were very good—Dick Roth, my old roommate in Tokyo and the Olympic gold medalist in the individual medley; Greg Buckingham and John Nelson, two of our best freestyle men. Many people rated Nelson the best 200- and 400-meter man in the country. Neither Poland nor Russia was considered strong in swimming, and we didn't anticipate trouble beating either of them.

After a brief stopover in Paris we landed in Warsaw on July 9 to compete against the Polish National swimming team on the tenth and eleventh. Then we would go to Moscow.

We worked out in the pool the first morning and then went out to see the city. To me Warsaw was bleak and depressing. It had been 90 percent destroyed in World War II and was rebuilt into just a city of modern slums, dirty and overcrowded. Buildings only twenty years old were already falling down. The people seemed devoid of emotions. They rarely smiled and they moved in a plodding way, as though always carrying a load on their shoulders. Their clothes were drab—the brightest colors I saw in Warsaw were the red and blue blazers of the American swimmers. Even when the sun shone, the city was depressing.

And yet I still remember a couple of very pleasant hours that first afternoon in Warsaw. I met a girl, a university student who spoke fluent English and she took me around and showed me the sights. She wasn't a pretty girl but very warm. She smiled a lot—one of the few people I saw who did smile—and she told me a great deal about Poland.

Late in the afternoon we saw some soldiers in a park and I asked her if they were Polish or Russian soldiers.

Her smile vanished. "Russian soldiers wouldn't dare appear in Warsaw in uniform," she said with hatred in her voice. "Do you think we like the Russians?"

"Well, I don't really know," I said, "you're allies."

Then she opened up and told me how the Polish people felt toward the Russians. During the war, when the Russians were driving back the Germans, they got all the way to Warsaw and then they just stopped and camped on the other side of the river while the Germans burned the city to the ground. "The Russians said their forces were overextended and they couldn't go on until their rear ranks caught up. But the Polish people felt the Russians just sat there and let the Germans burn Warsaw. They could have helped us but they didn't." Once the Germans were gone, then the Russians advanced. There was still a terrible hatred among the Poles for both the Germans and the Russians, she said—and I could hear it in her voice.

At the meet that night I swam the 200 free in about 2:01, not a very good time but I wasn't pressing it and no one was pressing me. But there was a happy twist to the story. I swam against Poland's best freestyler, and apparently I pulled him to a new all-time Polish record—the fastest he had ever gone. He just went wild and the crowd went wild and really applauded him. And they gave me a big ovation because they thought I was responsible, that I had inspired him to this new record. The next day the story was in the papers and I was interviewed on national television—all because this guy had lost to me by only two seconds.

Actually the Polish swimmers and swimming officials were very warm to us. On our last night in Warsaw they held a big banquet and told us they were proud to have had us in Poland. Then they said they hoped they'd gotten us ready to beat the Russians. They actually said this in public—that they hoped we would beat the Russians.

I felt that we created goodwill in Poland, the kind of goodwill that American athletes, given half a chance, can create among the people of other countries. This is one reason I feel so strongly that the AAU should do a better job of protecting our athletes while they travel abroad. If an athlete is exploited—if he is the victim of a setup for propaganda purposes or for reasons of national pride—he is put on the defensive. He resists the exploitation, he fights back against being setup, and this results in ill-feeling all around. Ill will among principals always reaches the press and is automatically intensified.

To me, the most valid reasons for sending American athletes abroad is to create goodwill among the people. Sports is an international language, the one area in which communication is possible across national, political, and verbal barriers. This is supposed to be the purpose behind the Olympics, although that purpose has eroded almost beyond recognition.

In Poland where we stayed only three days, this kind of communication took place. To me it was interesting that it happened so effortlessly in an iron-curtain country—with a people with whom, ordinarily, we had so little communication. I saw with my own eyes that even in countries where governments might follow a hard unfriendly line it is possible to reach the people and to find them responsive to friendship and goodwill. We all felt this and we were in great spirits when we left for the airport to get the plane to Moscow. Then, at the airport, we had some sobering news. We learned that a Russian-American track meet, scheduled for about the same time as our swimming meet, had been canceled. The Russian track athletes had issued a statement: they refused to compete against Americans until the United States stopped its war of aggression against the people of Vietnam.

24

When we boarded the plane for Moscow, we honestly didn't know what would happen when we got there and we were worried. We didn't know whether the swimming meet had also been canceled, or whether it would be canceled. We didn't know whether, if our meet was canceled, we would leave Russia immediately or be asked to remain there. Worst of all we still didn't know what was really behind the track meet cancellation, whether there was more to it than the Vietnam War—some new diplomatic tension, possibly, between Russia and the United States. We just didn't know anything except that Russia had canceled the track meet and had, apparently, used some sharp language. Back home, if you heard that Russia had canceled a track meet, you would probably figure it was just another propaganda stunt and forget it, but we were on a plane going there. We were fifteen kids, and at twenty I was one of the oldest. Some of the girls were only fifteen or sixteen.

We landed in Moscow in the evening. Except for customs officials and security police the airport was deserted. I had always thought that dark, empty airports in Communist countries were just things you saw in American spy movies, but that was the way Moscow airport looked. We went through customs, although in foreign countries visiting athletes are often waved through.

The Russians who met us were a sharp contrast to the Poles we had known. The Russians were just plain unfriendly—not rude or impolite—just cold and very formal. Very silent.

That morning, before we left Warsaw, we had had a practice session in the pool, and I had misjudged a turn and smashed my heel against a wall. When I got off the plane in Moscow I was limping. The Russian officials who met us noticed that, and one of them asked about it right away. He seemed overjoyed to think I was hurt—in fact, it seemed to be the only thing in the whole deal that pleased him. I could see the Russians still thought I was the man to beat, and I figured they hadn't caught up with my case of mono and my unspectacular career since the Olympics.

The Russian officials waited while we went through customs and then they showed us to the bus that was to take us to our hotel. Everything went very smoothly—no mix-ups, no confusion—but there was no effort to make us feel welcome. They were grim and serious about their jobs and they expected us to be the same.

We stayed at a Western-style hotel that had an elevator and decent bathrooms and a phone in every room. But the rooms were very small, and quite barren. They were furnished with small drab rugs, window shades but no curtains, no bedspreads, no pictures. But it wasn't the austerity that bothered us, it was the space. There were three of us in each little room, three beds along one wall, with just a small space on each side and a couple of feet at the foot of the beds. I shared a room with Dick Roth and Greg Buckingham, two guys I got along with very well. We were going to have to get along well because we were going to be living on top of each other, literally, for the next six days. I'm not sure the crowded accommodations were deliberate. It might have been the best they could do.

American swimmers are usually cool and very relaxed when they travel. Ordinarily they're thrilled to arrive in a new country. They're also curious; and they explore the hotel and look around the neighborhood. They horse around a little. They never go right to bed. That night we were worried and sober and very quiet. We all felt the tension and the coldness. When we got to the hotel we just went straight to our rooms and went to bed.

The sun rises around three A.M. in Russia during July. I was awake at four. Right away I realized that we were going to have trouble sleeping that week. In four days we had gone through four time changes—California to New York, to Paris, to Warsaw, to Moscow. We were tired from traveling and from training at different hours in different time zones every day. And now we would have to cope with nights only six hours long.

Greg and Dick were still asleep, and I just sat on my bed looking out the window, thinking. The day before we had picked up another piece of information. Just one week earlier the Russians had held their Nationals and some of their swimmers had turned in some amazing times. This meant two things: they were at the peak of their season, which we were not, and the Russian swimmers had come a long way since the 1964 Olympics. Comparing their times to ours if this meet came off, and we still didn't know that it would, we would have trouble taking it.

In Moscow at 4:00 A.M. the people are already going to work. I sat at the window and watched the city come awake. Moscow was drab, but not as bad as Warsaw. The buildings looked new and solid and the streets were wide. It was very quiet on the streets even though people were moving about—

no hustle, ho horns. Just people in gray overalls going to work, moving silently through the streets, not speaking.

And then as I sat there I thought suddenly, it's going to be a setup. I tried to remember details of what had happened in France. I could feel it. The accommodations were crowded and uncomfortable; the reception was cold. And holding their Nationals only a week earlier, showing us their times, letting us know they were at the peak of their season—that was the beginning of a psych-out. I wondered how many of our American swimmers had ever been set up, and I wondered whether I should say anything to them.

At breakfast I was even more convinced. We ordered eggs and they came to the table raw. We sent them back and asked that they be cooked longer. Again they came back raw. We sent them back again and they still came back raw. Finally we ate them, because we didn't want the Russians to think that we weren't eating. Later I learned that raw eggs are favored in Russia, so maybe the Russians had good intentions, but since we were going to compete, I think the AAU should have briefed them on a few basic items in our diets. More than once in Russia we just couldn't eat the food and many of us lost weight and strength.

At practice that morning we asked the Russians whether the meet was on and they told us that it was. We asked them why, if the track meet had been canceled because of Vietnam, the swimming meet had not also been canceled. They said that the track meet was a dual meet between Russia and the United States. The swimming meet was an international meet.

This was the first we'd heard about an international meet and they showed us a list of the competitors. They had invited one swimmer from each of three other countries: Poland, Norway, and Bulgaria. That made it an international swimming meet. It wouldn't be fair to the other countries to cancel it.

Then we began to catch on. The United States had a very strong track team that year. When we saw a list of the Russian track times we realized that the Russians had a very weak track team. And so they canceled the track meet because of the war; the Russian *athletes*, not the government, refused to compete against Americans. The Russian swimmers were strong and ready to go, and *they* had no bones about the war. Besides they had to think about all those other countries—the three swimmers from Poland, Norway, and Bulgaria.

By now we all realized that we had a problem. This had started out as a cultural exchange meet—a "training vacation." Russia was not supposed to have strong swimmers and nobody on the American team had intended to peak. Nobody wanted to peak. When we got home we had the Nationals coming up. Now this cultural exchange was turning into a major American-Russian competition and for this American team to have any chance at all of winning here in Russia it was going to have to peak.

I thought a long time that morning about my own problem. I doubted that I could peak now and then peak again for the Nationals. I wasn't in that good condition. And losing at the Nationals might finish me forever. Still, I couldn't accept losing to the Russians. For all of us it was becoming a question of our own best interest versus national pride.

At practice that morning a Russian woman turned up who haunted me for the rest of the trip. Wherever American swimmers go in foreign countries, people come out to watch the practices; this is not unusual. But this one woman seemed to be watching only me. I would reach one end of the pool and she would be standing there; I would swim to the other end and there she was. Between one set of repeats I took a good look at her. She was a tough, unsmiling woman, very businesslike. Then I saw a stopwatch cupped in her hand.

In racing it is so important to have seen your competitors swim, to know their split times, their pacing, to have watched their starts and their turns and to understand their weak points and their strong points. But we weren't training at the same time as the Russians so we had no way of knowing about them—and they had no way of knowing about us. I figured it was this woman's job to report.

I remembered that in 1965 several Russian coaches had toured the United States to learn about American swimming, and many American coaches had cooperated with them. This was one reason, I felt, that Russia's swimming had improved so dramatically between 1964 and 1966. And on that tour, I knew, they had seen or heard about many techniques that at the time were still in an experimental stage. Now, this year, those techniques would have been accepted or dis-carded. I decided that my Russian Mata Hari had more than one job. She was getting my split times for the benefit of my Russian competition, and she was watching my training methods and my stroke techniques for the benefit of Russian swimming in general. I wondered whether other people around the pool were keying off on Roth and Buckingham, too—whether we each had our personal spy. I was beginning to understand the reason for this "cultural exchange."

I was working up a burn. I had enough problems with-out being decoded by a Russian spy. Since I could judge my splits with my own internal clock, I began to slow down as I approached the wall. I began doing one-handed touch turns; by now the touch turn was archaic—the flipturn was stan-dard—and she knew it. Instead of breathing four strokes after coming out of the turn I breathed any time—after anything from two to six strokes—in any damn direction I felt like breathing. I kept changing my stroke. I went from a slow kick to a fast kick and then to just dragging my legs, hardly kick-ing at all. I could see Mata Hari beginning to boil.

That afternoon we asked for a tour of Moscow. We didn't think we should come all the way to Russia just to see a swimming stadium and a hotel. But it was very hot in

Moscow that July, and we knew that the usual guided tours can tire you out, so we asked that the tour be short.

That tour lasted from noon until six o'clock. We saw Moscow inside out—palaces and old churches, GUM's Department Store. We toured the entire Kremlin, visited historical sites, and listened to long stories and legends about everything. We were in and out of that damn bus all afternoon, walking dozens of city blocks, climbing up and down stairs and standing around in palaces. A couple of times we suggested that they wind it up, but they wouldn't let us go and we felt that we should not insist because we were supposed to be goodwill ambassadors. The longer they stretched it, the harder we tried to conserve our strength and the madder and more frustrated we grew.

After that we didn't ask to tour Moscow again. Many of us would have liked to have seen more, but from then on we just trained and stayed in our rooms and rested.

Practice that night was very quiet. You could feel the tension, partly because we were so teed off over that sightseeing tour and partly, I think, because each individual was deciding whether to peak. We had decided not to make the decision as a team but to leave it as a personal decision to each individual. We were all aware of the possible cost to everyone. That night, I think, the situation had jelled enough so that, in his own mind, everyone was wrestling with the personal decision—whether to say, "The hell with it" and just swim through the meet, or whether to reach a slight peak, or whether to psych-up and shave down and hit a full peak. I think we had all decided to give it a little more effort than we had intended—to at least try to pull even with the Russian swimmers.

My personal spy was back that night, following me up and down the pool. Then about halfway through practice I saw a familiar piece of equipment—a camera in a window at the bottom of the pool. Pictures would be even more valuable than reports. On the next lap the camera was still there and I dove for it. I finished my repeat and headed back. This time it was gone and I swam on by. On the next repeat it was back and I dove for it again. For the rest of the evening, whenever the camera was at the window, I either dove for it or flipped over on my back while I was in its range.

My training suffered from all this, but by now I was starting to think that I would ease off in my training anyway, and reach some kind of a peak.

After practice the Russian woman complained to Don Gambril, the coach, that they were trying to photograph me while I was swimming and that I was fouling them up. This was a cultural exchange, she said, and I wasn't cooperating. Don reminded me that the State Department had told us to cooperate, and he suggested that I let them get a few shots. I don't think he really meant it. I think he knew what was going on, but he was in the middle. I said that I didn't care what the State Department had told us, that these people were obviously setting us up, and that I would be cooperative out of the water but in that pool I wasn't going to show them a damn thing.

The next morning the woman was back—with her cameraman—and we went through the whole show again. In my own mind I tried to think of it as a game of cat-and-mouse—but it was getting harder and harder to laugh it off.

25

THE FOLLOWING MORNING, after practice, there was a new development: some Russian doctors wanted to give our whole team physical tests. The meet was two days away and they wanted to put us through tests for the whole afternoon.

This time Gambril said he couldn't allow it. The Russians argued and finally they asked for just one guy and one girl and Gambril said okay, that much he would do. For the guy they wanted me. When Gambril asked me if I would mind doing it, I said I'd be glad to.

That afternoon, they took me into a room filled with muscle-testing and coordination-testing equipment. On the wall were pictures of Russian athletes demonstrating the equipment. The Russian woman was there with the doctor who would be conducting the tests.

I nodded toward the pictures. "Are those swimmers?" I asked.

"Of course they're swimmers," the doctor said.

They were the most muscular swimmers I ever saw.

The first test was a jumping test. They asked me to jump as high as I could and to touch a board that measured the jump. I did so. I knew that jumping is not always an accurate measure of leg strength.

"You don't have very strong legs, do you?" the doctor said.

I just shrugged. As far as I knew, I had the strongest legs of any swimmer in the United States.

Next came a piece of equipment that I recognized—an isometric bar that measured quite accurately your back strength and leg strength. At Yale, I had murdered this machine, but now I felt that my leg and back strength was my business. I spotted the dial that measured the pull, saw that the numbers were lower, in kilograms instead of pounds. My norm on this machine was about 350 pounds, or around 135 kilograms.

They strapped me into the machine and I grunted and groaned and pulled the bar until the dial showed 100 kilos; then I let go.

"That's the best you can do?" I nodded. "Oh, come on, try again." I pulled again. 105 kilos. Again. 100 kilos. Again. 99 kilos.

"Step this way," the doctor said. I thought he sounded a little sharp.

The next machine measured arm strength. My norm was about 50 kilos. I gave them 40 kilos.

"You didn't try! Do it again."

I gave them lots of grunting and groaning—and 35 kilos.

"You can't be that weak!" the doctor said.

"We don't stress strength in the United States," I said, "we stress technique."

Enter the Russian woman. "Your girl tested almost that well."

"That's the best I can do," I said.

"That isn't true," the doctor said.

I stared at him. "That's the best I can do. Either you believe me or I'm going to stop right now."

The next machine was a small bar that you squeezed to measure hand strength. If they wanted to know how strong my hands were, that was okay with me. I'd never won a race because of my hands. I squeezed the hell out of that bar.

The doctor threw up his arms. "How can your hands be as strong as your arms?" I considered telling them I played baseball and baseball gave you strong hands. "I can only assume that you're not trying on these other machines," the doctor said.

"Look," I said, "we don't make a big thing out of strength in the United States. We rely on technique."

They gave me a few more tests and then they gave up and said they wanted to go out to the pool to take some pictures of me. At the pool Don Gambril asked if it had gone well.

"No, it did not go well," the doctor said. "He's very weak."

Don looked puzzled. "Well, I'm sorry," he said, but I think he was holding back a smile.

Then the woman said that now, if I would cooperate, they would take some pictures. I said I wouldn't cooperate—

I'd had enough. Don was embarrassed and suggested that I cooperate just this once. But there was no way that I was going to cooperate with these people. I got into the pool and changed my stroke and my kick and my breathing and finally the session was over.

Cooperate. All I heard during that entire trip was that the State Department had told us to cooperate. But nobody checked on whether the Russians were cooperating with us. Neither the State Department nor the AAU protected us against foreign exploitation. I suppose some people might criticize me for guarding my training secrets—for refusing to be clocked and tested and photographed. I felt that for us to share our knowledge with the Russians would be cutting our own throats. The Russians were making great strides in swimming—very quickly. The people in the State Department and in the AAU didn't have to swim against the Russians in international competition. I did. I was the one who would suffer if I lost and I decided that I just was not going to cooperate.

I don't think either the State Department or the AAU realizes how much Russia uses these athletic victories for propaganda purposes. Why else were they going to such extremes to set us up, spy on us, inconvenience us, tire us out? *We* felt it. We felt it so much that almost every member of our team was making his own decision—five thousand miles from home—that, regardless of the damage to his (or her) own career, he was going to do this for his country. Everyone was beginning to build some kind of a peak.

I remember that American team with a lot of pride. They were young and relatively inexperienced and they were taken completely by surprise by the unexpected strength of the Russian swimmers. The terrific pressure was increased by their own reaction to harassment, the desire to win because they were harassed.

On paper we were going to lose. Comparing times, out of seventeen events we were sure of winning only six or seven.

And winning the race was important because, unlike most meets, no points would be given for second and third places. Russia was only counting first places because she had a good front line of swimmers but no depth. And there would be no relays, because Russia didn't have enough depth for relay teams. On paper we couldn't win. And yet this American team, both men and women, stayed very cool.

I've noticed this about American swimmers at such other important international meets as the Pan-American Games and even the Olympics. American athletes hold up very well under pressure. Where another team might be quiet and very nervous and tense up against what we were facing in Russia, this team stayed very relaxed, and even tried to joke about it.

Greg Buckingham, for instance, kept a running joke going the whole six days with a "Mike" he was convinced was hidden somewhere in our room. As soon as we got there Greg decided that we were certainly being bugged and he began to talk to Mike. He addressed it as another person in the room; he would talk to Dick Roth and to me and to Mike. As the pressure built up, Mike became one of the guys. We'd come into the room and say, "Hi, Mike, we're back again, boy." Or, "Hi, Mike—Don's decided to swim the breaststroke tomorrow night, and Greg'll be swimming the IM and Dick's going to swim the women's 200 backstroke." We even told bedtime stories to Mike: "Listen, Mike, are you ready? Once upon a time, there was a capitalist, imperialist swimmer . . ."

It's a crazy story, but it relieved the tension and we were better off for it.

Originally I was scheduled to swim the 200 and the 400, but a few days before the meet Don Gambril and I decided I would drop the 400 and swim the 100 instead. We had two good men in the 400, Buckingham and Nelson. We were more worried about our chances in the sprint, and we needed every victory we could get.

Also, privately, I had another reason. The 100-meter free was the first race of the meet and the Russian sprinter Leonid Ilyichev was their big hero. The week before he had done the 100 in 53.8, just .4 seconds off my Olympic record. I doubted that I was ready to go that fast, and yet if I could beat him in that first event—it would be a tight race but if I could—I felt it might boost our team's morale and knock some wind out of the Russians. This is a common phenomenon in swimming: many times a team arrives at a big meet depressed and worried, and then in the first race one of their swimmers upsets the favorite or smashes a world record and suddenly everyone on the team is psyched up so that you can't stop them. The opposite is also true: beat the best man on any team in the first race and the whole team is deflated. I wasn't really confident that I could beat Ilyichev if he was swimming the 100 free in 53.8. But we were on the spot. We couldn't pick nine out of seventeen events and say we would win those races. To win the meet we had to bring in some long shots and I figured I ought to try to be one of them.

Actually, thanks to the Russians, I was getting really psyched-up about this meet. I had decided to go to a full peak and so had Buckingham and Roth. We had shaved down, we were resting a lot, and we were building the tension and getting excited about the meet. For the first time since the Olympics I really wanted to swim to win. It was the old feeling I used to have and it felt good.

Then, two nights before the meet, trouble struck.

Four of us—Don Gambril, Buckingham, Roth, and I— were sitting around, talking in our room. I was lying on the bed propped up on my left arm. Then I felt my arm getting numb so I raised myself up and suddenly as I moved it something in my shoulder snapped.

I knew at once what it was. I'd had this before; it has to do with a tendon next to the shoulder bone, and I'm not the only swimmer who gets it. It's not a serious injury and usually it goes away in three or four days, but meanwhile you can't raise your arm and it hurts like hell.

Within minutes Don Gambril had my shirt off and was rubbing down my shoulder with alcohol and telling me not to worry, that it would be all right in the morning; but he knew that it wouldn't be all right and I knew it, too.

In the morning Don rubbed it down again and I found I could move my arm a little, but not enough to swim. By the morning workout the whole team knew about it and was pretty depressed. My sore arm could mean the loss of two first places for the team, and this team was peaking only as a team—there was nothing in it for anyone as an individual.

That morning I worked in the pool for an hour using a kickboard. My spy was there, and she couldn't understand why the rest of the team was going through a normal workout while I was alone at one side of the pool just kicking. Apparently the Russians decided that this was my special training technique, and we let them think it. The Russian swimmers would have been ecstatic to hear that I couldn't lift my left arm out of the water.

By evening, after repeated rubdowns the swelling began to disappear, but the pain remained. The injury seemed to be following its normal healing process, which meant another three days, but the meet started in twenty-four hours. At practice that night I used a kickboard again.

The next morning, the day of the meet, my arm was more numb than sore—a dull ache left by the sharp pain. But for me, there was a big difference between an ache and a sharp pain, and I began to hope. I got a rubdown and went to practice, the last practice before the meet. My spy was there and I didn't try to swim; I just kicked and let her wonder. I slept in the afternoon and when I woke up the ache was gone and I could actually move my arm quite well. At five o'clock

Gambril and I went to the pool. I warmed up completely, just as I would before a race, and then Don just rubbed the hell out of my arm. I got in the water, and took a few strokes, and my arm didn't hurt at all. I couldn't believe it! I decided to try to pull. I pulled 150 meters before it started to hurt. I took another few strokes to see if I could move it in spite of the slight pain. I could. I stopped right away and got out of the water.

By seven o'clock the stadium was packed. The Moscow stadium was nearly as big as the one in Tokyo, and I estimated that as many as ten thousand people had turned out for this swimming meet. I looked at that crowd and thought there were an awful lot of people who were sure that Russia was going to win.

A few minutes later we had our first glimpse of our competitors. They were a very impressive looking bunch of swimmers—healthy, tanned from training outdoors, confident. On the whole they were a few years older than we were, and very muscular; they all looked like weight lifters, even the girls.

I looked over at Leonid Ilyichev, the Russian sprinter. Later I got to know Ilyichev and he's really a pretty nice guy. That night I saw that he looked very confident, but I saw, too, that he kept stealing quick looks at me. Then I knew he wasn't so confident and I realized that I had a psychological advantage.

I glanced down the bench at my teammates. We looked pale beside the Russians; we had lost our tans traveling, and I could sense the tension. There was more anxiety than you would expect in a team that had peaked. We looked nervous, and we were.

Suddenly I began to get mad about this whole setup—the hotel, the food, the spy, the tests, the guided tour, everything. I was *so* mad. Not just for myself but for the whole team. As for me, I told myself I'd been pushed all I was going to be pushed and that, whatever they had done, it hadn't worked. I was staking my career on this meet and I wasn't going to get bumped off by any Russian psych-out squad for the sake of Russian propaganda. God, I was mad. And suddenly I knew I was going to win. Whether my arm lasted or not, tonight I was going to win my race.

They announced the 100-meter freestyle. The gun sounded and I just blasted off the blocks. And everything clicked. It was one of the best races of my life. Going into the turn I was a half-body length ahead, a fantastic lead in the 100 free. Everything was with me that night: I got a speed turn that was absolutely perfect—something that happens very rarely—a turn that shot me even farther ahead. Then I started to pour it on. I didn't try to save a thing; I couldn't go hard enough. About 20 meters from the finish my shoulder snapped and I hardly felt it. The pain just blended in with the rest of the pain and that night I felt completely at home with the pain. I finished as strongly as I'd started.

My time was 53.2 seconds—.2 seconds faster than my time in Tokyo. Steve Rerych, the other American sprinter, finished second with 53.7. Ilyichev came in third.

A little later Charlie Hickcox from Indiana University won the 100-meter backstroke. This meet was the beginning of a great career for Hickcox. We lost the men's 400 free that night, the 200 breaststroke, and the 200-meter butterfly. Our girls did better and took three of their four events. At the end of the first night the United States team was ahead, 5–4.

The next night we wrapped it up. Charlie Hickcox had a great victory in the 200-meter backstroke, swimming it almost four seconds faster than he'd ever gone in his life. I took Ilyichev again, in the 200-meter free. Dick Roth walked away with the 400-meter individual medley, and Ross Wales from Princeton came through in the 100-meter butterfly. Martha Randall from Wayne, Pennsylvania, and Judy Humbarger from Miami took their races again that night, becoming double winners, and we won the meet, 11–6.

The next morning the Moscow newspapers only reported that two Russian girls had broken world records—in the 100-meter and the 200-meter breaststroke events—and that was true enough, but they didn't mention the other events at all. They reported the meet very briefly in a small article on an inside page.

After we left Russia I thought a great deal about what had happened there. Strangely enough my greatest resentment was not against the Russians for what they did to us but against our own State Department and AAU for letting it happen.

I remember thinking: they send us abroad, they hand us over to the host country, and they do absolutely nothing to protect us against harassment or exploitation. They make a token inquiry ahead of time about how we will be treated or what will be expected of us and then they drop it there. They establish no minimum standards or maximum demands. In a foreign country we are like sitting ducks with no one to intercede on our behalf. We represent the United States, and from the moment we arrive we have to fight for a fair chance to do it.

I came home from this trip with some new thoughts about amateurism and professionalism.

The thing that I resented *least* was the fact that we were amateurs competing against professionals. Certainly those Russians were professionals. That was their job—competitive swimming.

But as we spent time with them we realized that their attitude toward competition was not very different from our own. They were just as nervous, just as excited, just as eager to win as we were. They were happy when they won, upset when they lost—just as we were. In the United States you hear so much about the amateur who competes just for the love of the sport, as though you could not love the sport if you were not an amateur. As we got to know those Russians we saw that they loved the sport as much as we did.

I have competed in a lot of places against a lot of people and one thing I have come to believe, absolutely, is that no one can be the best if his only incentive is money. Amateur or professional, in the end it's the competition that counts. A winner has to *want* to compete, he has to love the sport, he has to love the winning, or he can't be the best. All the rules and regulations can't change that.

I think that the AAU should worry about whether the competition is fair and equal, and about whether an athlete is being exploited, and they should care less about whether he is making a few dollars on the side that, presto, turns him from an amateur into a professional.

In the sport, in performance, at the top level there is no distinction between amateur and professional. At the top, in performance, everyone is a professional.

More and more I think we should reexamine the criteria by which these labels, amateur and professional, are established. What makes a professional? Excellence? Experience? Time invested in the sport? Or a few dollars, earned not in the performance of his sport but in talking or writing about it? Amateur, professional—the difference is the cake with or without the frosting. The cake is the same.

26

WE LEFT MOSCOW on July 18, stopped for a night in Brussels, and arrived back in Santa Clara on July 21. The Nationals would begin in Lincoln, Nebraska, on August 18.

People who had followed the results in the papers knew

that I must have peaked in Russia. They knew, too, that peaking was not part of the plan because the Nationals were so important and the Russian meet was not, and many of them wondered why I would pull a thing like that with the Nationals only a month away. (I was the guy who, only two years ago, had had enough cool not to even peak for the Olympic Trials.) You couldn't explain; you had to have been there in Moscow to understand.

Now I had twenty days to get into condition before starting another peak.

For the first time since 1962—four years—I wasn't going to the Nationals as defending champion in any event. By not competing in 1965 I had lost all my championship titles by default.

One side effect of the Russian meet was that I felt I was as good as ever. When they talked about my being over the hill and trying for a comeback, it didn't bother me so much anymore. Still, I had three championships to recapture and it wouldn't be easy. In 1964, when I had won them—in the 100, 200, and 400—many people had not peaked. They had preferred to save themselves for the Olympic Trials. This year everyone would peak. And there was a whole new crop of tough young swimmers.

We trained in Santa Clara until August 14 and then flew to Nebraska. It was hot in Lincoln that year, a good excuse to just stay in the air-conditioned motel room and rest when we weren't training. And that's all Mike Wall and I did—train and rest, that whole week. In many ways Mike and I had the same problem: we were both trying to prove we could still hold our own against the younger crop.

In the 200 and the 400 both George and I felt that John Nelson, a high-school senior from Florida was my strongest competition. Nelson had been with us in Russia but he didn't win and George thought that he probably hadn't peaked. He felt that if Nelson had peaked he would have done better in Russia. I thought that Nelson had made a good try but that his mind was too much on the Nationals to push himself psychologically all the way in Russia.

The first event was the 400 free—on Thursday, August 18; the heats were in the morning, the finals at night. I still held the world record in this event, set at the 1964 Olympics, and I was in the final heat. About halfway through the heats, we all began to realize that everyone was going very fast times for heats, much faster than two years or even a year ago. Then, in the next to last heat, Nelson tore out and broke my world record, a record that, for two years, no one had come close to. My record was 4:12.6 and Nelson went 4:11.8.

People went wild! I was stunned. A world record is rarely broken in the heats. And I had to swim in the very next race.

Before my heat George came over to me and said, "You're going to have to *go,* Don."

"But I don't want to go all out this morning," I said. I was really shaken. I had never gone all out in the heats. I'd never had to.

"Those days are past," George said, "you can't just squeeze by in the heats anymore. These guys are getting too fast. You may have to go all out this morning to qualify."

But I knew I wasn't in good enough condition to go all out in all the heats and then go again in all the finals. "George, I've never done it," I said, "and I don't want to do it now."

"Well, don't cut it too close," George said, worried.

I couldn't have cut it much closer. I was very much upset and I qualified sixth out of eight. I made the finals by .6 seconds. I think that many people wrote me off right then and there, after those trials.

Nelson had been a favorite in this race. Now he became a heavy favorite.

I went back to my room and I rested. I mean I *rested.* I

was going to need every ounce of energy I had for the finals that night, and all afternoon I didn't move a muscle.

That night the sky was overcast and the pool was very dark. I loosened up and felt a little better and then I sat down to think about my race. And suddenly I thought of a way I might win it. I could use the darkness and make it work for me. I was in lane two and Nelson was in lane five. With two lanes between us he would have trouble seeing me in the dark pool. I knew the kind of race that Nelson liked to swim. He liked to come on hard over the last 100 meters. I decided to try to get a big enough lead on him so that even if he went all out at the end he wouldn't be able to catch me. During the first 100 meters I knew he'd be looking for me, so I planned to try for just a small lead at first. Then, using the darkness, I wanted to slip out ahead during the second and third hundreds and build a lead too big for him to close.

The more I thought about this idea, the more it seemed a very good strategy. I had a feeling that it would work, and all at once I felt great. All day I'd been nervous and upset. When I stepped to the starting blocks suddenly I was very confident. Then the gun sounded and we took off.

Over the first 100 meters I picked up just a small lead, as I had planned. Over the second hundred, I opened up a little more. At the 300-meter wall I looked and saw that I had about a body-length lead. But now, with just 100 meters to go, Nelson was making his move, and I knew that this was where I could get hurt—on endurance—over the last 100 meters. I was afraid I would die first.

Before the next turn I caught another glimpse of Nelson and saw that he had begun to close the lead and that now he was going all out. After the turn I looked for him again, but I couldn't see him. The television lights were shining across the pool from lane eight, right into my eyes. Only one length left to go and I couldn't see him. But I knew he could see me, and that he would be able to see that he was closing the gap. I could hear people screaming; usually I don't hear the people, but that night I heard them plainly and I knew he was catching me. I tried again to find him and could not. I told myself that if he had passed me I would be able to see him but I wasn't certain of that and the screaming was getting louder. Then, about 15 meters from the wall, he pulled up to my shoulders and I saw him. Then I knew I could hold on, that he wouldn't pull any closer. Over those last 15 meters I gave everything I had. I finished in 4:11.6 and broke the new record that had been set that morning.

George never bets on a race but many of the coaches have a small betting pool and they try to pick the winner and the time. I heard that night that all the coaches except one had bet against me. From that race on, I heard later, they started betting with me again.

I anchored a relay for Santa Clara that same night and we set a new world record; I also picked up a second gold medal for the meet. There is nothing like the magic of victory, especially a victory in your first race. The next day, Friday, I won the 200-meter free, breaking my own world record, and we took another relay. And on Sunday I took the 100-meter free. I'd made five gold medals and was high-point winner for the meet.

Everybody was saying, "What a great comeback!" But I still felt that I had never fallen.

part four

New Thoughts on Old Institutions

27

I HAD MADE UP MY MIND to last until the 1968 Olympics in Mexico City and I was halfway there, and still holding on at the top; but the odds were against me and I knew it. The competition at the Nationals wasn't as tough as at the Olympics, and yet in 1966 it was harder for me to be a champion than it had been in 1964. I knew I was starting to run down.

At Yale I couldn't train properly and my major competitors—the guys at Santa Clara and other West Coast swim clubs and at the big universities—were training hard, with the latest techniques. In Tokyo I had won because I had worked so hard for such a long time. Now other people were working that hard and I was not. To keep pace I had to accomplish during June, July, and part of August what they did in a whole year. In 1966 I managed—I pulled it off—but I was getting old for a swimmer. Swimming is a young sport, with young competitors and young coaches who keep finding newer, better techniques for swimming faster, techniques I had to learn and master in those two summer months. And in 1968 the Olympic competition would be tougher, too. Swimming was becoming a prestigious sport. All over the world, in countries where athletes were professionals, swimming was making great strides. In Russia I had seen firsthand what could be done in two short years. Right now, swimmers everywhere, with an eye on the Olympics, were training four hours a day with the latest techniques. And I was training ninety minutes a day, from December to April, with outdated techniques. I told myself I couldn't expect to be up there when they passed out the gold medals in Mexico.

But in my own mind I couldn't compromise, I could not think of myself in terms of second best, even though my whole attitude was changing. In 1966 the thought of being a champion was less exciting to me than it had been in 1964. There were more interesting things in this world than winning a race. I didn't want to spend four hours a day in a pool, the year round. I felt it would be cheating myself of everything else that Yale could mean.

Now the press was writing that as long as Schollander swam, Schollander would win. And now *my* attitude had changed. I felt that I would win only as long as I *wanted* to win—*really wanted* it. I didn't want it enough, anymore.

Yale during 1966–1967 was a good year for me as a student, and a strange one as an athlete. I saw more and I thought more about what I had seen. I stopped accepting and I began asking questions, questions I didn't begin to answer until 1968.

I had ten roommates, ten guys who had their own lives to live and didn't give a damn about mine, except as another guy, a good friend. We worked hard and we played hard. That was the semester I started to learn something at Yale.

My roommates developed such expertise at screening my calls that even people I wanted to talk to couldn't reach me. "Well, why do you want to talk to him?" they would say. "Does he want to talk to you? Well, then why does he want to talk to you? Well, his room is way the hell on the other side of the house and I don't really feel like going for him, but I'll be glad to take a message." After a while they just said, "No, he's not in and I don't know where he is and I don't know when he'll be back. Who's calling? Can I take a message?" We went to Smith and Vassar. We argued about what color to paint the bar. We went to the football games and had good parties after them, good grain alcohol parties. We were known all over campus for our grain parties. And nothing bothered me—nothing except the AAU and the NCAA and swimming.

There was an incident that fall that crystallized some of the things I was beginning to feel and some of the questions I was beginning to ask about American attitudes toward sports and especially about the AAU.

During the previous fall, a men's magazine had come to Yale to photograph me modeling clothes that I had picked up over the years in different cities around the world. They brought along one sports jacket that they wanted me to model for the cover picture. The job took up a day's time and I couldn't accept a modeling fee so when they finished, the man directing the job told me to keep the sports jacket. I told him I couldn't keep the jacket. So when he left he just walked out and "forgot" the jacket in my room. When I saw it I said, "Oh, damn," because now I'd have to find a box and pack it and get it to the post office to mail it back to him. I kept putting it off and finally I didn't bother. It was such a little thing, a $130 jacket. But I had broken an AAU rule; the jacket was a a form of payment for a service asked of me as a result of my swimming. And somehow the AAU heard about it. A month later I was informed that the Pacific Coast Association of the AAU would conduct a full investigation. Over a $130 coat. You'd think I'd made a deal with the Russians to throw the Olympics.

I told them to go right ahead and investigate. I heard that they called the magazine, and then I never heard anymore about it. I remember thinking, If these guys are so on the ball when it comes to payoffs, why can't they take better care of the athletes competing abroad?

Then came this incident, in the fall of 1966. I was at a New Haven motel, reserving a room for my weekend date, and I met a man who turned out to be a former Olympic track star. "You must really be hauling it in," he said after a few minutes. "What do you figure you net in a year because of your name?"

"I figure I don't net anything," I said, "I figure I lose."

He didn't believe me. He thought I was protecting

myself. Then he said, "Well, swimmers never made that much, anyway. Us track stars used to haul it in. Of course, swimming wasn't that big a sport then. Hell, in my day, I knew runners used to charge a dollar a meter just to run at the county fair. Not to mention what we hauled in just for talking. I wouldn't even cross a city line for less than forty bucks." He shook his head, kind of regretfully. "I guess even the runners don't haul it in like that anymore. That was back before these amateur organizations took themselves so seriously."

I asked him if the track stars were still "hauling it in."

"Some do, some don't," he said. "I know some do. I'm still pretty active, you know. I know what goes on. It's like everything else—the big ones have to be careful. I can see how you'd have to be careful, but you've been in the business so long, I'd think you'd have figured out how to cash in; I'd think you'd be making ten, fifteen thousand dollars a year."

And the AAU had gone into a state of shock over a $130 jacket.

Around this time I started questioning the whole philosophy of amateurism. I had already begun to have some doubts about the AAU. When I first realized that amateurism was nonexistent in most other countries I had thought, That's unfair to American athletes—to make amateurs compete against professionals. I'd thought that the other countries, Russia and France, were wrong. Now I began to think that maybe we were the ones who were wrong, that maybe our strict definition of amateurism had outlived its usefulness, and that our organizations were closing their eyes to the facts of life in the world today.

I didn't think, Okay, let's all be professionals, subsidized by the government or by big business, paid to train and to compete. But I did think, What's really wrong with an athlete making a few bucks on the side in something not directly related to competing in his sport—like teaching or modeling or talking at the Rotary Club or the Elks if they wanted him? A top athlete today gives up a great deal for his sport. He invests a lot of money for coaches and training and traveling to meets. How does that kind of unrelated money make him more corrupt or make his sport any less honorable? I was just beginning to think about all this, looking around, asking questions. I didn't arrive at my own answers, right or wrong, until 1968.

A few months later I had another clash with the AAU.

I'd been invited to Ireland over Christmas vacation and George Haines was going as AAU representative. Actually I've always wondered whether the AAU knew about the sequence of these invitations. Usually the host country got in touch with me first to ask if and when I could come and I would set a date. Then they'd call the AAU and invite me for that date. Then the AAU would call me and say, for instance, "You've got an invitation to Ireland during Christmas vacation, 1966—can you make it?" And I'd say, "Great! Sure I can make it!"

That Christmas I wanted to leave the States early and visit London first. The AAU said okay, but George couldn't get away early so he was going to meet me in Ireland. I would be in England without a coach but I wasn't swimming in England. The AAU office in New York gave me the address and telephone number of the British Swimming Federation and told me to call there if I had any problems. So far, so good.

In London there was a message for me at the airport from a British woman reporter I had known in Tokyo. It turned out that many of my British friends from Tokyo were in London and wanted to get together to show me the town. She suggested that I stay at a nice little hotel near her apartment where she could get me a discount.

Since I was paying for this part of the trip myself, and

since it would be more fun to be near friends, I said, "Fine," and I canceled my other hotel reservation. For three days I had a great time seeing London with all my old friends from Tokyo.

On the last day I was there, the British Broadcasting Company called me and I taped an interview for them. About an hour later I left London for Ireland, where I met George and completed the swimming part of the trip and had a wonderful relaxing visit. On January 3 we came home and George went on to California and I went up to New Haven.

And then all hell broke loose.

I got a scathing letter from the AAU: What had I been up to in London? Why hadn't I stayed where I was supposed to stay? Why hadn't I gotten in touch with the British Swimming Federation? What was I doing talking to the BBC? Where was my sense of responsibility?

Apparently the British Swimming Federation had expected me to call them, but our AAU had only told me to call them if I needed help. The people from the British Federation reported that they had arranged to meet my plane until they learned that I wasn't on the plane I was supposed to be on. (I didn't know what plane I was supposed to be on, but I was pretty sure they'd gotten their information from our AAU, and an AAU man had put me on the plane, so I figured *he* should have known what plane I was on.)

Then I wasn't in the hotel, which was true. But nobody had told me that these people would try to get in touch with me. I'd assumed I was on my own. Then the British swimming people heard me on the BBC, and they still couldn't find me. (The BBC had found me all right.) But the swimming people got pretty mad and wrote our AAU which in turn wrote me at Yale, passing along the accusation and the blame for this terrible incident. Didn't I have any sense of responsibility? Here they'd let me go on a trip alone and look what I'd done!

I think what really bothered them was that I'd taped an interview for the BBC and they were afraid I might have taken money for it. I hadn't gotten paid; I was in too much of a hurry at the time even to think about it, but the AAU couldn't be sure and that was the kind of thing that bothered them more than anything in the world.

I wrote back to the AAU and explained where I'd been in London. Later they apologized for some of the things they'd written. But still, they repeated, this just showed that you couldn't let an athlete travel alone: he got into too much trouble.

28

By now competitive swimming was becoming drudgery. Yale had fifteen dual meets that year, which meant putting my reputation on the line fifteen times. Every Saturday I was swimming against some guy out to make the headlines by knocking me off, in front of a crowd that thought it had been cheated if I turned in some lousy time. When you're on top, people expect you to break a record every time you swim. I won my races and Yale won her meets and we moved into the postseason championships.

First the Easterns, which were held at Yale that year. Out of the seven Easterns that had been held, Yale had won six. We never peaked for the Easterns—just swam right through them, shooting for the NCAA Collegiate championships. At the Easterns I won the 500 and the 200. I lost the 100 to Mike Fitzmorris from Villanova.

Everybody in the stadium went wild. What an upset. The Villanova people were ecstatic. The cheering for Fitzmorris went on and on. For the awards, Mike was on the top tier of the stand and I was at his right on a lower tier. They announced the results and suddenly one voice in the stand rose above all the rest: "Now you've got him, Fitz! Now you're on top, looking down at him!" Mike, who is a good friend, was embarrassed and leaned over and said, "You know that's not true," and I wasn't concerned about losing. You can't peak for every single race, and yet after the race the press kept asking me, "What happened? What does this mean? Are you worried? Are you upset?" I couldn't get rid of them.

Suddenly there was an exact repetition of the events of the year before. At the Easterns somebody had brought a virus to the Yale pool and by Sunday night four or five Yale swimmers were in the infirmary, including me. Two weeks before the Collegiate championships. I was in the infirmary until Friday and the Collegiates started the following Friday.

Also, the same as the year before, Yale was having trouble with the NCAA over the 1.6 average grade rule.

I've criticized the AAU more than the NCAA because I've had to deal with it more, but the NCAA is even worse. The chief source of AAU power lies in its right to approve United States international teams and United States Olympic contestants in most sports. The NCAA's power lies in its control of college athletics. For almost fifty years these two organizations have engaged in a bitter power struggle that has included banning athletes from events for no reason except as a show of their own power. An example was the Olympic crisis of 1964 when for a while it looked as though some athletes would have to choose between the Olympics and their college scholarships.

Both groups make loud noises about their devotion to the quality and integrity of American amateur sports, but the record shows devotion primarily to the power struggle between the two groups. To gain the upper hand, each group has worked to strengthen its own power. The NCAA has moved to become absolute dictator over college sports. Toward this end, in 1966, it passed the ruling that athletes had to maintain a certain scholastic average—1.6—in order to be eligible to compete for their colleges.

To Yale this was an invasion of her academic autonomy and she refused to accept it. An average of 1.6 is the equivalent of D-plus, and at Yale a student with a D-plus average is ineligible, anyway. Nobody has a D-plus average very long at Yale. He flunks out. But this was a power play and Yale recognized it. The rule didn't really make sense. How could you compare the work at Yale with the work at some obscure college in the Deep South? And what about courses? How could you compare a guy taking nuclear physics at Harvard with a guy majoring in real estate at some small college in Texas? And would the NCAA be telling athletes next what courses they had to take? Or telling the colleges what courses they had to offer?

Yale refused to swallow this power grab, and in 1966 we were banned from all NCAA championship competition. Now, in 1967, Yale still refused to accept the rule. The other Ivy League schools fell in behind Yale, and they were all suspended. Then many other Eastern colleges threw their support to the Ivy League. By March, 1967, so many schools had lined up behind Yale on the issue of the 1.6 rule that the NCAA decided to reconsider it. In the meantime, Yale and the Ivy League could go to the championships.

Two years later, in 1969, the AAU–NCAA feud made headlines not in swimming but in basketball—in the Jack Langer story. The AAU and the NCAA were feuding enthusiastically on many fronts that year but they were slugging it out with special gusto for control of amateur basketball, an area where the NCAA is very strong through its control of all college basketball players, many of whom have athletic scholarships.

The Maccabiah Games, an innocent enough international competition for Jewish amateur athletes, were scheduled in Israel for the summer of 1969. Because this was an international competition, Israel dealt with the AAU, whereupon the NCAA announced that no college basketball players would be allowed to take part in the games. Apparently they saw nothing ludicrous or even inconsistent in the fact that other college athletes—swimmers, track men—would be allowed to participate. Only basketball players were singled out for this favored treatment.

Several Jewish college basketball players were offered places on the American team and except for Jack Langer they all refused, out of fear of being declared ineligible for their college teams. Jack Langer consulted Yale authorities, received permission and went. He was the only college player on the American basketball team. Yale pointed out that other Yale athletes would be participating in the games in other sports so it was illogical to refuse permission to Langer.

Because Langer played in the Maccabiah Games, when the college basketball season rolled around the NCAA declared him ineligible. Yale responded by letting Langer play. So the NCAA suspended Yale from all championship competition and the income derived from televising them for two years. Never let it be said that the NCAA let principle stand in the way of power.

I had been out of the infirmary for five days when we left for the Collegiates and the Yale coach, Phil Moriarty, scratched me from the 500 because I was in such terrible shape. The big threat in the 500 was Greg Buckingham of Stanford, my roommate from Russia who used to talk to the "Mike." Greg had been having a good year and now at the Collegiates he not only won the 500 but also set a new American record.

The next night I had to swim against him in the 200. I tried to jam the pace, hoping to force him to swim the race my way, nice and slowly, but I'd done that to Greg before. Greg knows me very well. And Mike Wall, who was also on the Stanford team, had warned him that I'd probably do just that. Greg went out fast and stayed ahead until the finish. He killed me. The Stanford guys went wild. The fans went wild. The press went wild.

After two days of competition I still didn't have an NCAA gold medal. Later, one of my roommates told me that on the television coverage of the meet all you heard was, "Schollander hasn't won a race here yet!"

The next day in the 100-yard free I went out very fast, got away ahead of everybody, then missed a turn and finished fourth.

That night, in the relay, I went off in fourth or fifth place and I finished in fourth or fifth place. No one caught me, and I didn't catch anyone.

The media said, "Schollander, who's been in the infirmary all week, hasn't won a race here yet, but he's not making any excuses!"

I'd been back in my room at Yale about ten minutes when a sports reporter called. "What happened to *you?*"

What happened! "You can read about it in the papers," I said.

"Isn't that the first 200 you ever lost?" Yeah, that's right. "Why'd you lose?"

"I guess someone swam it faster."

"You going to retire?"

"No, I'm not going to retire."

"Well, look boy, you lost the 100 at the Easterns, you backed out of the 500 at the Collegiates, and then you lost the 200 and the 100. Aren't you ready to call it quits?"

"Why'n hell should I call it quits?" I said.

The guy was quiet for a second and then he said, "You don't figure you're washed up?"

I hung up and wondered how much longer I would be

able to put up with all this—getting up for meets I didn't care about, having to swim them whether I was ready or not, reading my obituary every time I lost. The only reason I swam well, the only reason I competed, was because I enjoyed it. But it was becoming less enjoyable all the time. And if I didn't enjoy it? Then I couldn't swim.

29

AFTER SUCH A BAD WINTER SEASON I was eager to get to California that summer of 1967 to start training. I knew this was going to be a pattern with me. Winters I would fall behind and summers I would try to catch up at Santa Clara.

Then, a few days before I was to leave it looked as though I might not get there. My family had moved to Jacksonville, Florida, and while I was there, spending a few days with them, we learned that a typhoid epidemic had broken out at Stanford. Dick Roth and Mike Wall were down with it, and a few other Stanford-Santa Clara swimmers who, for the past month, had been using the Santa Clara pool.

When my mother heard about it she really raised a fuss about my going out there. She wanted me to stay in Florida to train. With my health record I didn't blame her, but I knew that I had to get back to George or I was finished.

I got a typhoid shot and took off.

Right from the start this year I felt like a stranger. I was early: the colleges were still in session and the Stanford guys were in the hospital. The only people at Santa Clara were a lot of high-school kids I didn't know. I had always felt at home, training at Santa Clara. Now, with these kids I felt old, and not particularly welcome.

These kids were hot; they were in great condition. I could remember when I was in high school and the college kids came back; they'd taken a break and I was already in shape and I'd kill them. And I could remember my attitude: no matter how well I'd been doing, when these guys arrived I shifted into high gear and did even better. Now I was on the other side of the fence.

I had always been the star at Santa Clara, the team leader; this gives you confidence. This team had its own star—a tall, thin, dark-haired high-school swimmer, with long arms and legs and, they said, a terrific lung capacity. He was already breaking American records whenever he swam, and the local newspapers were billing him as the next great American swimmer. His name was Mark Spitz.

From the beginning I think I was running scared that summer. Not only because I wasn't in shape at the start but because I sensed I had lost some of my interest in swimming. My motivation wasn't the same, and I knew this was bad.

Even worse, George was training us differently. We had always done a lot of overdistance early in the summer, the one kind of training I needed. This summer we started out with very little overdistance.

Another difference was that there were so many more people in the pool that George couldn't keep up with everyone. He was giving us less individual attention, less personal encouragement, and this was the thing that had made George great—the fact that he knew his swimmers so well. But it was more than just the increase in numbers. George seemed to have lost his old spirit. Other years he would walk along the end of the pool and ask every man for his repeat times. This summer, he would go days without asking for times. Other years he would walk up and down the length of the pool, talking to us at both ends. Now he would just sit in a chair at one corner of the pool. It was as though George had grown tired of the whole thing—swimming and coaching and us.

Finally, after a few weeks, I went to his house one night to ask him what was wrong. And I learned that George had been sick.

George Haines works harder than any man I know. He's at the pool at six in the morning and he goes at a fast pace all day, often until 9:30 at night. He trains the Santa Clara men's team, girl's team, high-school team, and the age group teams—the younger kids that he's bringing along. He has speaking duties and meetings with other coaches to exchange ideas and plan new programs. Finally, last spring, he had suffered a near collapse. He had had some kind of attack, not a serious attack, but he still was not well and his doctors told him that he had to slow down. He couldn't keep up that pace any longer.

What kind of a summer was it? It was pressured and frantic. Instead of one important meet, the Summer Nationals, for which you could build all summer, we were faced, within a one-month span, with three: the Santa Clara International Invitational on the Fourth of July weekend, the Pan-American Games at Winnipeg two weeks later, and then the Nationals the first week in August.

This was the first year of the Santa Clara International, destined to become one of the most prestigious international swimming events in the world. George had planned it in connection with the opening of the new $800,000 Santa Clara pool complex, partly to pacify a faction of the local citizenry who had objected to spending that kind of money on the Santa Clara swim club. The idea was that as an annual event this meet would bring profit and prestige to the city. And it did. Next to the Olympics, it became the biggest swimming meet in the world. Even that first year the best American, European, and Asian swimmers accepted invitations, and what had started out as a relatively small early June meet was shaping up as a bigger and tougher meet than the Nationals.

At Santa Clara by July 4 we would barely be out of preseason training, and we were going to have to swim against foreign athletes who would be in top condition because they trained the year round.

None of the college swimmers were ready for the Santa Clara Invitational, and they began to find reasons not to compete. The ones who had had typhoid had a ready-made excuse. Others just said they were sick, or that they couldn't do it. For me there was no getting out of it. I had to swim: for the publicity, for the meet, for the club.

I got out of the 400 because I knew I couldn't do it. And I wasn't too concerned about the 200. It was the 100 that worried me.

In Tokyo, in the 100 free at the Olympics, Bobby McGregor had been my toughest competition and when I beat him people had said that it was a fluke, that Bobby was still the greatest 100-meter man in the world. Now Bobby was coming to Santa Clara and it would be our first meeting since then. The race was getting a lot of publicity as a rematch—too much publicity, so far as I was concerned. Because of the Pan-American Games and the Nationals coming up, I hadn't peaked for the Santa Clara meet and I said so, but nobody paid much attention. I won the 200, although my time was terrible. And in the 100 Bobby McGregor beat me.

Our high-school kids were in great shape for that meet and did very well, especially Mark Spitz. A few weeks earlier, in the San Leandro meet, Spitz had broken my world record in the 400 free. In the Santa Clara meet he broke the world record in the 200-meter butterfly and set a new world record, for the second time that summer, in the 400-meter freestyle. More and more, people were now referring to him as the greatest swimmer in the world and to me as the "old pro," or "Schollander—the old man of swimming."

It was about this time, I think—not *because* of the Santa Clara meet, but at that time—that I began to ask myself whether I had made a mistake going to Yale, or made a mistake trying to continue in competitive swimming. More and more I felt that I should have made a clear choice, one or the other, that it had been a mistake to try to do both.

That was a summer of great psychological change for me. I had started the summer anxious and depressed because I'd had a bad winter season, saying to myself, subconsciously, at least, "God, I've got to get ready for the Olympics next year. I've got to *work* if I'm going to do well in those damned Olympics. And if I don't do well, then what?" Then, I suppose, my anxiety increased as I worried about having a competitor as good as Mark Spitz. Already people were talking about whether Spitz would win more gold medals at the 1968 Olympics than I had won in 1964—and the 1968 Olympics were still more than a year away.

I suppose all of this figured in my doubts about my decision to go to Yale. I had made the choice while I was on top; I hadn't really foreseen what it would mean. Until you have felt pain you can't imagine what it is like. That summer I still could not imagine the pain of not being the best swimmer in the world. The only thing I could feel was the *possibility* of not being the best. And I could ask myself whether I could cope with that. You get used to being the best, and having been on top doesn't make you feel better when you lose; it makes you feel worse. The higher you climb, the harder you fall, and I had to come to grips with the fact that I might fall. To have someone say, "Well, you were the best for a long time," is no consolation. It's like telling someone who is dying, "Well, you had a good life."

30

As we trained for the Pan-American Games, Spitz began to work out next to me. Every day he'd be in the next lane.

BEGINNING THE LAST LAP OF A 4 × 100-METER RELAY

About the only thing Spitz lacked for competitive swimming was a sharp sense of pace and that was something that I still had, as good as ever. I figured he wanted to pick up some pointers on pace from me and it bugged me to have him there. I'd get out of the pool and move over three or four lanes; a few minutes later he would follow. I'd move again and he would follow. Finally George got fed up and assigned us to lanes right next to each other and I felt let down that George would do that. If I'd been in condition it wouldn't have bothered me; I'd have been out to burn Spitz on every repeat. But that's how low I was—emotionally I was at absolute zero—that I'd let a thing like that bug me.

The Pan-American Games, which are like a small Olympics, open to all countries in the Western Hemisphere, were held that year in Winnipeg, Canada. The Spring Nationals of 1967 had counted as the trials for these games and, with the miserable spring season I'd had, I was entered only in the 200 free plus a couple of relays. My choice would have been to skip them altogether, but I was an Olympic champion and I was obligated to go. Then, since George wasn't going, he put me in charge of the Santa Clara swimmers because I was the oldest guy there. I was just about the oldest everything that summer. In fact, I was the only swimmer from the 1964 United States Olympic Team who was on the 1967 United States Pan-American Team. That was supposed to be pretty cool—to still be around and still be on top after three years. I thought it was pretty depressing—to be the *only guy that old*—like being the last alumnus in your class.

I have nightmare memories of those Pan-American Games, and not from the swimming. I felt completely alone. There was no one for me to talk to. I felt so old. These kids were of a different era. They had shaving-cream fights and grape fights and put peanuts in other people's beds. I had to yell at them to get them to bed.

I used to watch them and think about how swimmers

had changed. On the 1964 Olympic Team, so many of the
guys were interested in medicine or law or teaching; on this
1967 Pan-American Team, almost everyone was going into
physical education. This was a new breed. I think even then,
swimming was becoming so rigorous, so completely demanding, that guys with higher goals just couldn't give enough of
themselves to the sport to be champions. In 1964 swimmers
were very capable guys with great drive, even outside of the
pool—guys like Roy Saari, Steve Clark, Mike Austin. They
were more than just swimmers, and I thought that was why
they were such good swimmers. Watching these kids I used to
wonder. Even if they turned out to be better swimmers
technically, how would they shape up as competitors? Would
they have the drive and the cool and the brains to hold up
under real stress, the kind of stress that builds up at the
Olympics?

I swam my three events—the 200 free and two relays—
and, on George's orders, got back to Santa Clara without
waiting for the end of the meet. I broke my own world record
in the 200 free—I honestly don't know how—and my two
relay teams won, so I had three gold medals. Spitz swam in
five events, two butterfly and three relay. He broke one
world record, tied another, and with three relay wins, he took
five gold medals.

It was after I left that Spitz won his fifth gold medal and
drew a lot of attention. An AP reporter who interviewed him
sent out this story:

RIVALRY EXISTS BETWEEN SPITZ, SCHOLLANDER

by Will Grimsley

Winnipeg (AP) —The keenest swimming rivalry in the
Pan-Am Games is not between the United States and
other countries . . . but between young Mark Spitz,

the Yanks' newest water sensation, and Don Schollander, the old.

"The difference," one member of the (U.S. team) . . . said today, "is that Schollander talks about what he's done and Spitz talks about what he's going to do— then does it." This is an example of the sharp split in loyalties in the U.S. swimming camp. Either you're a pro-Spitz or a pro-Schollander man.

"Sure I'd like to duplicate Don's four gold medals in the Olympics and go him one better if I could," Spitz said. "I feel certain I'll try for four at Mexico City and, if the schedule permits, I could go for six. I'll swim the 100 and 200 meter butterfly and perhaps three relays. I could possibly throw in a freestyle event, if the altitude doesn't prove too tough. . . .

"Don reached his peak in the 1964 Olympics when he won four gold medals. . . . He not only won recognition as a swimmer but as an outstanding athlete. . . . Now he is trying to add to that. Instead he is going downhill." Spitz made a downward motion with his hand. "Me? I want to be the best. I want to win at Mexico City and maybe again in 1972 because they'll be my college years. But I want to quit on top. I have no intention of hanging on."

What can you say to an article like that? As far as I was concerned there wasn't any rivalry and I had never noticed that the team was divided into any kind of pro-Spitz, pro-Schollander camps. The part that burned me up was that statement that I talked about what I had done. For years I'd made it a point *not* to talk about that. And this summer I wasn't saying much about anything.

An article like that stirs up a fuss. The team was upset. Mark's father called George to say he didn't think Mark had made those statements. When Mark came back he said he hadn't made them, and George ordered him not to talk to any more reporters at the Nationals in Chicago; and he ordered me not to retaliate.

Retaliate! I wasn't even thinking about that. All I was thinking was that at the Nationals I was going to have to defend three national championships.

31

A WEEK LATER we were off to the Nationals. Even before we arrived in Chicago the press was playing up the Spitz-Schollander rivalry, focusing a lot of attention on which of us would do better in the national championships. They were building it up into a real feud and now Spitz fanned the flames. When people asked what events he would swim, he said he *might* swim the 400 freestyle. Now he wasn't going to swim the 400 free because it was the same day as the 200 butterfly, which he was definitely going to swim—and he knew it. This was kind of a cheap shot, as if to say, "I could win it, but even though I could win it, I might decide to swim something else."

The 400 free was my first event. I qualified second, which was good for me—I seldom qualify so high—and for a while I began to think that maybe I could win this race. But I couldn't believe how nervous I was. I hadn't slept at all the night before, and the whole day of the race I was on edge, which is always a bad sign.

That night, standing around waiting for the race to start, I thought (and I can remember the words) : Goddamn, I'm so nervous. I can't believe how nervous I am. And then: This is ridiculous. Why are you allowing yourself to be so nervous? It doesn't mean that much to you. It doesn't prove

anything. Why are you doing this? Then: Damnit, this isn't
fun, anymore. Why are you swimming this event? And as
soon as I said that, I had lost. I could have scratched. For the
first time I had blown my cool before a really important
event.

The race began and Greg Charlton took an early lead
and I let him go. I thought he would tire and I would over-
take him. At 250 meters I made my move and at 300 meters I
was with him. But by 350 meters I felt myself getting very
tired. Right after the turn the pain came—terrific pain and
too early—and I saw Greg pull ahead of me again. And I
realized that, for the first time since 1963, I was going to lose
a national championship race. It was like a piano falling on
me. I slowed up even more. Two other swimmers passed me,
and a third, and a fourth. I finished fifth.

The press made a big thing out of my loss. "Schollander's career turned a corner last night," they wrote.
Others just asked the same old question while suggesting the
answer, "Is Schollander through?"

At the end of the race that night, while I was still in the
water, George came over to me. "You're just not getting
enough overdistance at Yale," he said.

I was still sort of numb. Very depressed, I listened while
George insisted that there was nothing wrong with my swimming. I just wasn't building enough endurance the year
round to be able to last 400 meters. "You're not getting
enough training at Yale," he said.

"Well—" I said. I was very low. "Maybe I was wrong to
go there."

I half expected George to agree, or at least to say, "Well,
you're getting a good education, but for your swimming it
was a mistake." Instead he just looked at me hard. "You
know that's not true," he said, "and I don't ever want to hear
you say that again. That's the best school for you."

I knew George was right and I began to recover. Things

began to make sense to me again, and I knew that really, between an education at Yale and the capacity to win a 400-meter swimming race, for me there was no choice, and there never had been. My temporary lapse of sanity was over. By the time George finished talking to me and I got out of the water I wasn't at all upset. This is the sign of a great coach. When the reporters came around to ask me how I felt about losing, I said it didn't bother me much—and I meant it.

All summer I'd been depressed and uncertain and now, suddenly I was all right again. It was like a man who's been sick, running a high fever, and suddenly the fever breaks and he recovers. For the first time all summer I was in good spirits. The next day I went around with a big grin, which confused everyone. They had thought I would be down and bracing myself for a bad meet, and here I was walking around with a big grin, really relaxed.

The next night I won the 200-meter freestyle and smashed the world record. And the day after that, hardly a favorite anymore, I won the 100-meter free. With two winning relays I came out of the 1967 Nationals with four first places and a fifth. But I didn't take high point for the meet. Spitz had four first places and a third.

In retrospect, I think that summer of 1967 was one of the most important summers of my life. It was much more important than 1966 when I had made my so-called comeback after mono, because in 1967 I resolved certain things that had been bothering me for a long time. That summer I had had doubts about myself—for the first time in a long time—and I think the problem was that, although I had told myself in 1964 that swimming was going to come second to a good education, I hadn't really believed it. Deep down, I think, I had given them equal priority. I had told myself that I was going to do both, get the most out of Yale and stay on top in swimming. Now I realized that I couldn't do that. And

at the end of that summer I came to grips with myself and
with the problem.

I decided that I would never again let myself get caught
up in the drive to be the number one swimmer in the world.
I decided that I didn't care about what anyone else was doing
or how many other swimmers were keying off to try to unseat
me at the top. I said to myself, "What do you care if another
swimmer wins four gold medals, or five or six or a hundred?
What difference does it make whether you win more gold
medals than anyone else or whether you win the most gold
medals ever?" Others could set their standards by me, if they
had to. I had to be the one to set the standards for myself.

I had had my heyday in swimming. All I could do now
was my best. I promised myself I would do anything I could
do to win in the next Olympics. Almost anything. George had
told me that if I hoped to do well in Mexico in the fall I
would have to drop out of Yale for the spring semester in
1968 and begin to get into condition. For a while I had
thought of doing that. But at the end of that troubled
summer of 1967, I decided against it. I knew I couldn't do
it—drop out of Yale for the last semester of senior year and
leave it all behind—just to train for the 1968 Olympics.

Early that summer I had wondered whether I could cope
with not being the best swimmer in the world. At the end of
the summer I faced the possibility squarely that by the time
of the Olympics I might not be the best and I knew now that
I *could* cope with it. I didn't have to be the best swimmer in
the world.

It was a crossroads summer when one view of life ended
and another began.

part five

South Africa:
Politics and Sports

32

AT ABOUT THE SAME TIME I came to terms with my personal doubts, I began to think more critically and more constructively about the system under which I had lived and competed during my swimming career—the AAU, the philosophy of amateurism, the role of sports in international politics and the effect, in turn, of those politics on sports. And, I suppose because I was older and more knowledgeable, I began to form value judgments about them. Also, that year over Christmas vacation I took my final trip abroad under the auspices of the AAU—to South Africa. It was the worst, most confused, bungled up, irresponsible trip I ever had. And it was much more.

That trip turned out to be a sneak preview of the whole range of problems that developed during the next ten months, and that poisoned the atmosphere of the 1968 Olympic Games and nearly destroyed them. The 1968 Olympics, destined to be labeled the "Problem Olympics," were racked with every kind of difficulty: lack of communication, lack of understanding, international politics, organizational politics, commercialism, inefficiency, racial problems. When these problems boiled over, people rationalized sadly that they were the result of an unfortunate series of coincidences. Nothing could be more unrealistic. They were the inevitable conclusion to a progressive erosion in the world of amateur sports. The smoke was already visible when I was in South Africa. Shortly after my return it erupted.

In the summer of 1966, a year and a half earlier, a South

African swimming team had competed in the Los Angeles Invitational and some of their swimmers had asked if I would consider visiting South Africa. I told them that I could make the trip over Christmas vacation of 1967, but that the invitation would have to come through the AAU in New York.

A year later, in the summer of 1967, an AAU official called me to say that I'd been invited to South Africa over Christmas vacation. I said that I could leave any time after December 18 and that I had to be back by January 7. For a few months I heard nothing.

Then, apparently, a new swimming organization came into power in South Africa and wrote to our AAU to ask when I was coming. From here on, total noncommunication took over and inefficiency skidded downhill into complete confusion.

By November I still had no details about the trip—date of departure, date of return, the name of the coach, or even whether I was still going. When I told a good friend, John duPont—a pentathlete who trains for swimming at Santa Clara—that I was going to South Africa, he decided to pay his own way and come along. Late in November, when he called the AAU to make arrangements, he inquired about the dates and the AAU still didn't know them.

During the first week of December, I called the AAU to ask who the coach would be. They didn't have a coach yet. "If we can't find a coach, we'll have to cancel the trip," they said. A week later they found a coach, Dave Robertson, swimming coach at New Trier High School in Chicago. They still didn't know when we would leave. I reminded them that I could leave anytime after December 18 and that I had to be back by January 7. The AAU man said the South African people had planned events until the ninth. I told them again that I had to be back by the seventh. A few days later, the AAU called to say that if I couldn't stay until the tenth, the South African people would cancel the whole trip.

By now I was really curious about South Africa and I wanted to go there. At first I told the AAU to ask them to move everything up two or three days; then I told them to get me down there on the nineteenth and I would ask them myself. Two days before I left, I didn't know when I was leaving, when I was coming back, or whether I was going.

We finally left—Dave Robertson, John duPont, and I—on December 19 at 8:00 P.M. with a six-hour stopover scheduled in London. We landed in London at 3:00 A.M., New York time (8:00 A.M. London time) and had to wait until 2:00 P.M. for a South African Airlines plane to Johannesburg. With a six hour layover I went to a hotel near the airport and slept for four hours. It was the only sleep I had for three days. Because of international politics, South African Airlines cannot fly over continental Africa; the continental Africans shoot them down. So we flew a long roundabout ocean route with another stopover for gas in the Canary Islands. Late in the afternoon of December 21, two days after we left New York, we arrived in Johannesburg— cramped, exhausted, and very irritable from having missed two nights sleep.

Harry Getz, the head of the South African Swimming Union, met us at the airport and said, rather uncordially, "We're surprised you're here!"

"The last we heard," Getz said, "was that you had to leave on the seventh, and we wrote to the AAU that if you couldn't stay until the tenth, you should cancel the trip. We've heard nothing since then. We didn't know for sure that you were coming and we came out here to the airport just in case.

"We have a couple of bookings but since we didn't know for sure that you were coming, we haven't many that are definite," Getz said, accusingly, "and we've had trouble getting hotel reservations in some cities." Then he realized that John duPont was part of our party. No one had told him that John was coming. Reservations had only been made for two people. "Well, we'll work something out," he said. "In the meantime, we arranged a press interview, in case you showed up."

I told him that we hadn't slept for two days and had to get some sleep, but Getz said that the reporters were waiting there at the airport.

For an hour and a half I was trapped in a tiny room; the reporters finished in about thirty minutes and then the "press interview" became a reception for the officials of the South African AAU. I was bleary-eyed. Getz began to tell me about the arrangements. For a guy with "nothing definite," he was coming up with an awful lot of commitments.

"Tonight an exhibition . . . tomorrow night a race . . . then you go to Bethlehem for a race and an exhibition, then to Durban—two races, two exhibitions—then to East London, then Port Elizabeth, then to Kimberley, then Cape-town . . ."

It sounded like a touring vaudeville act. "Wait a minute," I said. I had been told that I would be expected only to demonstrate my strokes and to explain the fundamentals of our swimming and racing techniques. "I'm only supposed to put on a few clinics, to explain how we're training in the United States."

"Oh, no," Getz said, "that's not it at all. You have to compete."

"But I'm not in condition to compete every night. With all this traveling, I'll be dead tired. I'll be glad to put on exhibitions but I can't race in every town. And I'd like to see parts of the country," I said. "I'd like to see some gold and diamond mines, and Kruger National Park."

"No, no, there's no time for Kruger National Park," Getz said.

At the moment his biggest worry was that they couldn't hold an exhibition on Christmas Eve or New Year's Day.

Finally they let me go to bed for two hours and then woke me up to give an exhibition. I was pulled in as an added attraction to a water polo match.

The next day they showed us around Johannesburg and then drove us to Breckpan, a city two hours away, where I was scheduled to race.

The official in Breckpan assumed I was an idiot and spoke only to Dave. "We've got him entered in the 100-, 200-, and 400-meter freestyle," he said to Dave.

"All in one night?" I asked.

"We can get him into the 100 fly, too, if he wants to swim that," he said to Dave.

"I'll do the 200 free," I said, "and then if I'm not too tired, maybe the 100 free."

"He's going to disappoint a lot of people," he said to Dave.

"I'm sorry," I said, "but right now I'm not too concerned with that."

He snapped at me for being insolent.

"Any more lip from him and I won't swim at all," I said to Dave.

They told me that the best man in the race would be Brian Stuart and that he usually went around 2:12 for the 200. The others went slower—about 2:14. "Go 2:10 and you should be okay," they said.

When I saw Brian Stuart I recognized him. Nobody had bothered to tell me that I was scheduled to swim against one of South Africa's best freestylers the day after I arrived in the country. Another thing they had neglected to tell me was that Breckpan was at altitude. After the first lap of the 200 I was gasping for air. I couldn't get enough oxygen on a normal breath, and Stuart was two body lengths ahead of me. I didn't catch him until the last 5 meters of the race.

I went about 2:03 for the race; Stuart went about 2:05. If his normal time was 2:10, then he'd shaved off five seconds in a single race: he was certainly the first and last person in history to do that.

After that I refused to swim the 100. The crowd was furious and began to hiss; they had paid to see me swim in three or four events. The next day the press cut me to pieces because I'd said I was too tired to swim.

By now I had had it. Our AAU had not bothered to find out what I would be expected to do in South Africa and now I was being worked to death with no letup. At dinner that night I told the South African officials that I was going to take the next day off and go to Kruger National Park.

That was a bomb. "You have to be in Bethlehem tomorrow afternoon for an exhibition," they said.

For several minutes we argued. Finally, when they saw that I wouldn't give in, they said, "Okay, we'll cancel the exhibition tomorrow, but you've got to promise to be there the next day." I agreed to be in Bethlehem late the next day.

Kruger Park was so fantastic that I began to calm down right away. It was summer there, and very hot, and one of the guides said, "Don't expect to see too many animals. They've gone north for the summer." For a couple of hours we just drove, seeing no animals at all. Finally we saw some giraffes, and I said, just horsing around, "Okay, there are some lions around the next curve." And then, around the next curve, there were some lions! And then an elephant. And suddenly there were animals everywhere—every kind of animal you could imagine. John is a camera bug and we took hundreds of pictures. There is a small eating place overlooking the river and you just sit there, eating, out in the wilderness, and you see alligators, monkeys, gazelles, water buffaloes coming to the river to drink. And suddenly everything seemed worthwhile. My spirits rebounded and I was in a much better mood. That night we slept in the park in a camp of three-sided huts, with animals walking around all night; for the first time in Africa I got a good night's sleep.

John had hired a plane to fly us up to the park but the plane hadn't stayed overnight, so the next day we returned to Johannesburg by car, about a five hour ride, and arrived in the early afternoon. We went straight to the airport to fly to Bethlehem, where I'd been told I was supposed to put on an exhibition that night. At the airport two men came running up to us and said, "You're supposed to be in Bethlehem right now!"

"No, no," I said. "Didn't Getz tell you we were going up to Kruger Park and that we'd be in Bethlehem late this afternoon?"

"We didn't hear anything about that! Everybody is upset that you're not there. Come on. We're going to drive you there and we've got to get going."

Drive! It was a five and a half hour drive!

Now they told us that you couldn't fly to Bethlehem. You had to fly to a different city and then drive to Bethlehem, which took as long as driving from Johannesburg. So for another five and a half hours we drove to Bethlehem, arriving about seven o'clock. Without pausing for food, we were rushed directly to the pool.

"You're entered in three races this evening," someone told me.

"Races? I thought I was supposed to give an exhibition."

"No, no—there's a swimming meet."

I began to realize that nobody in one town knew what another town was planning. Harry Getz in Johannesburg had no idea what people had scheduled in Bethlehem, didn't ask, and didn't bother to advise them of any changes in our plans. Getz seemed to have no communication with people in other cities at all. Usually when we arrived they still hadn't been told that there were three of us. Most of them were expecting only Dave and me.

That night in Bethlehem, after riding in a car for over ten hours, it was just impossible for me to compete. I tried to explain and to tell them that they wouldn't learn much, anyway, if I just swam up and down the pool as fast as I could. "Why don't I just give an exhibition?" I suggested.

They were furious.

But a professional coach in Bethlehem, one of the few professional coaches in South Africa, came to my rescue and said they would all learn a lot more if I gave an exhibition.

The local officials weren't interested in learning any- thing; they were interested in money, but finally they agreed to an exhibition. Then the crowd was upset to hear that I would only give an exhibition. But Dave and I put on a good show and after a while the people settled down and enjoyed it.

After that, Dave and I decided that we had to straighten things out once and for all at the next city, Durban, where we were staying four days. At the airport the Durban swimming officials met us and began immediately to discuss my schedule—race, exhibit, race, exhibit, race, race. Finally we all sat down and I said, "I'm not going to compete in Durban. I'm just going to put on exhibitions. That's what I was supposed to do this whole trip, clinics only, and all I've been doing is racing. I can't race so often."

The following week, I knew, there was to be a big swimming meet in Capetown. Now I said, "I'll race one more time—in Capetown. Bring everybody in South Africa who wants to race against me to Capetown, and I'll take them all on at once instead of one at a time."

In Durban, when we brought things to a head we found out what was behind the chaos. The coach in Durban had been coach of the team that toured the United States in 1966, and when he heard what was happening, he undertook to straighten things out. Then I learned what was going on.

To raise money to bring me to South Africa the central office of their AAU, headed by Getz, had solicited the provinces, and each province had kicked in with the understanding that I would visit there to recoup their money. They had invested in me, like a racehorse, and they felt that once I got to their province, they could do anything they wanted with me to get back their money.

Durban had put up quite a bit of money because, as a resort area, it could make a lot of money back. But if I didn't race, it stood to lose a good sum. The coach called Harry Getz and told him that I couldn't be used this way, that I should only be asked to put on exhibitions. But he also said that with only exhibitions Durban should not be expected to put up all that money, that the national federation should foot the bill.

Getz exploded. *His* office wasn't going to pay for our entire trip. The next day he called Dave.

"We know what's going on over there," Getz said, "and we can't have it."

"We're sorry," Dave said, "but we don't think you're doing the right thing."

"Oh, no. You're the one to blame. It's your fault." Getz said that we had known all along that this would be a racing tour and Dave answered that we had not known—we had been told that we would only put on clinics. They argued for about ten minutes and finally Getz said, "Are you going to race in every town *or not?*"

At first Dave had been reluctant to argue, but now he was mad. "No, we are not," he said.

"Well, then, perhaps the rest of the trip should be canceled."

"You can't do that!" Dave said.

"You've broken the agreement, you might as well go home."

"Then we'll just stay here and pay our own expenses," Dave said. "We've got our return tickets."

"Oh, no. You can't do that."

A goodwill tour! I couldn't believe this was happening.
It was like a bad dream.

A little later Getz called again and this time I talked to
him. "Mr. Getz, if we leave right now you're going to lose
even more money," I said. "Besides, the whole thing is going
to look pretty silly. I don't ever have to come back to this
country; you have to live here. And you're going to have to
explain it all to the press."

The South African press had been giving my trip heavy
coverage. They were for me when I competed and against
me, at first, anyway, when I refused to compete. But as the
situation deteriorated I began to give them long, careful
statements explaining what was going on and why I couldn't
race every day, and more and more the press was swinging to
my side.

Also, by this time I had picked up another piece of
information. There was a political struggle going on in the
athletic federation, much like the struggle between our AAU
and NCAA. The Getz faction had strength in Johannesburg
and Capetown but it was unpopular in the provinces. That
was why there had been no communication where I was concerned; they were hardly speaking to each other. My abrupt
exit would not strengthen support for Getz in the provinces.

"You know the press is on my side, Mr. Getz," I said. "If
you order us to leave you'll look very bad." I wondered
whether this had ever happened in the annals of sport, that a
visiting athlete had had to fight for his own survival this way
with the local sponsor.

The next morning Getz called us back. He had a deal for
us. "I'll make sure that the best swimmers stay away from you
until you get to Capetown," he said, "if you'll just compete
against the local swimmers while you're out there."

These people had no interest in having their athletes
learn something from me or in giving them some experience:

they just wanted their money back. I didn't care. I didn't mind swimming against the locals; it would just be a workout for me. "But if I race, I won't put on exhibitions," I said, "one or the other." They had set up exhibitions in the afternoon and races at night.

"That means we lose money," Getz said.

"I'm sorry," I said, "but I didn't come down here to make money for you."

The battle was over. Getz resigned himself to losing money on me.

What I saw in South Africa was a classic example of the exploitation, by men in the power structure, of athletes they were supposed to be serving and protecting. These men didn't care a rap for their athletes, or for any athletes. They cared about their own power. They cared about making money for their organizations in order to perpetuate that power—and that is *all* they cared about.

The problem in South Africa was extreme, but hardly unique. For years I had seen it all over the world, not excluding the United States, where the feud between the AAU and the NCAA, openly called a power struggle, had been raging for years. A worldwide sickness had infected amateur sports and this corruption of purpose and ideals was one of the contributing factors to the problems of the "Problem Olympics."

In Durban, where we stayed for four days, I had time to inquire about a problem that everyone knew was going to boil up any day now as an Olympic issue. In 1964 South Africa had been banned from the Olympics because she refused to permit black athletes on her Olympic team. In February, 1968, one month away, the IOC was going to vote on whether to reinstate South Africa into the Olympic movement. While I was in South Africa I wanted to learn more about the apartheid situation. In Durban I asked questions, and received some careful answers. This was what I saw and learned.

In a "black" village that I visited the accommodations were similar to a low-income housing project in the United States. If anything, the houses maintained by the government were in better condition. Indian and Chinese people are part of a third group—"coloured." Japanese people are "white."

"It's a question of cultural development," I was told, "not a matter of race or color, but of being cultured—civilized."

I asked if they were saying that the great civilizations of China and India were less cultured than the white civilizations of Europe, and they replied that I just didn't understand. (I understood that South Africa carries on important trade with Japan.)

The race problems of South Africa are different from those of the United States. In South Africa there are two completely separate peoples with completely different cultures, and there is no cultural overlap. The black people and the white people do not even speak or write the same language.

South Africa has a dynamic economy, and black Africans filter into South Africa, seeking jobs in the diamond and gold mines. The white people want this labor. But when the black Africans arrive, they can't speak or read English or Dutch and they can't find work. To avoid the growth of slums, the South Africans have built camps and villages for the blacks, with adequate housing, schools, and athletic facilities. The people who live there are taken care of, but they *must* live there; they have no choice. They are separate and they are suppressed. They have no opportunity to improve their condition. If a black child were a genius in science or math he would still have to remain in the inferior black village school.

The blacks, who are a majority, have no say in the

government. The white South Africans say they are gradually giving the blacks a voice, but this is an extremely slow process and that voice is usually only symbolic. The people who showed me around said that these villages were the only solution to the problem of taking care of the black Africans until they could take care of themselves. The black people had to be acculturated, they said, before they could be incorporated into the society. The whites say that will take time. It is going very slowly.

From Durban we went on to East London and then to Port Elizabeth, where there were actually accommodations ready for three people! The American tennis team was there on tour, too, and, since tennis is such a big sport in South Africa, these amateurs could make more money for the tennis federation than I was making for the swimming federation, so naturally our rooms were not as good as theirs.

In Port Elizabeth I asked some of the coaches and athletes about professionalism and amateurism in South Africa and learned that amateurism is taken no more seriously there by the athletes than in most countries. Swimmers do well in South Africa, although not as well as amateur cricket players who, they estimated, made about $15,000 a year.

Next we went to Kimberley, the home of the De Beers diamond mines and of Karen Muir who, even then, at the age of fifteen was one of the great swimmers of the world. I cannot emphasize strongly enough what a wonderful swimmer this girl is. At the age of twelve she broke her first adult world record. Had she ever competed in an Olympics, there is no telling what she might have done.

Then we were off to Capetown, Getz territory, where I had promised to swim in one big meet. Capetown is one of the most beautiful cities in the world. It is on a peninsula with the Indian Ocean on one side and the Atlantic on the other, and in the middle of the city a huge mountain rises straight up, looking like its name, Table Mountain. When Getz met us at the plane, he was all smiles. "Gee, it's good to see you. How was your trip?" It was as though nothing had happened! Then he said, "We've been waiting for you for six hours. All the reporters were here but they got tired of waiting and went home."

"Well, you knew when we were coming." I said.

"No. You were supposed to arrive at two o'clock," he said. It was now eight.

"Mr. Getz, we've had the plane tickets for ten days. You bought them and gave them to us."

"You must have changed them; we thought you were coming on the other plane."

When John duPont got off the plane Getz greeted him like an old friend. "John! It's good to see you!" John just walked past, ignoring him, and Getz turned to me. "What's wrong with John?"

The next day the Capetown press blasted me for not telling anybody that I would arrive six hours late.

In Capetown, at the swimming meet, I saw again what a brilliant swimmer Karen Muir was, and later she came to the Capetown airport with some other swimmers to say good-bye. She doesn't speak English very well—she speaks Afrikaans—so just before we left she gave me a note to read on the plane. In it she asked if there was anything I could do to help get South Africa accepted back into the Olympics. All her life, she wrote, this was all she had lived for; all her life she had been training to compete in the Olympics. All she wanted was a chance to prove herself once in Olympic competition.

It was a very emotional and touching letter and I wished I could help her. I was beginning to see that in all the political maneuvering it was the athlete who got hurt.

From Capetown we flew to Johannesburg to London and then home. Our tickets had been changed over to BOAC and John upgraded them to first class, and we got to New York in ten hours less time than it had taken to go to Johannesburg.

At Kennedy Airport an AAU official met us. Dave had asked me not to be too outspoken because he had to work with the AAU so I tried to be restrained, but I did say that I thought they had really done a terrible job of arranging this trip. Then, after I left for New Haven, the AAU man accused John of not having gone to South Africa! I don't know where he got that idea, but this official had even called John's mother to ask why John hadn't gone to South Africa and then she began to worry because she thought something had happened to him.

When John heard this, it was the end. After all we had been through—all the problems, all the arguments—to come home to this! He had had enough. John can be blunt and outspoken and at that moment he was mad. This episode just about ended any goodwill he had had for the AAU.

33

THE SOUTH AFRICAN TRIP, in terms of organization, was the worst trip I ever had; and as a goodwill tour it was a complete failure: I've heard that my name is practically a dirty word in South Africa. The blame, I think, rested with both our AAU and with South Africa's AAU, and it's interesting that these two organizations are so similar in structure: they have the same inefficiency, the same petty rivalries, the same power-hungry top personnel. I looked at the shortcomings of the South African AAU and I saw my own AAU.

For a long time I had been thinking that there was a crying need to reorganize the administrative branches of

American sport. I think we should create a Federation of Sports—one organization with jurisdiction over sports on all levels: AAU sports, high school and college sports, professional sports. It should be partially subsidized by the government, partly dependent on private donations, and administered by salaried people who would be hired or appointed. The South African trip convinced me more than ever of this need, and while we were there Dave Robertson and I discussed it. Dave suggested that a secretary of sport would be a good idea.

Under our present system, which is splintered and disorganized, many of the top people are too old, too inefficient, and too far removed from the sport. They mean well—many of them are fine old men—but they're just too old. They're not promoters, they don't have the secretaries to help with the work load, and things are just a mishmash.

On the local level I would try to use mostly volunteers. It would be hard to pay officials on all levels and local problems are usually manageable; local volunteers tend to be enthusiastic and do a pretty good job, and on the local level you can put up with a little less efficiency.

The coaches are already professional but many, like George, are school coaches as well as club coaches. When George wanted to go to the preliminary Olympics in Mexico in 1967, Santa Clara High School wouldn't let him off because he was going to be gone so long in 1968. A government administrator could have asked Santa Clara High to let him go and reimbursed the school so that it could make arrangements during his absence.

Now both the AAU and the NCAA are run by volunteers and not only is there feuding between the two organizations but within each group there is a great deal of politicking and chicanery and maneuvering for power. There is jealousy and bickering between coaches, fights between young coaches and old coaches, fight for control among high-school officials, college officials, YMCA officials. There are squabbles between the AAU and the United States Olympic Committee. Some arguments are inevitable in any organization, but now it is excessive. If you had a well-organized federation, staffed by capable, salaried people you could do away with a lot of it. In South Africa, when Dave Robertson and I talked about this, we discussed the swimming situation in Chicago, where Dave is a high-school coach. This is a perfect example of how a bad situation can be created by the very people who are supposed to be serving the sport, and how in the end the athlete is the one who suffers.

Chicago has one of the best high-school swimming programs in the country, but it has serious AAU problems and in the summer the program falls apart. Instead of training their high-school swimmers in a club to develop them into national competitors, as George does at Santa Clara, most of the coaches spend the summer teaching younger kids how to swim. They want to make money and they want to develop more young swimmers in order to build a broad base for their high-school programs. The high-school swimmers are practically abandoned, and during the summer these guys, some with great potential, get wiped out. For a swimmer, the summer is the most important training time.

"Why don't the coaches at least let them train with somebody else?" I asked Dave.

"Because," Dave said, "the other coach then might take credit for him if he ever did anything great."

A strong federation could do something about this problem. An official with some authority could tell these coaches to forget their petty jealousies; he could shame them into it, and get some help for these swimmers. Now they won't admit they're hurting the kids. If they realized it, they would probably do something about it.

There is so much a Federation of Sports could do that would be of service not only to sports but to the country as well. Federation officials could organize health and recreation parks where they are needed and arrange with high schools and colleges for the use of their facilities during the summer. Now we have kids hanging around on city streets in the summer with nowhere to go and their frustrations building up until they riot, while many high school and college facilities remain closed.

There is nothing personal in my feelings toward the present officials. As people, I have liked some of these men very much, but many of them just can't do the job. I think that my trips abroad were indicative of this. Consistently, my best trips were to countries like Japan or Germany that had an efficient central sports organization—similar to a Federation of Sports. Those trips were a success because of the efforts of the organization in the host country. Which brings me to another job that I would really like to see a federation take over: the responsibility for hospitality toward foreign athletes who visit us. What happens now is just awful.

Whenever I traveled to Japan I had the best accommodations, the best care. It seemed that they just couldn't do enough for me. When a Japanese team came here to swim in the Los Angeles Invitational, our treatment of them was just terrible. They were housed in a dive, a dilapidated old building in a slum, with winos wandering through the lobby. They had to walk to the pool. When I saw the accommodations we had given these Japanese swimmers I was ashamed to be an American. When we traveled any distance in Japan, or in any other country, we traveled by plane at the host's expense. These Japanese swimmers traveled by *bus* across the United States from Los Angeles to Chicago and had the same kind of accommodations when they got there. The contrast between the treatment they received here and the courtesy we received in Japan was shocking. If a sports exchange program is supposed to create goodwill, the AAU just drops the ball completely.

I'm not saying that our sports structure should be reorganized all the way down to the local levels. Let the local communities handle their sports programs as they wish—with volunteers or with salaried employees, whichever they prefer. But at the regional, state, or national levels, where there is so much at stake, we must have better organization and less infighting. And I don't think that international exchange programs, whether we are the hosts or guests, will ever be handled properly by our present amateur organizations.

I am aware of the potential dangers of government intrusion into sports, and there should be built-in protection against politicians attempting to influence athletes or using sports in their own interests. But to me, this danger seems less of a threat to American sports than the politics and feuding and inefficiency that already characterizes our entire athletic system.

34

In February, the problems of the 1968 Olympic Games began to boil up. At the end of the Winter Olympics, in Grenoble, the IOC (International Olympic Committee) met to vote on the South African problem. Actually there were not many black athletes in South Africa since the country does not have many athletic facilities or coaches for either race, white or black; but many of the mining companies have provided recreational facilities for their black employees and a few very good black athletes have developed, mostly in such track events as running and jumping. In 1964, when the IOC asked South Africa to give its black athletes a chance to participate in the Olympics, South Africa refused and was banned from the 1964 Games. With this ban, the white people of South Africa were caught in a dilemma between their apartheid policy and their love of sports, which is very strong. In 1965 they yielded: they would allow black athletes to compete on their 1968 Olympic team. The trials, held within the country, would be separate but the team that traveled to Mexico would be integrated. This met the letter of the IOC request and at the meeting in Grenoble, South Africa's application for readmission was accepted.

The IOC does not even attempt to achieve equitable geographic representation. It is an autonomous, self-perpetuating body, a narrow, rigid elite corps selected mainly from western European countries, with some token Russians, North and South Americans, but as far as I know, no Asians or Africans, in spite of the growing importance of this bloc of nations. To black African nations, South Africa is identified with Europe, and the IOC was immediately and severely criticized for readmitting this European-oriented country in the face of objections from the African nations. Protesting the separate tryouts, the thirty-two Central Black African nations met in the Congo and voted to boycott the Olympics.

Immediately Red China, which doesn't even send athletes to the Olympics, loudly supported this protest and pointed out to the African nations that Russia hadn't said anything about joining their boycott. Now Russia was on the spot because Red China was becoming serious competition in the political courtship of these emerging nations. On the other hand, Russia really wanted to go to these Olympics because she expected to do very well at Mexico City's high altitude.

An athlete needs a long time to become conditioned to altitude. The IOC rules for 1968 called for only six weeks of altitude training, but a closed society can very easily ignore such rules and the Russians could train at altitude for a year and arrive at the Olympics with a very real advantage.

Actually Russia never came right out and said she would

join the boycott. She stayed on the fence and said that if South Africa were permitted to compete after holding separate tryouts, Russia would probably withdraw from the Games. And if Russia withdrew, it was hinted, the Eastern European countries would follow.

Suddenly the Olympics had been made an instrument of international politics, a tool by which to maneuver for satellites among the emerging nations.

Now Mexico appealed to the IOC. Half the world was threatening to withdraw from the Olympics, all because of South Africa. If they carried out their threat, there would be no Olympics; the entire movement was threatened. Wouldn't it be better to sacrifice one country than the whole Olympic movement?

So the IOC backed down and told South Africa that if she wanted in, she would have to integrate her tryouts. South Africa replied that she could not do that. And the fact is, she couldn't. Whether or not, morally, she should have, as a practical matter she simply could not integrate tryouts that year. Since 1965 she had been preparing the country to accept an integrated team with separate tryouts. To push harder at that time would have stirred up agitation at home by right-wing extremists.

But by now the IOC was completely caught in the cross fire of international politics. This was no longer a question of whether the blacks of South Africa were being allowed to compete in sports. It was a matter of cold war politics. In this eyeball to eyeball confrontation the IOC backed off. At that moment, when the IOC yielded to pressure and reversed its decision on South Africa, the Olympic movement entered the jungle of international politics.

It was the kiss of death. Once you let world politics dictate the policies of the Olympics, where does it end? How far does the proper area of intrusion reach? And why? If the IOC has the right to dictate to South Africa on a matter of inter-

nal affairs, could it in the name of integration tell the United
States that it must have equal numbers of black swimmers on
its swimming team, whether they are the best swimmers or
not? Or, in the name of antimilitarism, could it tell Russia
that its athletes must not serve in the Russian army? Or could
it order the satellite countries to hold free, two-party elec-
tions? How far can the IOC—this little self-centered group of
men, with no special qualifications, elected by no one but
themselves—presume to go in dictating the internal or international affairs of sovereign nations?

The Olympics are supposed to be beyond politics. They
are supposed to be dedicated to international goodwill. They
are supposed to be a means of communication between
people where other means of communication have failed.
They are supposed to build bridges between nations where
no other bridges exist—not more barriers, where there are
already too many barriers, to keep people out. In ancient
Greece and Rome, when the Olympics became entangled in
politics, the Olympics ended.

The day after the IOC yielded to this pressure on South
Africa, a new boycott was threatened—this time by American
black athletes.

The American boycott threat got rolling as a movement
to support the black African nations. In February the American Committee on Africa circulated a petition stating that the
undersigned would not compete in the 1968 Olympics if
South Africa was allowed to participate. Everyone on the
Yale swimming team, Olympic candidate or not, was asked to
sign the petition, and many did.

I refused to sign. South Africa had complied with the
original demands made of her, and I felt that now the athletes of South Africa, both black and white, were being
victimized by politics.

A lot of the people who were doing the shouting had
never been there to see what they were trying to change. I

had. I had seen it. And there was such a long way to go. You weren't going to bridge that gap with reprimands and punishments from the outside. Or by legislating it through bungling, well-meaning committees that didn't really have any idea what they were doing or why.

I *wanted* South Africa at the Olympics. I wanted some black South Africans there, as there surely would be, even with separate tryouts. I knew what gold-fever at the Olympics was like. Like every other country South Africa would want gold medals, and she would send her best athletes and some of the best were going to be Negroes. I knew how much those black athletes could do for their own people by proving themselves. (Look at Jesse Owens in Aryan Nazi Germany in 1936. Who ended up in a snit? Jesse Owens or Hitler?)

And who were the first black people in the United States to bridge the gulf between the races? The *individuals* in any field: the artists, the performers, but especially the athletes, because they were *good,* and they were respected because they were good. By barring South Africa, the black people as well as the whites were being hurt. And I felt that the athletes of both races were being forgotten in this fight. Later I learned that my signature had been forged and that it had appeared on the petition.

After South Africa was barred, the American Committee on Africa decided to use the Games as a vehicle for dramatizing the American Negro's problems and continued its boycott threat. I felt just as strongly, and for the same reasons, that this was wrong. I also thought it was very sad because international competition is one place where the American Negro absolutely gets a fair shake. At the Olympics, on the United States team or any other, there is no such thing as race or color: there are only athletes. For the Negro to boycott the one movement that is absolutely color-blind, in which he has always been respected and equal, to me seemed very sad.

Of course the USOC was upset over this threatened boycott because Negro athletes bring in about 14 percent of American gold medals and the United States gold-medal count would suffer if they didn't compete. According to the Olympic ideal, a nation is not supposed to be concerned with the number of gold medals it can win. The Olympic creed reads: "The most important thing in the Olympic Games is not to win but to take part. . . . The essential thing is not to have conquered but to have fought well."

The gold-medal count is not supposed to be important. The fact is that in everyone's mind it is the most important thing at the Olympics and it is getting more important all the time.

If I felt that the IOC was too quick to yield on the political issue, I was also convinced by this time that it was too unbending, as well as blind and hypocritical, on the matter of amateurism. My criticism applies as well to the USOC and the AAU since the definitions and rules are the same. For many years I had thought about this, questioning both the official policy and my own criticism of it, and I believe that the official definition of amateurism is obsolete, impractical, and unenforceable, that it encourages subterfuge, that it discriminates against excellence, and that efforts made to enforce it are unrealistic and overstrict.

I firmly believe that the amateur athlete should be allowed to make some money—in a regulated, controlled way—in areas that do not and could not involve any opportunity for less than honorable performance in his sport. That is to say, he should not be paid to race and he would not race for money. The prizes would still be trophies. But why should the amateur athlete be prohibited from making money in areas that are not directly related to his performance? Why should he not be paid to write an article or a book or to make a speech if anyone is interested in what he has to say? Only the few at the top would be offered this opportunity, and the fear that the opportunity would corrupt them is unrealistic. If they devoted too much to capitalizing on their fame, that fame would be short-lived and as success vanished, so would the opportunity. It would be self-regulatory.

The present rules penalize excellence. Why should a great swimmer not be allowed to teach? Many lesser known amateur college swimmers teach in the summer, sometimes earning as much as two or three thousand dollars. Technically, this makes them professionals, but the truth is there are very few amateurs in any sport today. The only real amateurs, who never earn a dollar in any way related to their sport, are the ones at the very top, the few who are too conspicuous, because of their excellence, to take a chance. A college swimmer who has to earn money in the summer should work to make a name for himself, but *not* to get to the top. Then his name will get him a summer job and he can make enough to see him through the school year. If he gets to the top he can't do that.

If an amateur champion is offered the opportunity to earn money by endorsing a product for an advertising campaign, why should he not be allowed to take it?

The Olympic eligibility code reads: "Among others, the following are not eligible for competition: If an athlete gets paid for the use of his name or picture or for radio or television appearance, it is capitalization of athletic fame. . . ." Then, in parentheses: *"Even if no payment is made, such practices are to be deplored, since in the minds of many, particularly the young, they undermine the exalted position rightfully held by amateur champions."*

And yet, in the winter of 1968 I received a letter from an advertising firm handling a dairy association account that wanted to build an advertising campaign around three American Olympic figures—figure skater Terry McDermott, track star Jim Ryun, and me. They asked me to sign a release giving them permission to use my name. The permission of

the United States Olympic Committee was also necessary and
the letter stated that the company intended to make a contribution of $300 to the USOC. The USOC gave its consent and
the company bought the use of our names at a very low price
because we were amateurs. The names of professional athletes of similar caliber would have cost them thousands.

But if the Olympic Committee believes in the spirit of
its own rules, should it have given permission for this ad at
any price? Is the "exalted position of the amateur" less
undermined if the Olympic Committee receives the money?
Does this, somehow, look better to "the young?"

Actually, I can't disapprove of the Olympic Committee
making money because it does support our Olympic Team. I
do object to the fact that they sell us out too cheap. These
large corporations save money by using amateurs in their
advertising campaigns instead of professionals. And I think
that the athlete should be allowed to make some money in
the same way. The USOC makes money on him, and the
AAU, and corporations, and the television industry—*why*
shouldn't he be allowed a share of all this commerce in his
name and his talent?

To avoid embarrassment or exploitation, endorsements
by amateurs could be monitored, especially if there were a
strong, interested sports federation to establish realistic
guidelines, such as prohibitions against endorsements of cigarettes or liquor or products directly related to an athlete's
sport. Track men, for instance, would not be allowed to
endorse one manufacturer's running shoes or skiers a certain
name ski.

To me, the argument that these limited opportunities to
make money would be so tantalizing that kids would say,
"I'm going into swimming (or any sport) to make big
money" is ridiculous. So few athletes, only those at the very
top, are able to capitalize on their fame. No one starting out
can be guaranteed that he will reach those heights, and if he
is in the sport only for the money, chances are that he won't

make it. Over the years I have known hundreds of swimmers, and one thing I know is that no one can give what it takes to be the best in this sport for any reason except love of the sport. If his goal is only money he will fall by the wayside. There are easier ways to make money.

When these official organizations—the Olympic Committee and the AAU—cling so stubbornly to these rules of amateurism they are ignoring some important facts of life. For one, they ignore the expense of the sport to the athlete or his family. When I trained at Santa Clara it cost $130-a-year fee, plus the expense of room and board while I lived away from home. Nor was that the end of it. The important meets—the Spring Nationals and Summer Nationals—are held all over the country, and when you travel to compete the swim club pays for the transportation but the individual pays for room, board, and other expenses. If you win a gold medal, the AAU pays all your expenses the following year. The AAU may claim that the amateur does not compete for monetary prizes, but I was always aware that if I could win at least one gold medal, I would save myself some money the following year. So I think the AAU is not being completely candid and realistic when it says that no money is involved. Money *is* involved.

It is a fact of life today that everything is expensive and often an athlete simply cannot get by. His sport is expensive and he cannot work in his spare time because he has no spare time. Amateurism today is a profession and it demands a full professional investment of time. Many sports have finally recognized these economic facts. In others, unless a more realistic attitude is taken, unless amateur athletes are permitted in some controlled way to make money openly and honorably, many are going to take money under the table. Many have already begun to do so.

Almost every rule of eligibility of the IOC is broken, and the IOC knows it and closes its eyes.

Consider this rule: "Among others, the following are not eligible for Olympic competition: An athlete who demands payment or expense money for a manager, coach, relative, or friend." On every trip I made abroad—to France, to Ireland, to South Africa—I was accompanied by a coach because the AAU absolutely required it, and the host country paid the expenses for me and for a coach. According to that rule, every American athlete who ever visited foreign countries at their expense is ineligible for the Olympics.

And consider this rule: "Among others, the following are not eligible for Olympic competition: Those who have capitalized in any way on their athletic fame or success, profited commercially therefrom or have accepted special inducements to participate, or those who have secured employment or promotion by reason of their sport performances, rather than their ability, whether in commercial or industrial enterprises, the armed services or any branch of the press, theatre, television, cinema, radio, or any other paid activity." That rule makes every Russian athlete ineligible. Also every other European athlete (except, possibly, British), every athlete in the army, and the hundreds of amateurs in this country who are hired because they are who they are.

Consider this rule of ineligibility: "Those whose occupation (studies or employment) has been interrupted for special training in a camp for more than four weeks in any one calendar year." That eliminates Australia, Russia, Britain—and how many others?

What about students? "Among others, the following are not eligible for Olympic competition: Anyone awarded a scholarship *mainly for his athletic ability*." That eliminates about 90 percent of American college athletes.

And, finally, "An athlete who becomes a professional in any sport or who has *decided* to become a professional or who plays on a professional team with a view to becoming a professional." Well, what is a professional? And when does a person *decide* to become one?

These are not the only rules—there are more, equally hypocritical and unenforceable—and yet this total package of "rules" goes to make up the IOC definition of amateurism, an amateurism that is nonexistent. The Eligibility Code describes an impossible set of conditions. If the IOC enforced the letter of its own law, about three people would show up for the Olympics. To me this had been apparent for four years and, as the 1968 Olympics approached, I felt that both the amateur movement and the spirit and goals of the Olympics were falling apart.

In the end, the 1968 Olympics were riddled with friction, payoffs, and scandals—and people were surprised. How, when the foundation was in a state of decay, could they have expected the structure not to begin to crumble? How could it have been otherwise?

35

As FOR MY SWIMMING that year? I stayed at Yale and did my best to train all winter.

While I studied for mid-years in January, I was aware that my competitors around the world—in Russia, France, Australia—were already going into special training camps. And, more important, that they would be training at altitude. I was aware, too, that this was the time of the year at which, George had said, if I hoped to win in Mexico I should drop out of Yale and begin concentrated training, not even altitude training, just good hard training at Santa Clara.

I continued training at Yale and then, although it was risky, in April I took a break. I felt that I needed it. I was getting tired of swimming, and tired of competing, and I felt that I just couldn't train for twelve solid months right through to the Olympics without some kind of break. I had already swum too many races. For me, now, there was only one meet left.

To keep my interest up that winter I tried to strengthen the Yale swimming program. I arranged for the use of the 50-meter pool during practice. I introduced circuit training and started twice-a-day workouts, an extra one in the morning for anyone who was interested. I went to morning workouts myself for the first couple of weeks and then I started cutting them, too. At Yale you just don't have time to work out twice a day. But I also cut many of the morning workouts just because I didn't want to swim. Long before the Olympics began, I knew that I was in trouble. I was going to have to push myself: not so much to make the Olympic Team, but to make myself want to try.

And yet I had said that I would swim in the 1968 Olympics and I was too close now to stop. I was disenchanted; I was tired of swimming—and I knew it. In 1964 I had been so eager to get into that competition and give it hell. Now I just told myself: Go out and do the best you can.

In June I went through graduation ceremonies with my class but I would have to return the next year to make up the semester I'd missed in 1964. It was a cold, gray day and it was a graduation without exuberance because so many men were going into the service and so many others had had to turn down graduate schools because of the threat of the draft. For me it was a strange, rather meaningless day. Everyone else was through with this phase of his life and at least trying to go on to something new. I was in limbo. I was going back to swimming, a part of my life that was ending and that I was ready to end; and then I would come back to Yale for a kind of epilogue to another phase that was ending. I wanted very much to move on from both, to step forward into something new, to get out into the world and get going.

It was in this mood that I approached the 1968 Olympics.

part six

The Problem Olympics:
Mexico, 1968

THE DRAMATIC START OF THE 100-METER FREE STYLE

36

AFTER GRADUATION I went directly to Santa Clara, arriving for my first workout on June 14, two weeks later than the year before. All the other college swimmers had been back at least a week, the high-school kids had been training since May. Right from the start I felt I was behind; I felt that I had missed something, just from coming a week late.

I lived with the Walls again that summer. They had moved to a new house that was on a golf course, where you could take long, silent walks. Or you could climb a nearby hill where, on some days, you could see all the way to San Francisco Bay, fifty miles away. It was very quiet, very beautiful, and this is the way I remember that summer: the stillness of it, the beauty of it, during the hours I was away from swimming.

At the pool I felt like a stranger. Every year there were more new faces and fewer familiar ones. Except for Gary Illman and Mike Wall, nobody from Santa Clara who had been on the men's Olympic Team in 1964 was around anymore. They had all long since retired. I felt old—not physically old, just that I had been around so long.

If Mike hadn't been there, I probably wouldn't have made it. We had the same problems that summer, Mike and I; we were both making a bid for our second Olympics, both facing the enemy of age in a young man's sport. I was fighting to stay on top. Mike was fighting just to stay around, to make the Olympic Team. And he had a tough fight because his event, the 1,500 free, is really a young kid's event.

But there was a difference between us. Mike had always been his own man. He always swam for himself, for his own personal satisfaction; he always remained a little aloof from the fever of competition. Now I realized that I could learn something from Mike. I kept a diary that summer and when I'd been back a week I wrote in it: "Inner Strength—the need for inner strength. You don't have to be the best in the world—just do the best you can. Become inner-directed, like Mike."

In retrospect I call this my philosophical summer. I spent a lot of time walking, particularly at sundown. When it began to grow dark and everyone had gone home, I would walk out on the golf course, usually alone, with only the Walls' dog, Shag, for company.

I did a lot of reading, not as escape from the routine of swimming, as I had done other summers, but because I was full of questions and trying to find answers, trying to put my thoughts in order. I read philosophy—Hermann Hesse, existentialism, books about Far Eastern religions. I read *Magister Ludi* and *Siddhartha*. Sometimes late at night I would go out on the golf course and just sit and think, or count how many different sounds I could hear simultaneously, or see how far my mind could reach out from something I had read that day. For me, it was a very, very beautiful summer—when I was away from the pool.

At the pool there was such a contrast between this summer and the pre-Olympic summer of 1964. Every year swimming had become a little harder, not just because I was getting older, although that was part of it, but because the sport itself was advancing so rapidly. In 1964 we had averaged about 8,000 meters a day. This summer we were doing about 12,000 meters a day; this is almost eight miles and is comparable to running thirty-two miles. The workouts were not only tougher; they were monotonous, and, to me, incredibly dull and boring. The sport was demanding more of me than ever before and I had changed and was less willing to give up so much of myself to it.

George had changed that summer, too. I felt that he didn't really enjoy coaching anymore, that he was tired of it. His enthusiasm, which had once been so infectious, was gone. He had been so dynamic, moving up and down the pool, shouting orders, seeing everything, kidding you when you were tired, changing the workouts to keep them lively. To me his spirit had been his greatest strength: it was fun to swim for him. Now he never kidded anyone, never moved from the block on which he sat throughout an entire workout, watching and talking from there. The workouts were always pretty much the same. He even assigned permanent lanes—there were so many people in the pool, it was easier to know where everyone was. But that only added to the boredom. I was always in lane two, Spitz was always in lane three, Mike in lane one, Illman in lane four. After a while this really got to me and I'd go over to lane nine, way over on the other side, just for a change of scenery. I hardly knew the kids in lanes eight and nine; halfway through the summer I still didn't know their names.

I used to ask myself that summer whether George had really changed or only my image of him. Probably it was both. He seemed to be in a bad mood so much of the time and his moods would affect the whole team; we wouldn't work out so well and then he would get grumpier. I don't think it was just my reaction because swimming wasn't fun for me anymore. I used to look at him and think that he was almost a mirror of my own attitude. This wasn't fun for him anymore, either.

In 1968, swimming was more important to the public than it had been in 1964, and we had the press on our backs that whole summer. Every week, it seemed, somebody else was there, watching the workout and taking pictures—*Sports Illustrated, Life, Newsweek,* ABC–TV. This continuous audience added to the tension. You couldn't concentrate totally on your swimming when you were worried about who was watching you and was going to report on how you were doing. You couldn't give it everything because you were aware that if you pushed yourself into the pain barrier and at the end your face was twisted with pain, someone might snap a picture. When the *Life* people were there, in order to get some special shots they set up a big crane at poolside and swung a guy in a box out over the pool, about fifteen feet above the water. What the hell! You'd swim down and you were afraid the thing was going to fall on you.

I kept waiting for George to say, "All right, get out of here. You guys can all come back for three days at the same time." But he never did. He would gripe to us and say, "Why can't these people leave us alone?" But if he didn't want them there he could have told them to leave. Hell, we had everybody there so many times.

And yet, with all of this, I was completely serious about training that summer. The first week I was there, even though I was very tired from the workouts because they were longer and harder than ever before, I began to do special work with weights. I went out and got shock cords to build up my arms and pulley boards to build up my legs. Twice a day, in the morning before I went to workout and again in the afternoon, I did sit-ups. I took Tiger's Milk and vitamins.

I had almost no free time, and this really bugged me. More than in any other summer I didn't want to be regimented. But I accepted it. I worked as hard as I could, not because I wanted to, but because, as long as I'd come this far, I was determined to do this right. I told myself: "This is the last summer you'll ever be swimming. Give it one last total effort."

And I did. But it was a constant inner struggle.

37

FOR ME there was only one more meet and that was the key to every decision I made that summer.

The previous summer at the Nationals I had won the 100 and even set a world record in the 200 but I had died in the 400, and I felt the reason for that was I had been too careful. I hadn't risked swimming the 400 in competition until I was in shape for it, which meant that I didn't swim it enough before the Nationals to be really confident or to sharpen my sense of pace at that distance. This year I told George that I was going to swim everything that came along— the 400, the 200, and the 100—every time I could, whether I was ready for it or not. If I lost, I lost; if the press said I was finished, that was okay. I'd heard that before. The year before I was still trying not to lose; I was still protecting my image. This year I didn't care. I wanted the experience more than the image.

The San Leandro Relays were at the end of June, when I'd been back in training only two weeks. The first event was the 400 free, an added feature in this relay meet. I entered it and finished second behind Mark Spitz with a 4:18, which was not too bad a time for me, so early in the season. In the 4 x 200 meter relay I turned in the same kind of unspectacular performance.

The bright spot of the meet was the sprint relay. I went off behind, overtook the guy ahead of me and turned in a fairly fast time. Actually I was surprised to find that I could go that fast so early in the season and I felt pretty good about it. I was in terrible condition; I'd been training so hard and doing so much extra work with weights and cords that I was physically exhausted, but now I felt that I really had speed this year and that, once I built endurance, my 100 and 200 were going to be very fast.

A week later, the first week in July, was the Santa Clara Invitational, and I entered the 400, the 200, and the 100. But during that week I saw the list of events for the Olympics. I was amazed to find that they had scheduled the 400 freestyle and the 200 freestyle back-to-back—the 400-meter finals Wednesday night, the 200-meter heats Thursday morning, and the 200-meter finals Thursday night. The 400 and the 200—both middle-distance events—are a natural double, but scheduled so close together, at altitude, they were going to be a very difficult double. I wanted to talk to George about this but George was always so busy that summer. You couldn't just walk up to him to discuss something. I remember I went to find him and said, "George, can I talk to you sometime this week?" And George said, "Yes, you can talk to me Thursday." This could never have happened in 1964.

So on Thursday I told George how I felt about this back-to-back double at altitude. "I don't think I should try to swim them both," I said. "I think I should forget about the 400. The 200 is more important to me. And I'm still going to do the sprint."

"Well, I'm not going to tell you what to do," George said, "but that makes sense."

Now that I'd decided not to go the 400 in the Olympics there was no reason to swim it in the Santa Clara Invitational and my name was scratched from the event. It was a late scratch and people immediately commented that they weren't surprised: I probably couldn't make the 400 anyway. I didn't agree. I felt that if I trained for it all summer, I'd make the 400 at the Olympic Trials. But even if I trained and proved that I could still do it, what difference would it make? In Mexico City, for me, the 400 and the 200 would still be an impossible double.

Before the Santa Clara Invitational there was another development that was much more upsetting to me than hearing still one more time that I was over the hill. George decided to ease up on training and bring us to a small peak for this meet. "Some of you may feel we should keep working and just swim through this meet," he told us, "but I think we can do small peaks for this meet and for the Nationals, then a big peak for the Olympic Trials."

This strategy really threw me. I didn't want to rest; I wanted to work. I wanted to swim through this meet, swim through the Nationals (I didn't even want to go to the Nationals), and then peak only for the Olympic Trials and for the Olympics. When I told George how I felt, he just repeated that he thought we could reach small peaks. I have to assume that he really believed it. To me, knowing what I did about peaking, it seemed very risky.

"Well, I think the team needs confidence," George said. "If they can do well at Santa Clara and at the Nationals with small peaks, then at the Olympic Trials they'll have confidence. We may sacrifice work time, but everyone will have confidence."

I didn't need confidence. I needed work, work, work. I was angry and disappointed. I could remember the summer when I had been allowed to do it my way, a way that was different but best for me. This summer I had to fall in line and do it everyone else's way. I tried not to let it get me. I told myself, "Hell, it's going to be a long summer—maybe it won't make that much difference."

But I think it did make a difference.

At the Santa Clara Invitational I'd been back only three weeks and was still in my animal stage, still training too hard. I won the 200, and put in a very slow time in the 100 and took second.

The only important thing about that meet was that Spitz led off the sprint relay and turned in a really very good time.

He had real speed, and that was when he decided to try for the 100-meter freestyle at the Olympics. I think George had decided it long ago. I felt that he had had Mark lead off that relay to show him—and to show me—what he could do, and so that later George could say, "Look how fast he swam it; it doesn't make any sense not for him to enter the 100 free."

People were saying now that Spitz would take five gold medals at the Olympics, and possibly six.

I settled down to wait for the Nationals. I was always waiting that summer: waiting for the morning workout, waiting to go to sleep, waiting for the evening workout. Finish this workout and wait for the next. Wait for Saturday, wait for Sunday. Wait for the next meet.

To fight the boredom, I went through a number of different stages during these months. The philosophical and intellectual stage lasted intermittently throughout the summer. The others began and ended abruptly. First came the "animal stage" when I worked out with weights and ate health foods. This lasted about three or four weeks until I couldn't take it anymore; I was tearing myself down so much that at workout I was coming in way behind on the repeats.

Then I went through a creative stage, when I tried to write and paint—both new activities for me. Obviously I was bored to desperation, for these were rapid, abrupt changes. One day I was an artist, the next I was reading books on the stock market. I studied the market for a week, and then said, "Oh the hell with this," and forgot it.

And the waiting went on. Four weeks until the Nationals, eight weeks until the Olympic Trials. And the longest wait of all, the wait until my final swim at the Olympics in October. Then it would all be over and the wait that had been going on since Tokyo would be finished. Then, for the first time since I was fifteen, I would retire to a normal life.

We trained for three more weeks and then we began to peak for the Nationals. And again I was upset because I didn't want to taper off. I wanted to work. My choice would have been to miss the Nationals. A little meet like San Leandro was one thing but I hated to go to the National Championships knowing that I was not going to try to win. And I had already decided just to swim through them. George was peaking the whole team physically, but so far as I could control the situation, I wasn't going to waste anything on the Nationals. I wasn't going to shave down. I wasn't going to peak psychologically. I wasn't going to try to win.

But an intention not to try is something you do not announce. When I came in fourth in the 200, it didn't bother me; I knew I could win at the Olympic Trials, even though everyone said, "Fourth! What happened? The first 200, outdoors, that you ever lost!"

Then came the 100-meter freestyle where suddenly I was beginning to feel threatened. All that day Mark Spitz was like my shadow. He rode to breakfast in my car, ate next to me, even rested in my room. He never left my side. I didn't feel that he was trying to psyche me out. By now he was shooting for the 100 free in Mexico City and I felt that he was just studying me. And I let him do it. I thought I might kill him with love.

Even though I hadn't shaved down or peaked psychologically, this was a race I was going to try to win, for psychological reasons. I felt that the toughest competition in the 100 free at the Olympics was right here at the Nationals—Zac Zorn and Don Havens from Los Angeles, Spitz and myself. In the heats I qualified first and Spitz qualified second, with almost identical times.

That night on the blocks, waiting for the gun to go off, I glanced around and thought again that the race for the 100-meter freestyle gold medal in Mexico City was right here tonight between Spitz, Zorn, Havens, and myself.

The gun went off. At the 50-meter wall Spitz and I were in the lead, and so close I couldn't see who was ahead. Then I made my move. I came out of that turn swimming for my life. I just lunged off that 50-meter wall. At the 75-meter mark I had half a body-length lead. Later Mike said, "God, we thought you were just going to kill *everybody*." Then I started to die. I just didn't have the endurance yet, and Spitz had it. He gained and gained until he closed the gap and we touched the wall almost together. We looked around and everyone said, "We don't know who won, it looked like a dead heat!"

I turned to George, and George pointed "number two" to me and "number one" to Mark. He was right. Spitz was accelerating and I was decelerating, and his hand just barely touched the electronic plate first. About the race I only thought, Okay, I didn't peak. I'll get him the next time. When I got the endurance, I knew I could take him.

But about George I thought, That close? Could George really have seen it? Or was that the way he wanted it?

Suddenly it hit me that George wanted very badly to have another four gold medal winner (or better) at the Olympics, and he didn't think I could give it to him.

I didn't blame the press or the public for writing me off. I expected it. I hadn't turned in a spectacular performance all summer. But George knew what I was doing; I had discussed it with him. George knew I had started training late, that I hadn't peaked for any of these meets.

Now suddenly I realized that George, too, thought I was finished. Already the press was saying that Spitz could take five gold medals—or possibly six—in Mexico. George liked the idea. I felt that George had made his choice. He had written me off; Spitz was a better bet. And the irony of it was that I was the one who had given him the taste of glory.

38

AFTER THE NATIONALS George was as irritable and depressed as I had ever seen him. We had peaked for the Nationals and we hadn't done that much better than anyone else. People were beginning to doubt him and he must have sensed it. He would just come to the pool and grumble, "Get in the water." The whole team reflected his mood. We would get in the water and do our laps and get out.

Then suddenly at the Olympic Trials, everything changed. The girls' trials were held a week before ours and the girls really came through. George was a changed man. He was in a great mood, joking around, full of energy; he was like the old George. And immediately we changed, too. Our spirits picked up overnight. This was a dramatic example of how close a team is to the coach, and how much it reflects his moods. It shows, too, the importance of the right psychological attitude. I'm convinced that winning is 20 percent physical and 80 percent psychological. We had finished training for this meet but overnight we were a new team. When the Olympic Trials began in Long Beach, California, we were ready to go.

Now, for the first time that summer, I really peaked—physically and psychologically. I shaved down. I rested. I stayed in careful control. I was really up for this meet. I wanted to get into that pool and just go.

My first race was the 200, and I really went out, even in the heats, which is something I never do. I always save something for the finals. But I'd held back all summer and now I really wanted to swim. The world record was 1:55.7. It was my record and I broke it by almost a full second. I went 1:54.8.

After the race, everybody flocked around, saying, "God-damn, what a great swim!" George came up to congratulate me and he seemed just so happy. George's old swimming coach was there and the guy had tears in his eyes. He said, "I'm ready to die now; it was just so beautiful."

In the finals that night, I swam the best race of my life and broke the record that I had set that morning. I went 1:54.3.

Now I felt that I had done it. I'd held on for four years and I was still at the top. I'd done it my way at college and caught up summers. I'd done it my way this summer, racing when I wasn't ready but refusing to peak, not trying to win, taking it when the fans and the press said that I was finished, that at the Nationals I hadn't won a single race, not even my race, the 200.

In 1964 in Tokyo I had told myself to try to stay in control, to try not to let anything get to me, to do what I thought was the right thing for me, whether or not it was right for anyone else, and to have the courage to stick to my own decision. I had said it all to myself again this summer. I hadn't done it the "right" way, but I had done it the way that was right for me. And now I felt that I had won.

The next day the news people said, "Don Schollander, the old man of swimming, proved last night that he is not over the hill . . ." And I felt that I had proved it. I *knew* now that I was still the best in the world. I was sprinting faster than ever before and now that I had endurance, I could do no wrong. I was better than I had ever been in my life. I said to myself, "Wait till that 100 free comes along. I'm going for that world record, too."

For most of the sprinters—Zorn, Havens, Walsh, Rerych—the 100 free was their first event and they were just waiting for it. In the morning, I was in the final heat and my strongest competitor was Zac Zorn. Zorn had beaten me at the Santa Clara Invitational and I had beaten him at the Nationals.

At the 50-meter mark Zorn was almost a body length ahead of me and I thought, Oh, man, I'd better get going. But I had confidence now because I knew I had endurance, and in the second length I really took off. I just let it go. I didn't even see when I passed Zorn but I touched him out and turned in a time of 52.89, the fastest anyone had ever gone anywhere in the individual nonrelay 100 free.

People rushed up to me at poolside. Reporters flocked around, talking as though I'd already won the finals. Around me I heard people speculate that now I could take five gold medals in Mexico.

I went home and rested. I wasn't worried about the finals; I always go faster in the finals.

Then suddenly things began to go wrong.

That whole afternoon the telephone rang: press people calling to talk about the morning race, asking did I think now that I could take five gold medals in Mexico. It never stopped. I was trying to rest and every ring began to jar me. I told myself to hang onto that old "control"; I'd just gone the fastest I'd ever gone in my life. But by midafternoon, as the phone kept ringing, I was very edgy.

By evening I thought I'd pulled myself together. I went over early to loosen up in the pool and I told myself I felt great. The water was cold and when I got out of the pool I could feel a night chill in the air. I put on my sweats and I stood there a minute, thinking, God, it's cold here. Should I go take a hot shower? No. It's better to sit here and rest. Just keep your body warm.

So I sat there, but I just couldn't get warm. I was shivering. Then I thought, Damnit, I should have gone over and taken a hot shower. Now it's too late. The race was scheduled to start in about five minutes, at eight o'clock. I moved around to try to get my blood circulating. When it was time I walked up to the starting blocks. I still felt that I was really ready for the race. But I was still shaking.

Then for some reason the race was delayed. I waited and waited. I just stood there in my wet suit, shaking—waiting, looking around. I glanced around the pool. I looked at the others—Spitz, Walsh, Zorn, Rerych—all waiting. Then for the first time I saw that all the big TV lights had been taken down. The race was not being telecast. This made it a different pool from the one I'd gotten used to and planned for. The turns would be much darker. Suddenly I thought, Oh, God, if I can't see the wall, I wonder if I'll hit that turn right. And I started to worry about the damned turn!

After all those years I knew better than to let myself do this. I struggled to check it. I talked to myself. "Come on, keep your cool—relax—relax." Trying to relax, I turned away from the pool and looked around the stands. I saw Mr. and Mrs. Wall and they saw me looking and waved. I waved back—something I had *never* done before! Mike's sister, Kortney, said with her lips, "Shag says good luck." I laughed. In convincing myself that I was relaxed, I had stopped concentrating on the race.

And still the start was delayed.

At last, ten minutes late, the words came: "Swimmers take your marks." Still shivering, I stepped up on the block. I have always dreaded that instant when I hit the water because I get so cold, but multiply my aversion that night to the nth degree because I was already chilled to the bone. I even shrank from leaning forward, for fear I'd go into the water. I was back on my heels.

Then came a twist. For a long time afterward, there were arguments about whether there was a false start. Many people in the stadium that night, and many who since then have seen the films, believe it was a false start. To me, when I saw the films, it looked as though Walsh started too soon and once he did, Zorn, who has a very fast start, anyway, went off, too. And so did everyone else. For the first time in my life—ever—anywhere—I was one of the last off the blocks. Even in the water, I expected to hear the gun to call us back. In a frame of the picture of the start, Walsh and Zorn were out of the picture—only their feet showed—when my hands were just cutting into the water.

I was way behind and as I went down, I said to myself: "Don't panic, don't try to catch them now—you'll have a strong second length." In the heats that morning I had made up a body length coming back, and I believed I could do it again that night. At the wall, in the bad light, I flipped a bad turn—my only bad turn of the meet. Now I was so far behind I was in the backwash. I stepped up my pace and shortened my stroke, which was a mistake. I was less streamlined. Halfway back, I had hardly closed on Zorn at all. I wasn't even looking at Spitz to my left; I was just trying to beat Zorn. Suddenly, about halfway back, it hit me that I wasn't going to do it. I don't even remember what happened after that.

When I touched and asked where I finished, someone said, "third or fourth." I groaned.

Zorn was first, Walsh second, and it seemed to be between Spitz and me for third. I waited. A chance for three gold medals hung on this decision: not only the sprint, but the sprint relay and the medley relay.

I looked at George. "What do you think?"

"I don't know. I think Mark got third and you got fourth."

"Oh, Goddamn."

"Just watch what you say," George warned me.

"Watch what I say!"

"Just be careful what you say." He walked away.

And I thought, Is that all he has to say to me! Watch what I say! What does he think I'm going to say? Something derogatory about Spitz? Or that it was a bad start? What's he afraid of? I still don't know what he was afraid of. At that time, I hadn't seen the films and I didn't know it was such a bad start.

Still we waited for the results. There were two types of judging machines in use at these trials—a Ritter machine on either side of the pool and an electronic clock. On the Ritter machine, when you touch, a hole is punched in a piece of paper. On the electronic clock when you touch the plate, the clock stops. More weight is given to the clock, but because some swimmers miss the touchplate the clock is backed up with a Ritter machine and with human timers.

Suddenly George came back. "Wait a minute," he said, "on the Ritter machines, left and right, you're third!"

We waited and waited for the official results. At last, because I was chattering with cold, I went to the locker room to take a hot shower. When I came back, I didn't see George, I didn't see Mark, I didn't see anybody. I sat down at the end of the pool to wait. Then at the other end of the pool I saw Zorn and Ken Walsh, and their coach, Don Gambril. And Steve Rerych and his coach. And Mark and George. And I thought, What the hell? What's that? Someone sat down beside me and said, "Hey, Don, I saw the results as they handed them to the announcer. You're third."

I said, "Are you sure?"

And he said, "Yeah, you're third."

Still I waited. Then suddenly the announcer: "The results of the 100-meter freestyle: first place, Zac Zorn; second place, Ken Walsh; third place, Mark Spitz; fourth place, Steve Rerych; fifth place, Don Schollander."

Fifth! No one had told me that I might be fifth! Fifth eliminated me from even the sprint relay.

The official times were Spitz, 53.30; Rerych, 53.35; Schollander, 53.40. 53.4 was exactly my winning time in the 1964 Olympics. And only that morning I had gone 52.89.

Suddenly I wondered what went on while I was in the

locker room. And yet I don't know that anything went on. I thought, How could the Ritter machines be that wrong? How could both Ritter machines have me third? Had that guy actually seen the results given to the announcer, showing me third, as he said he had? Nearby I heard someone say, "Bad start, false start." I heard someone agree with him and I thought, They had such a big start on me, and I still came so close. If it *was* a false start, what would have happened if we'd gone off together?

These doubts really hurt, but I guess the thing that hurt most was that on the way to the award stand, George and Mark were laughing.

During the awards, the crowd was absolutely silent. There was no applause.

I got dressed and stayed around for the rest of the events, trying not to show how much it hurt. Later, when I was alone back at the motel, it hit me how disappointed I was—not only in the race and in myself, but in George. Because George hadn't had anything to say to me afterward.

Then, even though it was all over and there would never be another chance, almost automatically I began to go over the race in my mind—just because I had always done this—to figure out why I had lost.

As I was sitting there, I saw a note being slipped under the door. When I opened the door, an old friend was standing there—Robert Riger, who had been with *Sports Illustrated* and was now with ABC.

"I was just pushing this thing under the door," he said. "It's such a sad thing; I'm so upset I can't talk. Here, this says what I want to say." He picked up the note and handed it to me and left. It read:

Dear Don,
   The loss hurts tremendously, I know. And it will hurt the team. I think the silence in the crowds during

the awards when you were missing was a tribute to you. Have faith that life changes, and a chance for one gold medal this year can mean as much as four did in '64. I wish I could do something to pick you up on a night like this, but know that we care, and chalk up one for the tall men. It is the price you have to pay for being there so long.

Fondest regards,
Bob Riger

I can't describe the healing effect of that note. I decided that life was not going to end right there after all, and I got a smile on my face and went out to a party with some old friends.

39

AFTER THE OLYMPIC TRIALS, it was never the same again. The team moved into the Long Beach State dorms for a week to continue working before going to training camp in Colorado. On the last day of the Trials, I'd had an argument with George over an exhibition relay race. When he asked me to swim it, I agreed, but then he wanted me to go all out and I protested. I hadn't been told I was to swim it, I was tired, I'd been out late the night before, and I just didn't care enough to get up for it. George and I had a bitter argument, and by the end of the Olympic Trials we were hardly speaking.

That whole week I just moped around so depressed I couldn't even work out. I'd swim a couple of lengths and get out of the pool and go down to the beach and just think. I knew I was still one of the best 100 freestylers in the world, and I still felt that I could have won the 100 free at the Olympics. I was better, faster than I had ever been in my life, and I was in condition now, ready to win. I had the mental ability and the experience in Olympic competition and I believed I could have won. The terrible frustration was that I was never going to have the chance to prove it.

Training camp that year was at Colorado Springs, selected because of its altitude. We lived at 6,500 feet, in a dormitory near the Broadmoor Hotel, and trained at 7,500 feet, at the Air Force Academy.

After the Trials George went home for a week. When he rejoined the team at Colorado Springs, he went out of his way to try to patch up our relationship and I tried, too. For a while we both pretended that we were getting along as we used to. But the hurt was there. We would never be the same again.

This was the most lackadaisical team I had ever seen. At first we had to take it easy because of the altitude, but the truth is, we never picked up any real steam. People were constantly looking for excuses to skip workouts—a sore throat, a bad leg, fatigue, exhaustion. There were about thirty-two guys on the team and usually for any one workout about twenty-two showed up. Nobody really seemed to care very much, not even the coaches. Don Gambril, the assistant coach, went home once, and George twice. The prevailing mood was one of monumental boredom.

In 1964 none of this would have touched me. I'd have found a way to get on top of it and work. This year I didn't care, either. Some days I would have great workouts; even though we were at altitude, I had some of the best repeats of my life. But I wasn't really interested anymore, and most of my workouts were just mediocre and some were bad. I skipped workouts along with everyone else. I don't think the coaches really cared whether I showed up or not. They figured I would win my one event—the 200 free—and hold my own in the 4 x 200 relay, so there wasn't much reason for me to train hard, and I thought the same thing. I figured I could win by at least three seconds.

When you think about it I suppose it's funny to be considered an old man at twenty-two. But that's the way it was that summer. Riding back and forth to workout, some of the young kids would ask about my times "way back then," as though I were a relic. "What did you do way back when in the 100 fly?" And then they'd be surprised at my times. "You couldn't have gone that fast way back then. People weren't swimming that fast." A hundred years ago. This was the only way I could communicate with these kids, talking about times. The times "back then."

Looking at these kids just coming up, I used to think they had an enormous advantage over us in swimming. They were using techniques at twelve that we didn't hear about until we were sixteen, many that we had developed for ourselves. Steve Clark perfected the whirling start, down and away in one motion. And Roy Saari and I were among the first to develop a sense of pace and make it work for us. We experimented with it and now pace is an accepted part of swimming. When the flip turn came in, I had to experiment to find out that it worked best not to breathe for four to six strokes after the turn: now that's common knowledge and standard training technique.

Yet I think this relentless progress in swimming was what was behind the terrible boredom that hung over training camp that Olympic summer. The sport has become so much more demanding. The workouts were so long and so hard that they left you absolutely exhausted physically. They consumed so much time and so much energy that, in the few hours left to you, you could only rest or watch television. Your life was so dull, so mechanical, so impoverished emotionally and intellectually, that you began to feel like a robot.

In 1968 we were spending so much more time in the water that the chlorine was beginning to affect our eyes. For the first time guys were wearing goggles for protection. And during those long training hours a kind of one-upmanship developed. Everyone was trying to get an edge with special gear. Guys were using leg bands, hand weights, goggles, ear plugs. We were starting to look like freaks in the water, like swimming machines. We didn't just live like automatons: we looked like them.

I think that in the next few years it will become impossible for the sport to accelerate. Something will have to give. They'll have to figure out how to train swimmers effectively in fewer hours, or else they will have only swimmers with low intellects. An intelligent guy could live like that and work like that for a while, but he couldn't sustain himself over a long period of time. He'd blow his mind.

After about two weeks, some of us were asked to move to ski cabins at a higher altitude and for me this turned out to be the best part of the summer. It was so remote and beautiful up there and I was so tempted to just forget about swimming and enjoy it. One Sunday we rode horses way up into the mountains, although that was supposed to be bad for our legs. Actually it didn't do much harm and it was so beautiful.

Another day we climbed the mountain on foot and *that* we did feel in our legs. Our cabins were right on the side of a mountain peak, and one morning I decided that I wanted to climb to the top of the peak. So, four of us—Don Gambril, John Nelson, Mike Burton, a 400-meter freestyle man who is a good friend and an excellent swimmer, and I—started out after the morning workout one day and climbed it.

This was really an experience, because that mountain was *high*. And we weren't just walking up an easy grade, we were climbing up the side of a cliff. On the top of the mountain we planted a flag: "United States Olympic Team, 1968, Don Gambril, John Nelson, Mike Burton, Don Schollander." Then we climbed back down. The whole thing took us over three hours. For the next five days my leg muscles ached so that I could hardly walk. But it was a break in the terrible monotony and the kind of thing everyone was really hurting for that summer.

All during training camp there was a lot of talk about the Olympic schedule, most of it centering on the relay teams, especially the 4 x 200. The problem was that this relay was scheduled for the same night as the 100-meter butterfly event and Spitz was supposed to swim both, with only one race in between. A lot of the guys, myself included, felt that at altitude this would be an almost impossible feat. We discussed it with Don Gambril and Gambril spoke to George. A few days before we were to leave for Mexico City, they called a team meeting.

"Listen," George said at the meeting, "You guys should have faith in me. Some of you think that Mark shouldn't swim on that relay team. I want to win that relay, too, and even though he has to swim the 100 fly two events earlier, and even though he will be tired, I think that in the relay Mark can give us a 1:58."

The fact is that at altitude very few people were going to swim 200 meters in 1:58, let alone doing it right after swimming the 100-meter butterfly.

"But we can wait and see," George said, "If we get down there and we see that he can't do it, then we won't let him do it."

He changed the subject to the medley relay, in which, it turned out, he *was* thinking of making a change. (Shades of 1964 when Counsilman had bumped me for Steve Clark in the medley relay.) But this year it was the breaststroker who was in question.

"The medley relay is going to be a tough event to win," George said. "We're really worried about it. We need our fastest swimmers on that team. And we're worried about the breaststroke." At the trials two very good breaststrokers had failed to make the 100-meter team and George thought they were better than the three guys who did make it. "So here's what we're going to do," George said. "We're going to decide based on times. The guys in the 100-meter race will have their race times, but in Mexico we'll give special time trials to these other two men, and the man with the fastest time will swim breaststroke in the medley relay."

"Wait a minute!" someone spoke up. "If you're doing that for the breaststroke, why aren't you doing that for the others? How about the guys who didn't make it in the 100 free—why can't they have special time trials, too?"

"Well," George said, "they already had their chance."

"How about the backstrokers?" someone asked. "Do they get time trials?"

The coaches were in a corner because they knew they were being inconsistent and a real argument blew up. Finally George said, "Well, we won't hold this time trial for the breaststroke unless we have to, and we probably won't do it. But just in case we have to, we want you guys to know about it."

But the argument still went on. "You can't do that," the guys said. "It's not right."

Then Spitz, who expected to swim butterfly in that event, spoke up. "In that case, you should give Don another chance to swim freestyle in the relay."

That threw them a little. "Well—" George hedged, "we don't want Don to have to swim another time trial."

"He's already swimming in the heats of the sprint relay," someone said. "Let him lead off and use his time in that."

To which George said, *"Well, that's not really fair—to let someone have a time trial leading off a relay. I think Don would be the first to admit that what we did in Tokyo was not really right.* When you swim lead-off in the relay you're not under as much pressure, you don't have the waves, you go faster."

I just looked at him. I thought, Oh, great! The exact same situation, but now he's jumped the fence! Now, four

years later, when it could mean a crack at another race, he
screws me again.

George looked at me. "Isn't that right?"

"That's right," I said. "Leading off a relay shouldn't
count as a time trial." I thought it was wrong in 1964, and I
didn't think it was right in 1968 just because it was me.

Then they got back to the subject that started it all—the
breaststrokers. They decided to wait and see what happened
in Mexico in the 100-meter breaststroke race. If the regulars
didn't do anything, which is what they expected, they would
give the other two men a time trial.

What actually happened in Mexico City was that Don
McKenzie, one of the regulars, came through with a great
race and was the Olympic champion. That's how little communication there was that year between the coaches and the
team, how little feeling the coaches had for the potential of
individual swimmers.

After the meeting broke up, I spoke to George about it.
"You've got to be consistent, George," I said. "You can't do
one thing with one relay and another thing with another
relay."

Then another Santa Clara man stepped up and told him
point blank that he was jeopardizing the 4 x 200 freestyle
team for the sake of Mark Spitz. George blew up. "Do you
think I'd favor one guy over another?" he said. "I resent that
you'd even say that."

But I think he knew that the issue was splitting the team
into factions.

40

THE OLYMPIC GAMES were not revived by the Baron
de Coubertin merely to give contestants a chance to win

medals and to break records, nor to entertain the public, nor to provide for the participants a stepping stone to a career in professional sport, nor certainly to demonstrate the superiority of one political system over another. . . .

Among the Olympic goals:

To demonstrate the principles of fair play and good sportsmanship. . . .
To create international amity and good will, thus leading to a happier and more peaceful world.
From *Objectives of the Olympic Movement*

The problems of the "Problem Olympics" that began in February with the South African crisis continued through the summer and into the fall, right up to the opening of the Games—and beyond. In the United States, the threatened boycott by black athletes went on. In August, Russia invaded Czechoslovakia and settled her tanks on the streets of Prague, and Sweden, following the spirit of the action against South Africa, protested that the Soviets should be barred from the Olympics.

South Africa *was* banned; Russia was *not* banned. In the end the American black athletes called off their boycott on September 1, but they were troubled and unhappy. Before our arrival there were riots in Mexico City, student activists barricaded themselves on rooftops, there was shooting in the streets—all said to have been triggered by the impending Olympics.   Revolution—repression—racism—communism—imperialism. Before the Games even began the whole vocabulary of world dissension had attached itself to the one event designed to foster goodwill.

On October 3, thirty-four people were killed and hundreds wounded as Mexican troops opened fire on student demonstrators.

The nineteenth Olympiad would open on October 12.

41

When I stepped off the plane in Mexico City I was amazed to find myself surrounded by reporters, photographers, and even fans. The foreign press bombarded me with questions. "How many gold medals this time, Don?"

"You gonna make it five this time, Don?"

"I'm only swimming two events this year."

"Two events? Why only two events?" They couldn't understand why I wasn't in the 100 free; going into the Olympics I had the second best time in the world in the 100 free (Zorn had the world record from the Trials). Well, why wasn't I even in the sprint relay? They couldn't understand that one bad race could knock you out of everything, and it was sort of depressing to try to explain.

On the bus into town I could still hear those press questions. How many this time, Don? Five this time, Don?

This emphasis on an individual gold-medal count was already much more extreme this year than it had been in 1964. For two weeks the press had been beating up a gold-medal count as though it were the only reason for the whole deal. And partly, at least, I was probably the cause of it because I won four gold medals in Tokyo—the first time in twenty-eight years that anyone had piled up four—and revived the drama of a big individual winner.

And, I thought, Where does this kind of thing end? In Tokyo I could have had five if they'd let me swim that medley relay; I could have had six if there had been a 200-meter freestyle then, which there wasn't. (The 200-meter freestyle was included for the first time this year.) If you're just going to count gold medals, where do you stop? Why not run the Olympics twice as long and pile up a couple of dozen? Already the whole thing was getting out of hand. Gold-medal fever was becoming an epidemic. And yet even while I considered this, another part of me said that it would have been nice to have had a shot at my own record and go for five.

Then, still riding into town on the bus, I thought about Karen Muir, the world record holder from South Africa, who couldn't even come to the Olympics because of politics. And about Greg Charlton, another world record holder—in the 400-meter freestyle—who was sick the week before the Trials and didn't make the team at all. And about Gary Illman, who had held on four more years after 1964 as I had, who hadn't made the team, either. And I said to myself, "You're on the team. At least you're here."

Did I feel sorry for myself? I did. Because I still felt I was the fastest 100-meter freestyle man in the world.

Still—the warm reception at the airport pleased me. For a moment it was almost like Tokyo, but only for a moment. These Olympics couldn't be the same for me.

And yet, in a strange unexpected way the 1968 Olympics became very important to me.

Perhaps it was because I was older now and because over the past four years I had seen so much. Perhaps it was because this time I knew what to expect and was looking for it. I know that it was partly because this time I was only swimming two events, in which I became increasingly less interested. At any rate I spent very little time thinking about myself and my races and a great deal of time thinking about what was obviously happening to the Olympics and where it would lead.

The new problems did nothing to dissipate the old ones. They were all still there, full-grown and twice as ugly and it took only a day or two to see them.

Nationalism and politics were riding high again. With hardly a lost day the arguments began. The East Germans wanted to be called the Democratic People's Republic of Germany; West Germany didn't seem to care much what it was called. The men on the IOC remembered when Germany was Germany and, typically, clung to the illusion. They just called both sides Germany. The North Koreans, who were referred to simply as North Koreans, protested that they were the Democratic Republic of North Korea.

The pressure by nations on their athletes to win was running amuck. For the first time this year there were to be tests for drugs. The same as with a racehorse, that little pill can drive you harder, harder, harder to win—win—win.

Also this year there were chromosome tests to prove that women competitors were really women. A Polish contestant failed the test and was rumored to be near suicide. There was a rash of scratched entries, especially among women from iron-curtain countries. We heard that a Russian woman track star and her sister were staying home. Sister? You began to wonder what the hell to call them.

Mexico was caught in the gold-medal fever. In their own country it was a matter of face. They pinned their hopes on their swimming star, Guillermo Echeverria, who held the world record in the 1,500-meter freestyle. He was swimming the 1,500 and the 400, too, and the Mexicans believed that he would become their first Olympic gold-medal winner in swimming. On the streets of Mexico City, because I understand Spanish, I heard it everywhere—Echeverria would win for Mexico. Every day, it seemed, I read it in the papers. Mike and I used to talk about how unfair this was because, according to our calculations, the guy just wasn't going to make it. His only advantage was that he'd lived his whole life at altitude, right there in Mexico City. But the Mexicans had pinned their hopes on him and the poor guy was under so much pressure. Later when he lost, it was terrible. Unless he leaves Mexico, I think he'll have a hard time living it down.

The beautiful Olympic "spirit" was everywhere. East

Germans were avoiding West Germans; Czechs were avoiding Russians. The press stepped up the gold-medal predictions. There was a rumor—unverified—that a Japanese runner had committed suicide because his country was counting on him and he knew he couldn't win.

Back home people said, "Go down there and let 'em have it; we gotta win those Olympics, boy!"

> The most important thing in the Olympic Games is not to win but to take part, just as the most important thing in life is not the triumph but the struggle. The essential thing is not to have conquered but to have fought well.
> *The Olympic Creed*

42

MEXICO CITY was like a fiesta, gay, crowded, colorful. I used to think that the Olympic Village was like a carnival, just as colorful and with the same aura of impermanence. We lived in high-rise, apartment-type buildings constructed of rather flimsy material that had a thrown-together look about them. Mike Wall and I roomed together—just the two of us in the room—but next to us there were three men in a room and four and even five in rooms down the hall. On the whole the place was pretty crowded and seemed dirtier, I suspect, than it really was.

With the facilities they had, they did everything they could to make us comfortable. The separate dining rooms were there to cater to native tastes, and for Mexico the food was good. There was a very good international building, one of the things that really worked in this Olympics. The athletes gathered there more than they had in Tokyo and made a real effort to communicate with each other.

One of the best things Mexico did was to revive the idea
of a cultural Olympics along with the athletic program. The
Village was filled with art—paintings, statues—early Mexican,
modern Mexican, European, Far Eastern. When they exca-
vated for the buildings, they unearthed pre-conquistador
pyramids and restored them and left them where they were,
so that turning up unexpectedly all over this modern Village
were these handsome, ancient monuments. Mexico invited
performers from all over the world—orchestras, singers, ballet
groups. This was one area where she really extended herself
with very exciting results.

On the minus side was the unbelievable lack of organization. Most people don't realize the amount of behind-the-
scenes planning it takes to run an Olympics properly. The
Mexican facilities were scattered all over the area. In swimming, for instance, they had one good 50-meter Olympic
pool—still unfinished but usable—and besides that, in the
main building, only a small practice pool where nobody
really wanted to train. Seven or eight other pools were available but they were scattered all over Mexico City, some of
them more than an hour away. One of the large pools assigned to us was so far away that after a few days we found
that we were getting too tired from spending so much time
on the bus. On the days that we were assigned to that pool,
we just skipped the workout.

We would each get one assigned workout a day in the
50-meter Olympic pool, and then we would spend the rest of
our time trying to sneak into it for more workouts. I used to
go there alone and find old friends on the teams of other
countries, and jump in to work out with them. I would go
days without seeing some of the guys on my own team; I
don't remember one workout for the whole team together in
the Olympic pool. George and Don Gambril would work
with twelve guys at one time, twelve guys at another time,
whenever they could. They were at the pool most of the day

just trying to get in workouts for everyone on the team. Aside from a short daily workout, I hardly ever saw George. There was no thought of training even close to the hour of your race—the schedule was such a mess.

Olympic transportation around Mexico City was unbelievable. One night, going home on a shuttle bus, it hit us suddenly that we were wandering all over Mexico City. At first we thought the driver must be taking a new route, but after forty-five minutes we realized that he was way over on the outskirts of town, where, a few minutes later, he stopped the bus. A girl got out, and the driver turned the bus around and headed back to the Village. He was just giving his girl friend a ride home. In Mexico we could get home tonight—or get home mañana—what was the difference?

But on the whole, everything on the surface in Mexico seemed to be fine. What was going on beneath the surface was another matter.

After only a few days in Mexico I began to feel that, unless something was done soon, the Olympic Games were going to die. If not with this nineteenth Olympiad, then with the twentieth. This year's Olympics had come very close to being canceled. Next time they might not be saved and that would be the end.

When I mentioned this to a couple of coaches, they just shrugged it off. "Then we'll just have world championships," they said.

They didn't see that it wouldn't be the same. They didn't see any purpose to the Olympics—except to win gold medals. To them it was just a championship meet. The thought that the Olympics could actually die didn't bother them at all. It bothered me.

I suppose you could say that it is naïve and unrealistic to think that this direction can be reversed. To do that nations and individuals—both athletes and coaches—would have to change. How are you going to tell an individual to compete for the sake of competition when his autocratic government, which supports him, orders him or woos him to compete to win? How do you tell the Communist nations to change? How do you tell nations to be less nationalistic?

I think there are places to start. Certain things have crept into the Olympic ceremonies that shouldn't be there. When the medals are awarded, the flag of the winning country is raised and strains of its national anthem are played—every time. This has a propaganda effect and tends to whip up the gold-medal count and intensify nationalistic rivalries. This flag-raising and playing of national anthems and gold-medal counts have only recently crept into the Olympics. They haven't always been there and they don't belong there. They should be eliminated.

A medal should be awarded to an individual. You wouldn't know whether he was Russian or Hungarian or what. You would just know his name. This would make it harder to squeeze propaganda out of the victory. Certainly the press could still find out the national origin of the winner and other countries could keep tallies and publicize the news, but I think eliminating the nationalistic aspects from the ceremonies would have a cooling effect psychologically. Perhaps not at first, but gradually, I think, the competitive frenzy among nations would begin to die.

This would be a start. Once we recognized that this deflation of the nationalistic balloon was a healthy thing, we would begin to find other ways. Then victories wouldn't be worth quite so much to a nation and the Olympics might again become what they were intended to be.

The biggest problem for the United States Olympic Committee in 1968 had been the black athletes. At the time of the threatened boycott they appointed a board of consultants to act as a liaison between the athletes and the Olympic Committee. They were passing the buck but it was just as well. The United States Olympic Committee never had much communication with the athletes—any athletes. Very few of them knew how or what the athletes were thinking or why. They didn't know when something was going wrong until it happened. This board of consultants was made up of some very good men, including former Olympic athletes Jesse Owens, Billy Mills, and John Sayers of *Pace* magazine. These men cared about the problems and were sensitive to the needs of the athletes.

Once the boycott threat had passed, there was no real reason for them to remain in Mexico except that they had already been invited. For their part, these consultants decided that they wanted to stay in touch with the athletes.

Many of them, especially Sayers, Owens, and Mills, knew that the black athletes were still unhappy, and they knew that there were other problems, too. They decided to hear the athletes out, listen to all the complaints that no officials ever heard, and then make recommendations to the United States and international Olympic committees.

Before long I sensed a widening gulf between the consultants and the United States Olympic Committee. In an elevator one night, an Olympic Committee member turned to John Sayers and said, "What's our team doing? Are you keeping those guys in line?"

John said, "I'm not supposed to keep them in *line!* You're on the Olympic Committee. Why don't *you* know what they're doing?"

The guy just smiled and said, "Well, I guess they're behaving themselves as much as the officials are."

Out of the thousands of people at the Olympics who should have cared—officials, coaches, athletes—I felt that these three consultants were the only ones who sensed, as I did, how wrong things were going and how close to the end it might be.

43

AT EVERY OLYMPICS there are two different Olympics going on: the regular Olympics of athletic competition that the spectators watch and the world hears about, and the other Olympics for the Olympic Committee officials and their friends. The officials go to events to hand out medals and then they go to cocktail parties and dinner parties every night and that's their Olympics. It has very little to do with the athletes.

One evening, a few days before the 1968 Games started, John Sayers took me along to one of these cocktail parties. It turned out to be a rare close-up of the whole upper echelon of the Olympic movement. They were all there—most of the men on the Olympic Committee, officers, directors, all those people who held the power and made the rules and did or did not enforce them, all those people who ran the show. Plus a handful of famous Olympic athletes.

I walked in, people greeted me, people said they were glad I was there, nobody remembered that I hadn't been invited.

I stood off to one side and looked at them. They were so far removed from anything that had to do with the Olympics! The contrast between the Olympic Village and this cocktail party was almost beyond description. In the Village we were part of the world of tough black athletes churning with frustration, tough hardheaded iron-curtain athletes with a lot at stake, tough black athletes from emerging countries fighting for their place in the world. And these men were part of a world long since gone by that hardly existed anymore outside this room.

They were old—they had that tired, soft, withered look of old men—confident, self-satisfied old men. They were elegant and very courteous and they smiled and laughed and sipped their wine—this power elite that hadn't thought for a long time, if they had ever thought at all, about where their power was coming from.

I moved through the crowd, hoping someone would ask me about some of the things on my mind. Nobody did. That whole evening I didn't hear a word about the problems of the Olympics.

What I heard was internal politics. They had a presidential election coming up in the IOC and that was their main event. Avery Brundage was up for reelection and a first vice-president from France was running against him. To me there was little choice between them. They were equally unqualified for the job. They were both old, both rich, both totally out of contact with the athletes, without the slightest insight into their needs, the slightest concern over changing conditions. The only thing any of these men seemed to be concerned about that night was their own power.

I was aware that they gave a lot of time to the Olympic movement. And they worked for nothing—it was their hobby. Certainly my objection was not to age alone. It was to stultification. Their age and, perhaps, their other interests were getting in the way of honest observation and communication. All around them sports were changing, the whole world relating to the Olympics was changing, and they had no idea that it was happening. They didn't get out to look. That whole night nobody talked about the actual Olympics— the Games. Nobody talked about what was going on at these 1968 Olympics. Nobody asked me how things were going in the Village.

Another year I might not have noticed, but that night I was bursting to talk to someone. I knew how much things had gone wrong and that they were getting worse and I wanted to tell them.

Then I thought, How could they ask? They didn't have a clue that anything was wrong. They wouldn't ask anymore than they would ask, "How's the measles epidemic?" There wasn't any measles epidemic. For them there wasn't any trouble. The fire was smoldering but they were too far away to feel the heat.

These men on the IOC honestly didn't know ahead of time about the problems that blew up in their faces. In the Village we knew that the black athletes were still searching for some way to express their feelings. They hadn't been able to agree—some guys wanted to do more than others—and they had split up into factions. But they knew they were going to do something and we knew it, too.

They never did agree on a single plan and in the end they left it that each man would do his own thing. Some wore Afro-American clothes. Some spent a lot of time hanging around the entrance to the Village, to keep their protest in evidence. Some kept completely apart, segregating themselves from the rest of us. They held meetings and they talked a lot in small groups about reviving the boycott. And later, Tommie Smith and John Carlos bowed their heads and raised black-gloved hands during the raising of the American flag.

Actually there wasn't nearly so much excitement about this in the Olympic Village as there was outside it. We knew how committed Smith and Carlos were to these problems. We knew they were going to compete and try to win and we knew, too, that they felt they had to make some kind of a gesture. The public made a lot of it, and it was a big item with all the news media.

Apparently the IOC had no idea that anything was going to happen. And when it did, they were stunned. Then they got excited and said that Smith and Carlos had embarrassed not only the United States, but Mexico and the whole Olympic movement. In the Village we heard that all the fuss that followed originated with the IOC; they told the United States Committee that if they didn't kick out Smith and Carlos, the entire American team would be disqualified and sent home. That put the USOC in a bind and they ordered

Smith and Carlos out of the Olympic Village and within three days the two guys were back in the United States. Everyone thought our USOC had instigated the action and our committee took the blame for it, but in the Village we heard that the IOC forced them to do it.

When you come right down to it, whatever you may think about Smith and Carlos, if Russia could protest against South Africa and if the IOC respected the protest enough to keep South Africa out, then why couldn't Smith and Carlos protest? Both protests were dragging something into the Olympic Games that didn't belong there. The difference was that the IOC could handle Smith and Carlos.

Another problem that blew up at the 1968 Olympics that the IOC men seemed to know nothing about that night at their party was the payoffs. In the Village for days we had heard that Mexico City was crawling with manufacturers' representatives who were ready to make payoffs to athletes if they would agree to use their equipment in Olympic competition. We heard they were slipping $500 in cash under the table to athletes of all countries. Later we heard that it was $1,500. There was even a wild story of an athlete who tried to cash a shoe company check for $1,440 right at the Olympic Village.

In the Olympic Village nobody doubted that money was changing hands under the table. It was an open secret— hardly a secret at all. Everyone knew. In a post-Olympic article, *Sports Illustrated* said facetiously that the reason so many athletes walked so slowly out of the stadium was that their shoes were filled with money.

The IOC, alone, seemed not to know. And when the rumors finally caught up with them, they set up a howl of righteous indignation and announced that there would be a thorough investigation.

Did it ever even occur to them, I wondered, to consider how much they had contributed to the situation by their failure to adjust to the times? Many of these athletes—especially the track men—had jobs. Many were married and had children. To compete in the Olympics, they had to leave their jobs for at least two months—six weeks of training and two weeks at the Games. That meant, in most cases, two months without pay, plus the money they had shelled out already just to keep up with their sport, and the time they had put in for years, training twenty hours a week or more, during which time they might have made more money. The Olympic Committee reimburses them for none of this, not even for lost salaries while they compete. And it expects them not to take payoffs under the table.

As for college students, while they don't sacrifice two months' salary for the Games, they do sacrifice a semester of college, which means another year that their families must support them. Otherwise the cost has been the same—the cost of keeping pace with the sport, traveling to meets, and having no spare time in which to earn some money.

When these Olympic Committee officials were young, an Olympic athlete trained three or four hours a week. Now Olympic athletes train up to ten times that much. The simple fact is that when a man has worked so hard for so many years, with every legitimate opportunity to make money closed to him, and when someone offers him $1,500 under the table the temptation to take it is very strong.

The IOC cannot understand this because they have no idea how much amateur sports have changed or the size of the personal investment the amateur and his family must make for years if he is to reach the top and stay there. The loftiest goal of the IOC is still the preservation of an amateurism that in fact no longer exists. They are worshiping a corpse. And by refusing to admit it, they create the conditions in which under-the-table deals can flourish.

Aside from the nasty possibility that an amateur might make some money, the IOC thought that everything else about the Olympics was fine—A-OK. They couldn't see for themselves—and there was no new blood to tell them—that the Olympics were not fine. I felt they were never going to see until something happened to shake them up. And then it might be too late.

I think the only hope is to get the athletes some representation on the board so they can keep the board in touch with what is happening and give them some idea of the real spirit of the competition. Only the athletes can know why they're competing, whether they're there for medals and money or for the Olympic experience. Now the IOC is running the show without any idea of what's happening. The brain doesn't know what the limbs are doing. The general is making the decisions without knowing what's going on at the front.

44

Peace would be furthered by the Olympic Games. . . . But peace would be the product only of a better world; a better world could be brought about only by better individuals. . . .

The foundation of real human morality lies in mutual respect—and to respect one another it is necessary to know one another.

The Olympic goals—
quoted in the Olympic Manual

I left the party that night too churned up to go to bed, and for a long time I just walked around the Olympic Village thinking, going over in my mind all those things that had been bothering me for a year and, more than ever, these past few days.

Those words about the Olympic goals sounded great, but they had a hollow ring. How long since anyone had really

thought—or cared—about what they were trying to say?
Coaches, athletes, the press, the public, the men of the IOC
back at the party I had just left, who had the power and the
responsibility—anyone? The Olympics were supposed to be
person to person—*individual* to *individual*—completely removed from politics, so far removed, in fact, that ideally even
a war, cold or hot, should not affect them. The fact was that
the smoke of international politics over the Olympics was so
thick that nobody could even see the original ideals anymore,
much less think about how much had been lost when they
were abandoned.

The problem of politics in the Olympics had been going
on for a long time, but in 1968 with the South African affair,
it became much more sinister. For years now governments
had understood the propaganda value of Olympic victories
and had been using the Olympics as a propaganda tool. But
in 1968 something was added. With the South African affair,
the Olympics also became a weapon, a lever against existing
governments to force a change in political policy. Red China
had forced Russia's hand and had changed the Olympic
movement. And the IOC had let it happen.

When the black African and the Communist bloc nations threatened to withdraw, the IOC should have said, "All
right, we're sorry you won't be there. We'll hold the Olympics with half the world, and when you're ready to come back
you will be welcome."

It would have been painful and Mexico would have
suffered, but wouldn't the Olympic movement have come out
stronger? If the IOC had held its ground and maintained that
politics had no place in the Olympics, and then held the 1968
Olympics for anyone who would come, including a biracial
South African team, wouldn't the Olympic movement have
been enhanced? Then it would have been on Olympic
grounds that white South Africans and black South Africans
lived together for the first time. Then, if a black athlete from
South Africa had won, white and black South Africans, alike,

might have said, "Our man took first place." Then, South African blacks might have said, "It was there—at the Olympics—that we took the first step."

In that eyeball-to-eyeball confrontation, when the IOC backed down, they gave to any large bloc of nations—whether morally right or wrong—the power to end the Olympics. This year there was real doubt about whether the Olympics would be held. If, in 1972, another issue blows up six months before the Games are to begin, and once again they hang in doubt—and again in 1976—won't the Olympics inevitably die? Will athletes train all those years only to have the ground cut out from under them by politics? Will nations spend millions of dollars to host a party that might not take place?

Take it a step further. In 1968 we saw the Olympics used as tools of international politics in two ways—as propaganda and as a lever. Doesn't it follow that the Olympics are going to end when the Russian bloc can gain more from the lever than from the propaganda? If at any time Russia feels she will lose badly at the Olympics, she will find a reason to back out and go for the political gain. In 1968 Russia felt she would do extremely well and she had no desire to back out. But if the day ever comes when the Western nations gain complete superiority over the Eastern bloc, then Russia will boycott the Olympics and she will find a way to turn her boycott, rather than her victories, into propaganda.

In the 1968 confrontation the IOC yielded because they really thought there was something to lose. To me all you had to do was look around Mexico City to see that there was little that was worth saving.

The original purpose of Olympic competition was to bring people together. Now the competition—and the *winning it*—had become the purpose. The means had become the end.

Baron de Coubertin, the founder of the modern Olympics, was a sociologist—not an athlete—who thought that athletics brought out the best in people. Now there had been such a perverse twist that more and more they seemed to bring out the worst. To De Coubertin the importance lay in mingling cultures, not in competition. Now it was just the reverse. If the athlete had to make a choice, mingle or win, there was no question. He chose to win. If De Coubertin had decided that rock and roll dances were a better way to get people together, he would have suggested dances. It was beginning to look as though it might have been a better choice.

And yet, in a way, the Olympics are man's last chance, the only place where the people of the world can get together, regardless of race, religion, or ideology, and make an effort to communicate and begin to understand each other. If we let the Olympics die, there is nothing to replace them. Individual nations may enter into cultural exchange programs, groups of scientists may meet, artists and musicians may become interested in other cultures. These are the few, not the many. But anywhere on earth, people from all nations however different can come together on the universally understood level of sport. One athlete can compete against another athlete and respect the man through his performance. Only through sports can *individuals* of the world begin to know each other and to develop mutual respect. And if we can't believe that there are better *individuals* even in the countries whose political philosophies we oppose and whose actions we dispise, then what can we believe? If we give up the hope that the better *individuals* of one nation can still reach the better individuals of another nation, and somehow make a beginning toward understanding and respect, then what is left? If we close this last bridge between people who are kept apart, where do we find another?

The next day, at a meeting of the United States Olympic Team, an Olympic Committee official stood up to give us a pep talk. "We know why we're down here," he said, "and we've got everything going for us. We've got the best medical attention, the best facilities, we've trained hard, our whole country is behind us, they're depending on us, we've come down here and we're going to do well, and . . ." and he yelled, "AND WE'RE GONNA WIN!!!"

I couldn't stand it. I just walked out.

Somebody had to do something. Somebody had to call attention in a dramatic way, so that people would notice—and the IOC would have to notice—what was happening to the Olympic movement. Nobody was going to reach those men on the IOC. Nobody could talk to them. And they weren't going to suddenly wake up by themselves. Somebody had to dramatize the Olympic problem publicly. I decided that I was the one to do it.

My campaign in electing myself came down to four reasons. (1) I was probably the best-known figure at the 1968 Olympics so if I did something, people would notice. (2) For four years I had had the opportunity to see so much. Many less successful athletes do not have so much exposure to the problems, and sometimes the better athletes are beguiled by the preferential treatment they receive and do not see the hard facts beneath the surface. I felt that I had had a chance to see what was going on and that I understood it and cared. (3) I felt that in four years at Yale I had acquired enough mental discipline to think the problem through honestly and that I had become articulate enough to say what had to be said. (4) I felt that I had a debt to pay. The Games had meant so much to me. They had changed my life, and I felt I wanted to do this to repay some part of what the Olympics had given to me.

This was the year of the protest and now I decided on one of my own. I found Mike and told him, "I think I'm going to quit." I said, "I'm going to call a press conference tomorrow and make a speech to tell them everything I've been thinking about the Olympic movement." Mike knew what I was talking about; we'd been discussing it all week. "And then as a protest, I'm going to retire immediately, before the Games begin."

I felt very strongly that I should do this. I had had plenty of glory in 1964 and glory didn't mean much to me, anymore. That night Mike and I wrote down all our ideas and talked them over and I started to write the speech. I stayed up until about two o'clock and then got up at six the next morning—Friday, the day before the opening ceremonies. I wanted to do it that day, before the Games began. I didn't want to steal the limelight from any individual performances during the Games, and I didn't think it would be nearly so effective if I waited until the Games were over.

When Mike got up we talked about it again—whether it was the right thing to do, whether it could possibly work, what the repercussions might be. I knew I would have to give my speech and leave Mexico City. I didn't know how I was going to get home; I didn't have enough money. I was concerned about the effect it would have on my parents, who had not yet arrived in Mexico City. I remember that Mike and I discussed whether people would see me only as someone who deserted the Olympic Team the day before the Games began, or as just a dreamer, who had thrown away his name, career, and reputation for a naïve and totally unrealistic ideal. If I couldn't pull this off, I would have a very bad name. But I felt I could do it. And I felt I had to do it. I don't think I had ever felt like this before.

And then we talked about George. In spite of everything that had happened this summer, I felt I owed it to George to tell him before I did it.

Mike had to go over to the pool, and after he left, I went down to breakfast. While I ate, I thought, This may be the last breakfast I'm going to eat as an Olympic swimmer. I went back upstairs and read the speech again.

Then I braced myself and went to look for George. I

found him in his room and handed him the speech. He read the speech through without a word and while he read it I watched him. He was so tired he looked sick. He started to read it again and I thought, Why doesn't he get out of this business? Obviously he doesn't enjoy it anymore—why doesn't he find someone to take over and get out?

George read all the way through the speech twice. Then he looked at me and said, "Don, if you did this, I think I'd pack my bags and go home before the Olympics even started."

And as soon as he said that, I knew there was just no way I would be able to make that speech.

For a long time George talked to me, giving me the reasons why I shouldn't do it—I would create such a sensation that I would end the Olympics right then and there; I couldn't pull this off alone; I should work through the AAU and the Olympic movement. I hardly heard him—to me his reasons didn't make sense. The thing I kept thinking over and over was that George was tired, disheartened, and sick, and that he had said he would go home. I felt that this would be the final blow, and I couldn't do it to him.

When Mike came back at 12:30, I was still talking to George. Later he said that when he walked in and found me there, he knew it was all over.

This is the speech I didn't make.

"I have asked you to come here today—the day before the Olympics begin—in order to announce my retirement from the sport of swimming, from the United States Olympic Team, and from the 1968 Olympic Games as of today, October 11. It is with deep personal sorrow that I announce this decision. Yet I feel this is something that I must do. I do this alone, without the knowledge of my parents, my coaches, or my teammates, and I alone will take the consequences of my action.

"Ever since the Tokyo Olympics, I have been growing more and more disturbed about the direction in which sports and, especially, the Olympic movement, are going. For al-

most a year, controversy and crisis have surrounded these
1968 Games. Here in Mexico City, for two weeks, I have
watched the spirit of this nineteenth Olympiad and have
compared it to the original spirit of the Olympic Games.

"The Olympics Games are intended to be an athletic
contest for people from all over the world, competing against
each other in the best spirit of competition, in the hope that
politics, ideologies, racial and religious prejudices will be cast
aside. It is intended that individuals will compete as individuals and come to understand each other as individuals, not
as Russians or Americans or Africans.

"Mexico has intended to host a cultural and sporting
event for the entire world to promote understanding and
brotherhood, peace and good will. These are the ideals, and
these ideals should be uppermost in the minds of everyone in
any way associated with the Olympic movement. What has
happened and what is happening now is very far removed
from this Olympic ideal.

"I am not trying to lead a rebellion. I am trying to bring
about an honest, sincere reevaluation of the Olympic spirit
that has been killed by people who have lost sight of its
potential and its goals. . . ."

I talked about my feelings on South Africa, about the
threatened boycott, about all the questions that had dragged
politics into the Olympic movement. I talked about commercialism, and about national leaders who demanded victories
and gold medals, forgetting it was participation that was
important. I talked about the officials of the IOC who were
too much concerned with perpetuating their power and too
little concerned with Olympic goals.

"I feel that the very future of the Olympics is at stake.
The Olympics were not intended to be a political arena. No
matter how much we may disagree with any nation or sympa-
thize with any people, the Olympics must not be used as an
instrument of politics.

"As we get further and further away from the Olympic

ideal, the risk of the Olympics being discontinued increases. The fault lies with nearly everyone—officials, national leaders, the athletes themselves who, too often, are concerned only with winning. I, too, have wanted to win. And I still have respect for excellence. I think the athletes are less to blame than anyone else. I have seen them at night in the international center, making attempts to communicate with each other in spite of language barriers. Every night they try to exchange pins, listen to each other's music, they laugh together at the Village auditorium. They are at least trying, and this is what the Olympics are all about.

"You people of the news media, with your gold-medal counts and trumped-up rivalries, are partly to blame. And the people who pay athletes to promote the sports products that they manufacture and the general public, too, are all at fault. Everyone, to some degree, shares in the guilt.

"The Olympic Games should be open to everyone who qualifies, regardless of race, religion, or color, whether professional or amateur, no matter what country he is from. This is a competition for individuals, and the only person who is hurt by politics entering into the Games is the athlete himself. Many of you will say that I am naïve to think that in the world as it is today we can still believe in an Olympic ideal that has become antiquated. But somehow, something must be done.

"If we hope to contribute to world peace through sports and through the Olympic Games, we cannot permit the present trends to continue. We must act now to change the direction of the Olympic movement. We must recognize what is going on. We must rethink our purpose. We must put the Olympics back on course. It is the only way we can preserve the Olympics and the contribution they can make to international understanding and goodwill.

"My action is not intended as a boycott. It is not intended to embarrass anyone. I apologize to the people of the United States and to the people of Mexico. I am trying to save something that I truly believe is worth saving and that I feel is more important than any personal success I might gain. I only hope that something constructive will come out of my protest, and that my actions will not have been in vain."

I still think it's something that should have been said. Later it was too late and I was never able to say it. And I'm sorry.

The next day the nineteenth Olympiad began, with student activists in the fields around the stadium and armed soldiers in front of it. A few athletes collapsed because of the altitude, there were some attempted defections and, of course, the payoff scandal, and Smith and Carlos raised their fists. Otherwise everything was fine.

We waited a week for the swimming events to begin. In the 100-meter free Mike Wenden of Australia came in first with Walsh next and then Spitz. I had to wait an extra few days for my events, and about two weeks after the Olympics began I swam my first race—anchor man in the 4 x 200 meter relay. I turned in a very fast time—1:54.6—and the event gave me my first and last gold medal. Even I was surprised at how fast I went, and two days later in the individual 200, I had slowed down. Also, by the next day I was telling myself with joy, "My last race!" The race went to Wenden. I expected him to die over the last 50 meters and he didn't, and I came in second in 1:55.8, 1.2 seconds slower than the day before.

On the whole it was a good Olympics for our swimming team and there were some fine performances. Charlie Hickcox and Debbie Meyer each won three gold medals, the most that any American swimmer took in those Olympics.

I would have liked to have gone out a winner, but at the closing ceremonies that was not very much on my mind. I kept thinking I was glad it was over, and then I began to think about all the other things while I looked at those blindly optimistic words: "Munich 1972."

Epilogue

I DO NOT THINK that the IOC, as it is presently constituted, will ever undertake the necessary reforms. I think the impetus must come from all over the world, from the athletes themselves.

I am only one of many United States athletes who have suggested reforms in our own sports program. I have advocated the creation by the government of a Federation of Sports with paid executives to administer our entire program. I would also envision an advisory council to this federation (similar to the President's Council on Physical Fitness), represented by active or recently retired athletes.

I believe that the purely American benefits from this federation would be very real. But far more important to me would be the effect that a strong, dynamic United States sports federation could exert on the Olympic movement. If we can put our own house in order, we can make effective changes in our own United States Olympic movement. In time, we could change the IOC and that, to me, is absolutely essential if the Olympics are to be saved. I would like to see former athletes, not only in the United States, but in all other countries as well, stay involved in their nation's sports program and work to improve it, with the ultimate goal, even though it would take time, of bringing about changes in the international Olympic movement.

Finally, I would like to call for former athletes to reconvene every four years during the Games and immediately afterward to discuss what is happening to the Olympics and to organize groups to try to bring about change more rapidly. Former participants are the people with special feeling for the athletes and for the Olympics. Their voice should be heard and would be effective.

I hope the first such meeting can take place in Munich in 1972. *I would like to issue a call for all athletes who are interested to come to Munich to organize a worldwide movement.* It is time to begin.